YOU COULD HAVE SAVED ME

Elisabeth M Goodchild

First published by Nielsen 2024

Copyright © Elisabeth M Goodchild

The moral right of the author has been asserted.

All rights reserved.
No part of this publication may be reproduced, stored in a retrieval system, or transmitted, in any form or by any means, without the prior permission in writing of the author, nor be otherwise circulated in any form of binding or cover other than that in which it is published and without a similar condition including this condition being imposed on the subsequent purchaser.

For privacy reasons some names, locations and dates may have been changed.

ISBN 978-1-3999-8202-3

Book cover illustration by Elisabeth M Goodchild
Book cover design by Eva Bittar

Foreword

I don't remember 'before'. At least not much. And what I think are memories may just be the memories others have created for me.

Occasionally, now, I get a fleeting image of something. Or the memory of a feeling, a smell, a word even, brings some 'thing' from before to the surface just long enough for me to notice its presence before it sinks and is gone again.

I go 'there' more often that I realise. There isn't a 'where' – it's so much more than that – it's the sadness, the anger, the inevitability, the lack of power, the fear, the loss, the theft, the 'undoing', the revisiting, the loneliness, the years of feeling worthless, ... the sheer weight of the acknowledgement of it all.

But I keep hearing the voice – this is my time. It's now. I don't need anything or anyone to tell me how to live, but I do need to tell my story.

Catch the wave. Jump in. Both feet. Don't leave anything unsaid.

Remember how hard you've had to fight, and for how long, to find your voice, to believe your voice has a right to be heard, to want the world to know, to understand, to listen. It's time to shout this truth. To live my truth. Fuck the haters, fuck the people who didn't and don't understand, fuck the people who let me down – over and over again over the years – fuck the people who can't get over themselves, fuck the whole fucking world. I don't want to forget anything, to leave a thing out – it all took me there and brought me here. From the tiniest word or action that left me shattered to the monumental events when I felt nothing

*

I don't know where to start. I'm lost in a sea of 'where to starts'. Do I tread gently or do I launch in? Do I start at the beginning (which is the end) or the end (which turned out to be the beginning)? I don't know. But I do know it's been stopping me starting for a long time now. Maybe part of me wants to hold back - doesn't want me to go there. Thinks it's all just a waste of time. Is afraid no one will listen, no one will care.

Because they didn't care. They didn't listen. They shut me up.

*

I can feel it now if I close my eyes. I can go back there and feel the terror that was sitting somewhere in the middle of me as I sat outside the headmistress's office. I can tell you how I felt, what the room was like, the time, what she said, I can remember the smallest details. What I can't tell you is the exact date that the clock stopped. 1974 I think. I know I was seven. My mother can't remember exactly either. But she can tell you that one day I came home from school and the girl I'd been had disappeared but I couldn't (and wouldn't) tell her why.

*

She'd grabbed my arm and dragged me from the room. I remember I wanted to cry but was terrified – by what had just happened and by her reaction. The school was a strange hexagonal construction – like a honeycomb around the central hall. It had always seemed bright, with the classrooms getting the light from their windows and the central hall. But the area near the school offices was dark and the darkness stayed with me and became part of my nightmares. Mostly I remember feeling numb. I guess it was the shock. Terrified and numb. She whisked me into her office, shut the door, sat me on a chair, roughly tried to get me dressed and then disappeared into the headmistresses' office. I don't recall that she said anything much. As she went into the office she pushed the door to behind her as if they didn't want me to hear. I wonder if the sense of fear, of abandonment, will never leave me. I wondered for a long time about the 'what-ifs'. What if someone had put an arm around me. What if someone had told me not to be scared, what if someone had let me cry, held my hand, stroked my hair, brought me a drink, given me a biscuit, what if someone had done something – anything – that hadn't made me feel so alone and lost in the terror.

They were in there for seventeen minutes. Seventeen! When I found myself, about three, four, five years ago, involuntarily doing the horrible thing of going back to the past to try and get rid of it in the present I found myself living the memory of that hour over and over like a stuck record. The room was smallish, with a brown

1970s fake-wood desk that ran from the end wall to just before the door to the headmistress' office. This still happens sometimes – when I start to recall what happened my brain gets foggy and I can't remember words. It'll come to me. Opposite the desk, along the wall were four or five chairs – not quite adult-size but not child-sized either. They were grey, covered in that sticky, cold polyurethane material that seemed revolutionary fifty years ago. I sat on the chair nearest the wall. Just sat there. Frozen. Waiting for someone to come and tell me everything would be ok – which is what adults are supposed to do when children get hurt – isn't it?

They talked in whispers, occasionally raising their voices. I could just see the shadow of her moving around the headmistress' desk. Sometimes I think she may have wanted to help me, to come to me and comfort me, to say and do the right thing. Did she stand there with one hand on the door handle indirectly trying to indicate to the headmistress that they really needed to wrap up the conversation and check how I was, or did I like to imagine it?

But she didn't. Who knows why – was she worried about her job, could she not believe what she had seen, was she that unsure of herself she didn't want to put herself forward, did she simply defer to the higher authority so she could see herself as blameless, had this happened before?

She's still alive. I have tried so hard to remember her name. My mother can't recall it either. And I can't remember whether she was the school secretary or the deputy head. In a turn of fate that sums up my life for the forty-five years after that day, all the school records were destroyed not so many years back – eight or ten maybe – so I can't be sure who she was or is. I've spent a long time searching for her online. I think she may be headmistress of a school now, in the same area. I hope she's done a better job than she did with me. I hope the guilt was enough to make her the most attentive, human, kind headmistress possible. To never accept anything less than the most appropriate course of action for the children under her responsibility instead of thinking of herself.

I hope the guilt still catches her sometimes and makes her wonder if I'm ok. I'd like to know that she spent years wishing she had done the right thing, wishing she could apologise to me, wishing she'd had the courage to challenge that bitch of a headmistress.

After seventeen minutes the headmistress came out her office followed by her. I don't remember her as very tall. In that very 1970s middle-aged woman uniform of a blouse and pleated skirt. I was going to say I think she was wearing brown – but everything I remember of that hour is brown, grey, drab, like the colour was suddenly sucked from my life – which of course it was. As the headmistress stood with her back to the wall next to the door she stood slightly behind her to her right, hovering at the door to the headmistress' office as though she wished she could back right into it, shut the door and make it all go away. She visibly shrank into herself, and as she shrank at some level the seven-year-old me knew that the hope of reaching her shrank too. At some intuitive level I do believe she wanted to reach out to me. Even now, when I shut my eyes, I have that feeling if the headmistress hadn't been there she would have scooped me up, called my mother and everything would have been alright. But as I said, she didn't. Selfish coward.

As the headmistress spoke I felt like I was being told off. She used that tone of voice, speaking too slowly and enunciating too clearly.

'Elle, Elle, are you listening to me …'. A pause.

'Are you listening to me?'

I nodded.

I don't remember everything she said. She didn't say much. But what she did say was 'Elle, you've always been such a good girl, haven't you. Now, you're not to tell anyone about this. No-one. Do you understand?'

I was being told off. I couldn't work out what I'd done wrong, but I was clearly being told off.

'Do you understand Elle?'.

I nodded.

'You're not to tell anyone. Not even Mummy. Is that clear?' I nodded.

And her parting shot 'And anyway no-one would believe you if you did'.

And with that she asked 'the other woman' – whose name and job I don't think I'll ever remember – to take me back to class.

*

And so it began. The constant fear that I had done something wrong or would do something wrong. The constant feeling that I was somehow less than everyone else and that I tried desperately hard to disprove by constantly trying desperately hard to prove myself. The feeling of certainty that I what I did, said, felt, needed was somehow of no importance to the rest of the world – my needs would never be met, as they had not been met in that hour on that day, my feelings were not important as they hadn't been honoured in that hour, my words were not important as I had been silenced.

You stole my voice. You have no idea. To you it seemed the right thing – for you – at that point in time. Maybe there was some guilt for a while. Maybe you wondered whether you did the right thing when my mother came to talk to you to ask if anything had happened at school. Maybe you almost told her.

But you didn't.

You took my voice, you stole my life.

Every moment of every day was a fight to survive without realising that the enemy was inside me not outside. My enemy was fear, a fear that had come quickly with no warning, and never left. And that fear fed off every part of me, every thought, every action, everything I said and didn't say. It grew and grew and grew. I could feel the black tar of it swallowing me up until I disappeared – all except some microscopic pinprick of light that flickered dimly at the centre of me, barely perceptible, keeping me alive, generating just enough hope that I woke up every day and fought for my life again.

*

The classroom was noisy. I can't remember specifics. I remember what I needed to know to help me stay alive – how I felt, who said what, what was threatening me. We were gathered around the teacher's desk at the front of the class. I really don't know why. I know she was a new teacher. The previous teacher, with her old habit of pacing the rows of desks in a pair of fur-trimmed Derry boots as she recounted 'history' to us so fast we had to scribble frantically trying to write quickly enough to get every word down, had left. Retired I imagine. The new teacher was young, fashionable and wanted us all to be her friends. She gave off that sense of being interested in us that in reality was just a front and made her feel better about herself more than it did us.

Why were we gathered round her desk? Was someone taking an end of year photo? If the teacher was there how come we were all making so much noise? Yes, yes, it was a photo. Someone must have brought a camera in. Maybe they were leaving? The classrooms were dark. Or were they? So many rooms from my childhood are dark and dingy in my memory. I don't think I have any memories from my childhood – and beyond – of sitting somewhere with glorious sunshine streaming in. How can it have been dark - the classrooms had plenty of windows, lighting, so why was it always dark? Maybe it was grey and raining outside.

She wasn't careful with her words – so few people are. She was telling us where to stand - move to the front, switch to the other side, squeeze up. I had stood at the back. For someone who never really wanted to attract attention I was tall. Five foot ten since the age of eleven, I had learnt to make myself appear shorter, to minimise my presence. I stood at the back, waiting for everyone to sort themselves out, waiting to get it over with. I often got impatient with other people. Even after everything I'm not sure I understand why … had I set myself such a high benchmark that I expected other people to do the same, in the race to fix myself did I need to rush from one thing to the next and didn't have the time to waste waiting for others to catch up. Was it even impatience? Might it have been despair, at the futility of it all? Constantly riding waves of expectations and knowing I'd always be let down. Wanting to let go and enter into the moment but by this point believing nothing would every change, so why bother. Then just wanting to get whatever it was over with and return to the inevitability of my life.

The fun of the moment had gone. I got fed up waiting, perched on the desk behind me and, un-noticeably, extracted myself from the laughter and chitchat. 'Elle, stop hiding your light under a bushel and stand up' came loudly from in front of us. Everyone turned around. Everyone looked at me. My hell. I had nothing to say, no funny comment, no retort, no smile. I was straight back there. Singled out, being told what to do. Shut up, Elle, do as your told.

I stood up. I had a big mop of dark curly hair – it was the eighties – and someone said 'yes, Elle, stop hiding your light under that bushel' pointing at my hair. And some of the girls laughed with her as they pointed.

And they weren't to know. And I didn't know – not until recently – how the fear and the self-hatred and the feelings of worthlessness had burrowed so deep that every moment like that took me back there, re-ignited the fight, flight, freeze reactions of that hour in 1974, and pulled the straps of my straight jacket just a little tighter as I sought to protect myself and my emotions from the world.

*

I have so much to say. But I don't know if I have the patience to take the time to tell my story. I've spent my life running at life, fighting life, doing my best not to waste my time on feelings, emotions, details. And yet these are the very things, when I stop and let my mind wander, that gave my life purpose and meaning, that shaped my existence outside of the mundanity of the everyday. An everyday that I tried so hard to attain, to cling to, and to tether me to some point of 'normality' that might over-ride the subconscious knowing that I had that my life had been and would always be shaped by something that was not – WAS NOT – 'normal'.

I must write it – I know I must. Every time I come back to the question of why I am here, what I should be doing with my time, what I will leave behind, it is words. Always words.

So, I shall write. Forgive me the spikes – the paragraphs I might spit out with no context, no background. Forgive me my getting stuck down rabbit holes of whys and why nots, forgive me the lack of detail and too much detail, forgive me the then and the now … forgive me as I write to forgive myself, to forgive my life, to forgive my present and my future.

But never forgive them. NEVER FORGIVE THEM.

The ethos of 'forgive and forget' does not apply here. There is nothing to be had from forgiving. Plus I cannot forget – so why forgive. I have been through the process of trauma recovery. I have dealt with the anger, the sadness, all the feelings – feelings which I have only let myself feel for the first time in my life as part of that recovery process. But I cannot make it un-happen. I can accept it. I can understand the myriad ways it has affected almost every aspect of my being and my doing. But it will not go away. I can't banish it to some dark recess of my mind – I did that and look what happened. I can't pretend it didn't happen – it did. And I will not –

WILL NOT – forgive them. I will not embrace forgiveness. I will embrace my life, my freedom, my heart, my mind, my soul, my body, my thoughts, I will embrace love. I will not embrace forgiveness. My emotional, spiritual and physical well-being lies on the path of embracing ME – not the path of absolving others from their evil.

I worry will I have the strength to write - to remember, to return, to tell that sadness, that anger, the loss, the missing-ness of so much of the last four decades.

Then I remember that my voice, my words, are my strength.

*

I don't remember the fifteen, thirty minutes directly before. No matter how hard I try whatever comes into my head I know is my thoughts imposed on the memory rather than the memory itself. And the events themselves – time stopped by my hippocampus going off-line, fear, and those words like a death sentence 'don't tell anyone' – were buried for years in my subconscious.

There would be the odd uncertain moment when they would show up in the here and now. For example, a friend recounting a story, in the girls' loos in the college campus pub, of some older boy feeling her up when she and her parents lived abroad. Or another friend recounting a similar story, when we were out for drinks, of a pool boy on holiday making a pass at her.

And, of course, any time I was having sex.

We must have been waiting on little chairs outside the room. You know those ones that had a metal frame and a plastic seat. I guess we were called in alphabetically. I am going to say he was around sixty-five – so difficult to tell with a seven-year old's eyes. He opened the door to let one child out and called my name – Elle – and I got up and walked in the room.

It was a sort of mid-brown colour. Everything about the room in my memory is this rather sickly deep tan colour. Was it wood, or maybe some sort of 1970s Formica?

I was already in my underwear – regulation school pants and a white vest. There is something disturbing to me about the fact the school made us take most of our clothes off and sit around waiting. When you visit the doctor they don't make you undress in the waiting room – why was this acceptable for seven-year olds? Did we somehow have less dignity, less shame? Do they still make kids run around in pants and vests for gym classes? Urgh.

He had on a dingy brown suit. An off-white shirt – maybe cream. A drab tie – maybe brown. Glasses. He smelt. I can remember the smell as I write this. Not a pungent or unusual smell – just the smell of a person and their clothes. No aftershave to cover up the smell of him. No popular 1970s shower gel or deodorant – no

Brut or Old Spice. A slightly musty smell to his clothes – maybe he smoked. I can't be sure.

He asked me some questions – nothing substantial. I stood on one of those things that measure your height and then on some scales to weigh me.

I sat on the bed – you know, like one of those treatment beds in doctors' surgeries and consulting rooms, more of a shelf than a bed. He took his stethoscope in his right hand. The other he put on my left shoulder. He may have lingered a bit. Then his right hand moved down, into my pants, and his left moved up, across my collar bone. His fingers moved inside me. I WAS SEVEN YEARS OLD. I was terrified. I froze. I couldn't speak or make any noise. His hands moved my pants down further. With his left hand now across the base of my neck he undid his trousers and took his old man's penis out and started to put it in me. I WAS SEVEN YEARS OLD. He barely spoke. He made the odd noise. He told me to be quiet, to be a 'good girl'. I WAS SEVEN YEARS OLD.

There was a tap at the door, and it opened a crack. It was the other woman. In a nanosecond she registered what was happening, reached in, grabbed me by the arm, and dragged me out of the room. I don't recall what she said to him – it's never been important.

She pulled me around the corner and into her office and pushed the door half to. She sat me on a chair, still in a state of undress, asking me if I was okay. I couldn't speak. I just sat there, feeling smaller than I was.

The room was oblong, with the door on one short end. I don't remember a window. I just sat there. Diagonally opposite me was the second door – into the headmistress's office.

Seventeen minutes! Seventeen minutes to reach the conclusion that it was easier, better (whatever the hell 'better' means) for them to have this swept under the carpet. What did they talk about for seventeen minutes? Were they disagreeing? Were they so wrapped up in their own shock that they forgot about me? Did they have a cup of fucking tea? I mean – seventeen minutes. For God's sake – why the hell didn't you think about me?

And where was he? What was he doing for that time? Seeing another child? Doing it again? Preparing some sort of excuse – although there wasn't one and never will be? Praying for his life? Feeling guilty? Wishing he could turn back the clock just thirty minutes? Hating himself? And did he spare a thought for me?

Did anyone spare a thought for seven-year-old me?

NO.

*

There is nothing from Before. Nothing. A rare sense of something – happiness, laughter, parents, smiling – will, very occasionally, pass fleetingly through my thoughts. But nothing more. I don't recall my first day at nursery school, my first day at junior school, days at the beach, piggy backs with my father, birthdays, treats, tears, or anything.

That's not quite true – I have one or two memories. I remember being at nursery school. We had to sit quietly in a circle, cross-legged, to drink our morning milk, out of tiny glass bottles with a straw. I laughed. I always laughed. I still do, when I'm nervous or fearful. I start to talk, about anything and everything, find the humour, make myself laugh, make the other person – or people – laugh. And then stop. If I keep prattling on, keep laughing, no one can steal my voice.

That day at nursery school I laughed when I was supposed to be quiet. The teacher came over, told me off and as 'punishment' I had to go and sit on the stage – we were in some sort of local church or community hall, I don't exactly recall – on my own. I felt a curious mixture of shame and the absurdity of being somehow in the wrong for laughing. The rest of the children were shocked into the quietest silence imaginable out of fear that they be shown up in the same way. Even then – Before – my understanding of right and wrong couldn't make sense of the un-necessarily hierarchical and authoritative way the teacher had admonished a five-year-old for laughing.

My mother tells me that all I did Before was laugh, and smile. I was the happiest child. People would comment on how happy I was, how delightful. When my Uncle moved to France and my father worked for an airline I was apparently flown, at less than a year old, over to

Paris. Back in the days when standard airline tickets involved a table and drinks I am told I sat on the table the whole flight and the passengers and stewardesses all commented on my beautiful face – the rosy, chubby cheeks – my sparkling blue eyes, and my smile. I've often wondered whether this was a figment of my mother's imagination as I can't even comprehend being that carefree, perpetually happy little human being.

There are moments in life, with friends, old and new, when you find yourself talking about your first memory, things you did as a baby or child, your earliest memories. Less so the older you get, but somehow in your teens and twenties it's a thing. Maybe because at that age it is still our near past and we don't yet have enough tangible, significant, other experiences to fill the gaps in our understanding and search for who we are. I stole my memories from photos. Stole because they never felt like they were mine. They felt like they should be, because I could see myself in the pictures, but I had the sense I was stealing them from a past that didn't belong to me in the present.

In one photo I am wearing a pair of leopard print zip up slipper booties. I must be two or three. My mother tells me I chose them myself. Along with numerous other colourful choices from my childhood: the deep purple wallpaper with enormous lime green flowers, that superseded a wallpaper with multi-coloured foot high sixties-style cartoon cats; the purple shag-pile carpet; the little fake fur coat and red wellies. I tell the story as though I remember choosing those slippers – in reality I don't even remember having them.

In another photo I am playing at feeding my brother who must, at the time, have been about eighteen months old. My mother tells me that I hit him over the head with a tin opener. I tell the story as though I remember hitting him, and make a joke about that being the reason my brother has always been so mean to me – in reality I don't remember feeding him, I don't remember hitting him and, let's be honest, if I don't remember my life Before then I have to admit to not even remembering him.

Everything is changed by Then. The linear distinction between Before and After is visible from the farthest points of consciousness. Everything was stolen. To have to be told that I was a happy child, yet to not know that, is criminal. To have to be told that my parents were loving and caring because I don't remember it for myself breaks my heart.

Yet there are fleeting glimpses. I keep hoping that, like someone who has suffered a physical trauma to the brain, more memories will start to come back and I can connect with that joy and happiness from my childhood, can connect with what to me feels like the truth of a love of life that in the present often feels like it is manufactured, built upon blocks I had to make myself rather than the strong foundations that life and family should have given me but were taken away within the space of forty-five minutes in 1974.

There was a shortage of grandparents on both my parents' sides. A tough life meant that none of them made it past sixty-two. My Great Aunty Mary – the sister of my mother's mother – was around. And she was lovely. I mean, just wonderful. I don't know why I felt so close to her. I suppose I always felt safe and loved in her presence. And, the older I got, appreciated. When we were little she lived not too far away and I can remember having tea in her front room one evening. And laughing. And my brother was there. It's not much of a memory, maybe a split second of a feeling of joy, of feeling seen, cared for. But it's definitely there.

I have a vague recollection of walking along a corridor in a hotel in Mallorca when I was about five one night when my parents and Mary were having dinner downstairs. The hotel babysitting was a simple intercom in each room that someone somewhere kept an ear out. The memory appears in monochrome like an old black and white photo or movie reel – maybe the darkness of the corridor and the white of the walls fixed it that way in my head. A young woman, a girl, came up to me and asked me what I was doing out of bed. The memory stops there. According to my mother, who recounted the story some years later, I told the girl who came to fine me that a man had come into my room. Was this Before? Or was it After and a figment of the fear that manifested when I was alone in bed in the dark?

*

The pieces of the rest of that day are held together by my mother's words. She came home from work and her daughter was somehow 'gone'. The happiness drained from me. The excitement of being alive no longer there.

She can only tell me that I was changed. She asked me what was wrong and I wouldn't – couldn't – tell her anything. It breaks my heart – seven-year-old me screaming inside for her mother to wrap her up in the warmth of her love and safety yet silenced by a greater fear already instilled in me by that fucking headmistress. Her wicked spell cast me in a sort of concrete – stuck in fear, rigid and unable to express my feelings, my voice somehow constrained, enough room to breathe but words trapped inside me - unable to ask for help to pull me out before the concrete set and I was condemned for life. Frozen – forever? - in that moment. In the terror, horror, and helplessness. Trapped in a perpetual cycle of knowing I should be able to ask for help, knowing people should help, but believing no one will because the two women in front of me never did.

I wouldn't go to sleep that night. I couldn't. And I wouldn't tell my mother why. I couldn't. Thinking back now I have an almost insubstantial feeling of her love for me as she sat on my bed asking me what was wrong, stroking my hair, telling me everything would be okay. It's a curious thing – from that day, from Then, I stopped believing anything would be okay. Although it's not really curious is it. Really it makes perfect sense. My life stopped at the moment he raped me. It could have started again fifteen minutes later if the headmistress and the other woman had behaved as kind, caring, compassionate human beings. But they didn't. They broke me further. I was alive. I lived. I had a life – just not mine.

The sleeping didn't get any better. My parents bought me a beautiful Disney night light. I had to have it on all night. Not so long After I was invited to a friend for a sleep-over. Why do I remember the room so clearly – why that detail and not others? It was flouncy and frilly and floral in that synthetic 1970s way. I couldn't sleep. I could sense my friend's mother was getting frustrated with me after she had dosed me with Nytol and I was still awake. That inherent feeling that I was wrong, that I was being a bad girl because I couldn't sleep. Almost a feeling that I was failing. Who? Myself? My friend? Her mother? Or just failing to be 'good'?

Did her mother call my mother to come and collect me? Did I eventually go to sleep? I don't know. It's a theme through my life. Over and above everything else my mind prioritises memories of the worst of times when that feeling of fear – simultaneously of being abandoned and not being good enough, and all the multiple layers and layers of complexity that became a way of life, a way, ironically, of 'protecting' myself – were present.

Now I like to sleep, ideally, in the pitch black. Where once I needed to know the monster wasn't in the room as I grew older I wanted to block out the world, retreat into myself. Night time became a refuge – the only place where I was safe to let myself feel. How many tears did I cry on how many pillows over the decades of my teenage years, twenties and beyond. Safe in the knowledge that no one could see me, no one would judge me, no one could tell me to pull myself together, to get on with it, not to complain and that I wasn't being a bad girl for feeling sad and hurt and lonely.

Dear god – how I want to go back and hold the hand of that girl who grew into that woman in every moment of her life and tell her she was loved, she was worthwhile, she was right.

My mother became increasingly worried about me. She took me to the local GPs' surgery and we were referred to a doctor specialising in paediatrics. I have no memory of any of this. The doctor asked my mother a few questions, asked me but I was understandably quiet. Her advice to my mother – give the child some Calpol, she may be looking for attention.

I was looking for attention! Of course I was. But I was petrified that if I did I would somehow be doing something wrong. There was that time, not long ago, when I was frightened, hurt, shaking, didn't know what had happened but knew it had been wrong, and the people – those two women who ostensibly had a duty of care – who should have told me everything was ok, looked after me and made it better instead told me that I had done something wrong, that I wasn't to tell anyone, that I should be a good girl, that no one would believe me.

And so it began.

*

I couldn't sleep. And the more I couldn't sleep the more anxious I was getting. I'd had insomnia on and off all my life, some dark periods when I had had to contact the local doctor's surgery for sleeping pills or once, diazepam, and it had taken several weeks for my sleep patterns to re-set. It wasn't un-heard of for me to lie in bed listening to my own thoughts imploding as I went down a well-travelled rabbit hole of self-destruction. But this was different. The anxiety was coming in waves. I couldn't order my thoughts. Every time I lay down telling myself to breathe, to calm my body, to become aware of my presence - the bed beneath me, the weight of the quilt – the tears came like a tsunami. There was no quiet crying or silently sobbing into the pillow here. And the more I tried to mentally sedate myself the wilder my emotions became. I tried to tell myself everything was okay, I would be fine, this would pass, everything would be alright tomorrow, but the more I tried the more my mind rejected the thoughts as it started to build great monuments of self-loathing, like pillars around me that were becoming denser and denser as my own fear closed in on me and finally trapped me until all I could do was howl and scream.

Hours I spent like this. Hours. And hours. And hours. Until I can only assume exhaustion took me and I slept for a short while until the alarm went off and the obligation of work weighed heavily on me.

I was shaken, shaking. I felt un-solid, as though something had swept through me, disturbing everything, and in its wake leaving every cell in my body jolted and jostled out of place.

I was fearful. A fear about what had happened last night and some inherent feeling of fear that I couldn't shake off, or out.

It was as though I had been possessed. The shock waves of whatever I had been feeling had washed over me as I lay there, and quite literally lurched through me, my body following the tremors as it was pulled from horizontal to vertical so I could howl once more at the dark space around me and quietly scream and hiss – at what I didn't know.

It was the same desperate thoughts I'd had for years – for all the life I could remember – and the same prayers.

It's not fair. It's not fair.

I can't …. I can't … but never able to get beyond those two words to find out what I couldn't.

I hate my life.

Why me? What did I do wrong?

There's no-one. No-one … I need someone to help but there's never anyone.

Over and over on repeat. The soundtrack to my tears. The finale to the devastating self-talk that typically preceded the long periods of depression from my twenties and thirties and still, from time, crept up and took me by surprise just when I thought everything was okay.

I messaged work and told them I hadn't been well in the night and would have to see how I went with work during the course of the day. Any sane person would have signed off sick but I had my own complex set of equations to work through before I could ever arrive at that conclusion.

My next thought was fuck, I need to get some sleeping pills otherwise I'm not going to be able to cope. Never the other way around – I never thought, oh, something is up, I must take some time out, look after myself, practice self-care. Always the same – I must keep going, I can't fail, I can't let anyone down, I'll be 'fine'.

I called the doctor's surgery. I asked if I could get a repeat prescription, although it must have been a few months surely since I last called? She suggested the emergency doctor for the day should speak with me – I would receive a call. I sat, and I waited. I called or messaged my mother – I don't remember which – and said I'd had a dreadful night of not-sleep. The mobile rang and it was the GP. I explained I was anxious and not sleeping. Apparently this was an emergency – I needed to come into the surgery and talk to a doctor face to face. An appointment was booked for an hour or so later. I made myself look presentable and waited. My mother called back to tell me that they were going to drive up to be with me. They would be there late lunch time.

It's about a ten-minute walk to the surgery. It was Autumn but the sky was clear and the day was bright. I was not. I was in a sleep-deprived, anxiety-fuelled daze – a level of fuzziness that meant I could barely hold a sentence together in my head. Trains of thought went into tunnels that led into darker tunnels and never came out.

Count your steps. If all else fails, count your steps. One, two, three, four ... or one-and, two-and, three-and, four-and ... . Or into 4/4 time ... one-hundred-and-one, one-hundred-and-two, ... measuring distance, measuring time, measuring my thoughts so my mind couldn't escape and run riot again. I had counted steps for years. No idea when it started. I would often walk if I was feeling stuck in some negative cycle of thinking. On a good day just twenty minutes could set me free, most often forty, and then there were the days that no amount of walking would take me away from the thoughts I'd set out with. I had walked and cried – mostly behind dark glasses in the summer when it was safer – walked and ranted and then I realised, the quickest way to stop my thoughts travelling faster than a motorbike in a globe of death was to focus on counting my steps. Most days on the way home from work, from a line in the pavement slabs at one end of the street to my front door, I counted. A form of decompression. Never the same number. It varied depending on my shoes, my mood, the strength of my spirit.

I registered at the self-check-in and took a seat.

I was in a daze. The world around me playing out as it always did, the world inside me indistinct, unfathomable, lost. I could think of nothing – absolutely nothing. My mind could barely hold a word, half a sentence let alone a whole thought. I felt incredibly small yet with a force inside me that if I screamed could stop the world spinning. I felt so small it was as though I was only a miniature version of myself hiding somewhere in the centre of my chest like a tiny Russian doll. And because I was buried so deep inside me I sort of knew no one would hear that scream.

I waited and waited. At that point in time I would have waited all day, all week. After about twenty-five minutes the doctor came over to me, apologised, with what seemed like genuine concern, and asked if I would mind seeing a junior doctor - effectively the 'work experience'. I'm sure there is a more polite term but it escapes me. I was polite – "Of course, that's fine." What else, in the circumstances, was I going to say? The doctor assured me I shouldn't have to wait much longer and walked away.

Fifteen or so minutes later the board flashed up my name calling me to one of the rooms downstairs. I went down, knocked on the door, he called me in. He was obviously in the cheap seats – a consulting room with no window. He asked me why I was there and I explained, matter of factly, about the previous night, my call to the surgery, the suggestion I needed to come in for an appointment. Default, as ever, set to 'chirpy with a dollop of let's laugh about it on the side'.

I don't know what changed. I don't know what, on that day, changed. I can only imagine it came from the part of me that knew it couldn't cope any more, knew it couldn't carry on like this, pretending, trying, dying inside. He asked me if there was any reason I might have been feeling anxious.

I replied, trying hard to sound like I wasn't a victim, 'I was sexually abused when I was seven'.

The tears started – my face scrumpled as my eyes overflowed and my mouth stifled the loud sobs that I wouldn't let myself let out.

He asked me more. I don't remember the order the questions came.

Had I told anyone about it before? Had I received any help before? Could I tell him what happened and when?

I answered all the questions. Words that hadn't been spoken in forty-five years through that feeling of shame and the fear that no-one would believe me and I would somehow be banished – from what or who I didn't know.

He was sympathetic. There were tissues. He didn't take notes, didn't take his attention off me, he simply listened and asked.

I joked that this probably wasn't what he was expecting when on his first Monday at the surgery. I thanked him – too profusely? – for listening.

He asked if he could go and speak with the GP – he'd be back in five minutes. I told him not to shut the door. Alone, in that room, with the door shut, not knowing what anyone outside was doing or saying, I would feel trapped, abandoned, prisoner to everyone else's decisions about me.

He was gone ten minutes. When he came back he stuck his head around the door and asked if I could come with him to the GP's consulting room. I picked up my coat and bag and we moved.

There were three men in the room. Looking back I wonder if they had really thought this through. Details are so important.

Another work experience and the GP.

The GP wanted to briefly go over everything I'd disclosed again as he took notes. I saw those notes later – for all that he seemed to write copious notes that day there were no more than a couple of short sentences in my medical records. I recall him saying to me 'and it was a doctor at your school?' and him responding 'you've done a brave thing' as I nodded and whispered 'Yes' in reply to the question. The irony.

He told me I needed to talk to people about it. I asked how? He couldn't answer that. Just that it was important to let people know what was going on, how I felt, what was happening so I could have their support. I sat there bemused, angry – annoyed that he didn't realise that if I'd felt able to talk to family and friends I would have done that before. And in fact, on the few occasions I had disclosed it to anyone, had been shot down by their response or lack of response.

He said he would refer me to the Tavistock Centre for 'trauma recovery services'. I should get a referral assessment appointment within eight weeks and then be referred for treatment shortly after that.

I asked what I could do between now and then. I was petrified. I needed a lifeline – to know that someone was listening, someone was there, I wasn't going to be abandoned again at my moment of greatest need. He suggested I come in to see him in a couple of weeks – book the appointment at reception upstairs.

I was too grateful as I walked out. They had done no more than they should have done in the circumstances and yet I was grateful that they had done that. I laughed, smiled, joked about that being quite the hour and a half. I assumed that the worst was over.

I can't be sure if it was that first visit or a subsequent one but the GP made a passing comment that he liked my pink coat 'you always look so vibrant when you come in' or something along those lines. I think my reply was 'no one would ever know what's going on underneath'.

*

I walked home, drained, lost, shell-shocked, confused. My parents were sitting in the car outside waiting for me. I don't know if I was pleased to see them – I was at the same time both relieved not to be on own and not sure how to navigate any usual patterns of behaviour in the context of what had just happened.

I don't know how I made it through the next few hours. On no more than an hour's restless sleep, after the enormity of it all. Exhausted by all those tears, by the fear of disclosing what I had had to hide for all those decades, by the fear of reprisal. I don't even know what that means - surely he was dead, she was dead, there was no one to 'reprise' me. I somehow made it through a very late lunch at the café in Regents Park.

Things that come to mind: organising where to sit, going to the counter to order and then paying for lunch; being aware my father really didn't know how to have any conversation around this – and why would he – and would have done almost anything to avoid being there; not feeling like either of them understood the near-impossibility of what had happened just a few hours earlier and the almost unbearable weight of something; feeling like I was having to call time on proceedings as I was so horribly tired; desperately wanting my parents to leave so I could be on my own and have a cry but not, equally desperately, wanting to be on my own.

They left.

Nothing. Nothing more from that day except the expectation of bed and the apprehension around taking a sleeping pill.

I lay there, one zopiclone down, waiting. If you haven't had zopiclone I will do my best to describe them. They create this metallic taste in your mouth two or three seconds after you swallow them. When you aren't over-anxious or over-tired you have this vague sense of your thoughts losing order as they start to work – not immediately but over maybe fifteen or thirty minutes. I rarely look at the clock from the point I get into bed until the point I wake up – the time is not an insomniac's friend. The next thing you are asleep. On the lowest dosage you can get anywhere from a couple of hours to a full night's sleep depending how anxious you are. The next day they leave you feeling muzzy-headed, a bit like a hangover without any of the other symptoms. And that taste – it lingers. Every time I took one of those bloody zopiclone the taste the next day was a reminder that I had somehow failed, that I was somehow failing, that I 'couldn't cope'.

I hated them but thanked god for them. Without the sleeping pills I wouldn't have been able to keep going at work and subsequently wouldn't have been able to pay the mortgage and the bills.

I lay there that night waiting, waiting. Trusting it would kick in, worried it wouldn't. After what I guessed was forty-five minutes I was still awake, still fizzing uncontrollably inside with anxiety and now worrying about not being able to work the next day – I know, I know, such mis-placed priorities. I took another, at maximum dosage now, and, at some point fell asleep.

*

The fear of the dark, a fear of not knowing what or who was in the corners of a room, the need to be alert and protect myself, all were a constant subconscious accompaniment to my life for forty-five years. And the residue seems to linger, to have morphed. No matter how much I want or try to change things - perspective, places, people, patterns – sleep remains my Achilles heel. I know what, ultimately, will change it, but I don't know – yet? – how to get there.

As a child, in the years immediately After, I would go downstairs and sit in the lounge with my parents, safe. I don't remember the lying there, not sleeping, and I don't remember whether I was counting time, but at about half eight, nine o'clock, I would open the door, walk along the landing, down the stairs, and push the door so it was open an inch or two and wait until one or other of my parents spotted me. Maybe it was the same exchange each night 'can't sleep darling?' A shake of my head. And in I went to sit next to one or other of them, or between them, on the hideous 1970s tan leatherette sofas that squeaked as you moved, with the tiny holes in the arms where the cover, stretched taut, had split as ash from one of the cigarettes or cigars that my parents and their friends smoked 'on social occasions' had missed the ashtray.

I remember watching things, in that extra hour of television, that possibly an eight-year old should not have been watching. I fell in love with Spike Milligan. I couldn't tell you the first thing about the Q series now. I don't remember one sketch, one joke. But I remember him. Some connection was formed – maybe some shared despair as I learned more about the man growing up.

One night I came down and witnessed a doctor performing a tracheotomy on a patient. Rudimentary surgery with a scalpel on someone who couldn't breathe. Often I would get in to bed and little me would worry that my breathing wasn't right and that the same thing would happen to me. And it filled me with a terror. A terror I couldn't understand until I wrote that sentence and understood that I couldn't bear the idea of someone – a doctor – getting that close to me.

I still get in to bed at night and lie there breathing in, breathing out, wondering if I have cancer of the oesophagus, or a problem with my heart. Even after everything I continue to do this. Even after everything, all these years later, is there a part of me terrified that there will be some reason for 'him' to put his hand around my neck and do that to me again? I can barely see for the tears as I write this. How the fuck have I lived with all this shit and come out of it alive.

I have always hated having to share a room with someone. Not a boyfriend – that's a whole lot of complicated in its own right – but friends, family, anyone that might judge me.

I never slept well or easily. Over the years there have been so many rituals – getting into bed, getting to sleep, going back to sleep if I wake up. It's a lot. And people

– even people that call themselves your friends – can be so judgemental. If you've never had insomnia you'll not understand. I don't mean the odd couple of days when you've had a bad night's sleep because of problems at work, or because you broke up with your boyfriend, or because your cat has had to be put down. I mean the 'for absolutely no discernible reason at all' type of not sleeping. Either you can't get off to sleep, or you wake up in the middle of the night and can't get back to sleep, or you wake up far too early and another couple of hours eludes you.

The older I get, and especially after the last couple of years, the less I care what others might think, but as a teenager, when acceptance was so integral, sharing a room was a nightmare. I didn't – and don't – like noise before I go to bed. I need quiet, calm. I need to feel SAFE. For most of my life it would take me a long time to get off to sleep – maybe forty-five minutes, an hour, at a guess. If I was on my own I could toss and turn, I had a teddy bear or some other cuddly creature I could hug, I could put the light on and read a few pages of a book, I would have pretend conversations with someone who understood me, loved me and was sympathetic, caring and kind. If I was sharing a room I worried about making any noise or creating any disturbance that would wake the other person up, or being mocked for being childish and still sleeping with cuddly animals. It was always the same comments 'What is wrong with you!' 'For God's sake just go to sleep'. I wish I could turn back the clock and answer 'I was raped when I was seven' and 'I can't - I'm afraid of the dark and when I lie here and shut my eyes I get stuck in the terror of it'.

And they might have replied 'Oh my God Elle, I'm so sorry' and come over and put an arm around me and let me cry and cry and cry …

If you want to help someone in your life help them to feel safe.

It was as I approached my late twenties that the tendency towards restless and disturbed sleep began to distort into something more complex and impactful. I had been living with a boyfriend for a couple of years. We'd split up and through the generosity of the landlady I was staying on in the flat on my own. At the same time work was becoming more stressful – at the age of just twenty-six I had been appointed manager of a small team, very admin focused, low level stuff, keep the wheels turning – but with the arrival of a new director with great plans I found myself managing a team of twelve, working to support delivering projects into big clients. At one point I was working ten, eleven, twelve-hour days, and weekends, to get contracts signed ahead of un-movable deadlines. So I found myself, within the space of about eighteen months, living on my own for the first time, responsible for the running of the home, projected into the limelight at work and responsible for my team delivering successfully and on time, without a boyfriend that I had come to rely on for an extended social life – however much, in hindsight, we should never have been together – and with no one at home to make me a cup of tea and 'make it all better', or do the shopping, or take me out for dinner, or to talk to about how stressful work had been that day.

Every few months I would have one night when I barely slept at all and then over the next couple of nights it would reset and all be forgotten. I was younger – in your twenties you can get away with practically no sleep and somehow still bounce through the next day. I never tried to analyse why. It was just a thing. Another 'thing' to add to the list of 'things' buried deep in behaviours and beliefs borne from forty-five minutes of my life all those years ago.

As I headed through my early and mid-thirties I started to creak. Outwardly, tangibly, the strain of increasingly stressful jobs. Inwardly, and without my being aware of it, the stress of coping with hiding so much for so many years. The further I ran away from the monster the more the fear engulfed me. I began to have this recurrent image, always as I walked to or from the gym at the weekend, of the black tar running through my blood, my veins, my lungs, covered in it, making every step an effort, leaving a trail of it behind me. I had a nervous breakdown when I was thirty-six – I don't think anyone except my parents really knew. I somehow made it to forty. Then, at the age of forty-four, my world as I had created it and lived it started to end.

Who knows why things happen when they do – why the next bit of rubbish, no different from the last, tips the bin over and spills its contents. I was doing a ridiculously stressful job, contracting for a financial services organisation. My manager was leaving – did he resign or was he pushed? I can't recall. And I had, to all intents and purposes, been told they would make me an offer for a permanent position at a competitive salary, to replace him. I was working silly hours – in the office until seven pm or later – for months. I kept pushing to prove that I was worth 'it' – worth the investment - despite the fact that I was tired, stressed and probably well on the way to burning out. I finally got some time in the diary of the CIO – had he been avoiding me? – and he completely pulled the rug out from under me. No – I must have been mistaken – there was no job, there was no competitive salary. As I had no voice I sat there, with the tsunami inside of me unable to get out, accepting that this was the way grown-up, responsible, professional people behaved. Me …. I didn't matter. I just had to put up and shut up.

I got back to my desk, fuming, angry, wanting to cry at the unfairness of it all, somehow knowing that this was wrong but being powerless to express that, or to stand up for myself, or even to walk away. Not five minutes later I got a text message from a man I had met on holiday in the summer – tall, ex-professional sportsman, living in Spain, and a fan of Arsenal. He was in the UK and going to the match that evening. Did I want to meet for a drink afterwards? The anger was replaced by hope. The part of me that desperately wanted someone to love me, to let me know that I wasn't unlovable, and was on a careless search for someone to both prove me wrong and prove me right, said Yes. If he could get to my local tube station after the match I'd meet him there. 'After 10' came the answer. 'See you then,'

I remember what I was wearing. Indigo jeans, a vest top and a chunky beige roll neck sweater over the top.

In the perfect storm of everything aligning for one perfect, almighty fuck-up I had been for acupuncture the day before to stop smoking.

I messaged around half nine – something along the lines of hoping it was a good game, he was winning, etc. No reply. I messaged again just after ten. By now I had opened a bottle of red wine. Ten thirty – still nothing. I took the glass of wine and went and sat in my spare room with the window open and lit a cigarette. Eleven, I messaged again. Gone. I began the slow decline that had marked disappointments throughout my life and was my gradual lean into depression.

Depression – that unwanted guest who shows up out of the blue, hijacks my self-esteem, turns the setting on all my thoughts to negative and tries to make everything I do and am seem pointless.

I finished the bottle of wine. It was after midnight. Let down three times in the space of half a day – twice by other people and once by myself. Angry, sad, feeling like a failure, hating myself for a reason I can't comprehend or explain, drunk, agitated, I get into bed. I expect to go straight off because of the wine but I don't. I am fizzing but not in a good way. Trying to quell whatever uprising is going on in body and mind.

*

I didn't sleep for three weeks, at least not more than two or three hours a night. I'd get in to bed, exhausted, and my mind would crank itself up into a frenzy of thinking.

For most of my adult life bed was my relief and release. I don't know if it is anyway 'normal' – what constitutes 'normal' after all – but over the course of my teenage years and adult life I had a 'pretend' boyfriend. I don't want to use the word 'imaginary' – for some reason it makes me think of a lonely child with some undefined problem. But then I suppose that was me. This pretend boyfriend was so real to me. Maybe some part of me believed that one day he would turn up. Did I look for him in any man I became involved with romantically – possibly. From the age of about thirty, after I split up with my only ever 'long-term' boyfriend, the story I created around him was so clear and so detailed I probably could have passed him off as real if anyone had ever asked me about him. Anyway, who is to question what is 'real' and what is not. If our thoughts create our reality then he was part of mine.

He was the only person I knew who understood me.

Why do I feel so ashamed to talk about this? Will I be judged, mocked, pitied? Will anyone even think 'oh my god I didn't realise how lonely, how trapped, how sad, how desperate, she was'?

He lived in a large apartment about five minutes' walk from me. He was four years older. Tall. With a thick head of hair. His apartment was far bigger than mine, with two bedrooms, a terrace off both the main room and his bedroom. There were heaters on the main terrace and an outdoor sofa and we would sit there, drink a bottle of wine, and talk. I could be me. He didn't push me away or make fun of me if I was feeling sad or depressed. He wanted to help. He would put his arm around me and I would feel safe. He loved me – for no other reason than he loved me.

His name was Jay. Or was it simply J? I could never quite decide on that. Short for Jason. I'm not sure I'd ever known a Jason. Maybe that was why.

I would lie in bed and create the same scenario every night. In his kitchen cooking together, on the sofa talking, on the terrace talking. I craved the closeness with someone, I craved being loved, being supported, being cared for. I would imagine over and over telling him I loved him and him telling me he loved me too. He didn't lie. He didn't say one thing and do another. He wasn't a selfish, self-absorbed, inconsiderate prick.

When this insomnia started no matter how hard I tried I couldn't find him. I could get as far as being in his apartment, opening a bottle of wine, … but then the fantasy would begin to creak and fade. I tried to talk to him but he was distant, fed up with me. He tried to look after me but I could tell his heart wasn't in it. And one night I called out, over and over 'I love you I love you I love you I love you …' and there was nothing, no answer, no echo of those words and he'd gone.

I was so lost, so broken, so distressed that even my pretend friend didn't want anything to do with me. How much do you have to hate yourself, hate your life, for someone who isn't real to turn their back on you? How much hope do you have to have lost that your imagination can't conjure up even a flicker of faith?

Three weeks. Life was becoming impossible. Yet instead of doing the sensible thing and saying I wasn't well and taking some time out to look after myself I carried on working, dragging myself into the office every day, fuelling myself to keep going. Incredible how only ten, fifteen, or so years ago, in 2011, 'mental health' didn't exist in the context of work. It was still some bizarre admission of your inability to cope with your job if you took time out because there was something wrong with your mind.

And, of course, I couldn't 'fail'. Couldn't let the responsible adults, my so-called 'superiors' think I wasn't 'good' enough.

Three fucking weeks I carried on like that. I made myself walk six, eight miles on Saturdays and spend ninety minutes in the gym on Sundays to wear myself out – pushing my collapsing mind and body closer to the edge. I started to look like shit. I bought an insanely expensive eye cream as though that might help fix things. I told people I wasn't sleeping, they told me about the nights they hadn't slept, when their boyfriend split up with them or when they were ill. No one said to me – three weeks Elle, are you okay? What's going on? Do you want to talk about it, shall we take half an hour out and get a coffee?

I was having my hair done. I'd had the same hairdresser for aeons. Des. Every four or five weeks I get my roots done. Every eight to ten weeks I have a cut and colour. And, of course, a blow dry.

I sat in the chair and, as usual, he asked me how my hair had been. It's a strange relationship with your hairdresser – a long term friend but one you only see in the mirror as they stand behind you, never face to face. Did that make it easier to open the door, a tiny bit, so the edges of my emotions could squeeze through but safe in the knowledge that however weak I was feeling I could pull the door to or at least retreat behind it?

Or was it the human contact? I have had such mixed emotions about anyone touching me. On the one hand that innate subconscious terror that however kind or harmless they seemed, however well I might know them, however inappropriate it might be, that they would touch me like 'he' did. And on the other a fear that if anyone reached out and made the slightest contact with me when I was feeling vulnerable – which if I'm honest was one of the over-riding emotions that was always just below the surface – I might crack, break and never be able to put myself back together. I'd spent a lifetime pretending to be someone and something I wasn't, all the time with the real me screaming silently to get out, hoping someone would see her.

My eyes welled up. He asked, with that gentle Irish intonation, what was up? I told him I hadn't slept for three weeks. He put his hands on my shoulders, breathed a sigh of relief, and said something along the lines of 'thank God – I thought you were going to tell me you had a cancer' – or words to that effect. He advised carbs and a drink. When I left the salon ninety minutes or so later I went straight to the off-licence up the road and bought a bottle of booze (Disaronno – really!). I went home and ordered pizza. I never ordered pizza, never ordered delivery food. I almost always cooked for myself - another of the small but plentiful actions to prove my 'goodness'. Even as I write this I don't expect anyone to understand. Every fucking thing I did was to try and prove to that fucking bitch and her accomplice that I was good. That I was therefore somehow worthy. It's an exhausting and impossible way to live – trying to attain 'goodness' in someone else's eyes when you don't even know the other person's definition of it, and, let's be honest, that person's opinion of you really shouldn't be of any consequence to you anyway.

And the fear – the abject terror – that if you aren't seen as 'good' by that other person – be it family, your best friend, your colleagues, your boss, your teacher, every bloody person that you meet on your way through life to the point where you think people walking down the street or sitting on the bus are judging you – that they will reject you. And the times – oh so many times – when you reject yourself so you can avoid them doing it for you.

I ate the pizza. It was around ten o'clock and 24 Hour Party People was on one of the channels as I flicked through. Music and the odd tortured soul. Right up my street. Des had suggested I take a couple of days off work sick, so I watched until late, drank one (or two) too many and eventually went to bed about one. The alcohol didn't quieten my mind but it somehow slowed down my thoughts and confused them. I slept.

*

Alcohol – specifically the sweet digestif that is Disaronno that didn't feel as 'dangerous' as vodka or gin - became a sort of crutch over the next six weeks or so. I alternated between taking one of the disgusting Zopiclone the GP prescribed and drinking several large glasses of that sickly sweet almond liqueur. I woke up the morning of Christmas Eve and my body felt toxic. 'No more' I thought. My parents were coming to stay for Christmas. I rang them and said 'get here as soon as you want' I didn't want to be on my own – needed a distraction from my head and the sense that I wasn't alone.

I busied myself with moving the furniture around so I could set up the king size blow up bed in my six foot by nine-foot spare room. I made the trip to Waitrose at the end of the road to pick up what was surely the last shopping I needed.

We had a nice couple of days. I had one glass of wine with Christmas lunch and determined that I would get myself out of the seemingly self-destructive pattern I'd been in. No, I didn't get under the covers on my bouncy bed and fall straight in to a deep sleep but, somehow, I reckon I managed six or seven hours sleep. I could do this – I could reset. I had some time off work and I would sort myself out.

Over the next few years, as the insomnia came and went, there followed a very strange set of rituals that became the norm but seemed to keep my afloat. Stranger than the numerous tricks and tips I'd tried earlier in the month, which included: turning all devices, including the TV, off at nine o'clock so my mind could switch off – which of course didn't work because for the hour or so before bed I had no distraction but my thoughts; sitting with my feet in a large, cake-sized Tupperware thing (in the absence of anything else) full of warm water and lavender oil – I'd read somewhere it helped; and acupuncture.

Everyone seems to have a theory on how to 'fix' insomnia. In my experience none of them actually work. You can do your absolute utmost to relax, to switch off, but if you are suffering from a fairly decent bout of anxiety, there is nothing that can stop your mind whirring into action when you turn the light out at night. No amount of deep breathing or tapping or 'sensing the weight of the bed beneath you' can do more than dial the sound of your thoughts down a notch or two only for the volume to turn itself back up loud in the silence of the night. It's like taking propanalol for anxiety – hopeless. And more of that later – bloody GPs.

I had been having acupuncture for a while. I started when I got really bad psoriasis. I mean – really bad. I was covered from the neck down in small to medium sized angry red dots and circles of itchy flaky skin. People at the gym would stare at my legs. People on the tube would stare even when I was wearing fifty denier opaque tights. The acupuncturist I was seeing was lovely – kind, calm, gentle. I could walk in after work feeling like you could wipe the floor with me and leave an hour later feeling restored. The psoriasis didn't miraculously disappear but if I felt better I would take it.

When I got insomnia my regular acupuncturist had had to take some time out as she was pregnant and had been told to rest in the last trimester because of complications. I called to book and booked with whoever was available that Saturday lunch. The usual stuff – she asked what was going on, a multitude of questions, I answered and off we went. I'm sure there was a perfectly acceptable reason for it but she started a small bonfire somewhere near my navel. I can't remember what she used, but I do remember smelling the incense or whatever plants or herbs she had used burning. She left it there for a minute, maybe two, then magicked it away and we went back to the needles. But I was gone. The apparent nonsense had set me off and all I could think of whilst I lay there with tiny needles stuck in my energy channels was some hilarious meme of a duck that my brother had sent me. Nothing wrong with anything that makes you laugh. The more I've been through and the more I understand the human condition the more I truly deeply believe that laughter is one of the best medicines. Not a cure-all but close.

Yoga makes me laugh. I enrolled for beginners' lessons I think in about 2012. Oh yes, I thought, I would start yoga after that Christmas, after my 're-set'. The teacher was oh so lovely. I wasn't very flexible and bendy but I made it past beginners' and into a regular class. The teacher left. I joined another class but everytime I ended up in some position where my body was being stretched further than it had been stretched before I laughed. Not some bloody great guffaw but a quiet enough giggle. Did he think I was taking the piss? Anyway, oblivious to the words of the Dalai Lama and Thich Nhat Hanh on Laughter he told me I should 'take it seriously'.

Fucking hell. Life was serious enough.

And if I didn't laugh the likelihood was I would cry.

I tried another beginners' class at a studio near me and, determined not to laugh, I found myself lying on my back with my legs entwined in ropes up the wall desperately holding back tears. Desperately wanting the girl taking the class to notice, to come over, to ask me if I was okay.

I held firm. Resolute. Managed to stop the tears from escaping down my face – a skill I perfected over the years in an attempt to hide. Red, watering eyes could be many things – conjunctivitis, a stray eyelash, contact lenses gone awol – but tears running down the face had no other explanation.

I got into some groove of 'coping'. To be honest every part of my life became about coping. One of the first conversations I had with a psychologist about being raped at seven and being told to cover it up was around the record that had got stuck in my head on the words 'I can't cope'. Over and over again some evenings, on a bloody loop.

I can't cope. I can't cope. I can't cope.

I 'coped' until something threw me off balance. The trigger was always emotional. I was piecing it together but I still couldn't get past the surface of what was 'wrong'. The trauma was still buried so deep, still hadn't managed to find a way out. Years of control and twenty-four-hour surveillance on my part, had been working – I couldn't tell anyone, I wouldn't tell anyone.

But man alive it wanted to come out. My body, mind and heart were coming under constant fire as I fought to keep it buried and it fought to break out.

I met my brother for brunch one weekend. It was April, around his birthday, and the Easter after that Christmas. I'd been maintaining a steady course for the last few months. Some interesting quirks had developed, like the ritual of going to bed only to get up at midnight to smoke one cigarette and have a glass of milk then go back to bed and sleep soundly.

Here is the logic. Milk apparently helps you sleep. And for me, smoking is quite literally about 'smoke and mirrors' – a cigarette deflects me from seeing my thoughts clearly. Smoking has, sadly, been one of the strongest distractions through the last decades. I wish I could stop. One day.

We had a table at The Delauney near Covent Garden. Very nice indeed.

You know what – I don't remember the details. One moment we were having a nice brunch, the next something had been said that hurt me, emotionally, at my core. It's a horrible feeling – you are fine then suddenly, completely unforeseen, it is like your heart drops from your chest into your stomach, the blood drains from your head, there is a vortex of energy spinning and making you feel dizzy and light-headed, and you lose the ability to think straight. Some chemical and emotional reaction takes over. You start to feel like you are going to cry. I started to feel like I was going to cry. I was hurt and I was hurting. But I couldn't say anything, I couldn't speak up, I couldn't reply and say how I felt, I couldn't. I tried really hard but I was stuck in the terror of that moment all those years ago – if I want to be good, if I want to do the right thing, I have to keep my mouth shut and not let anyone know how I feel, how they have made me feel.

Not just my voice taken away, but the right to feel and express any feelings. Forty-five minutes of my life ruined my life. Unable to disagree - ever. Carrying around the weight of my own belief that I wasn't allowed to tell anyone if I was feeling frightened, angry, hurt, sad, upset, lonely, … . Hours and hours I've had to put in – days and even weeks or months – to letting myself feel those feelings now, in this second go at life.

What more is there to say about sleep, or the lack of it? Except that it is like some weird addiction – once you've had chronic insomnia you have to accept you will always be an insomniac. Any night you get into bed, stressed, anxious, depressed, you hear that little voice at the back of your head wondering if you'll get off to sleep … or if it's back.

*

I don't really know what any of my friends from my teenage years and twenties thought of me. I felt ugly, un-loveable and generally unlikeable. I was so grateful for any crumb of friendship that came way because I hated myself and my life so much. Everyone's life always seemed, to me, so much better. Other people, friends, seemed happy, more easy going, less concerned with everything. They dived into life and I always felt I was hovering somewhere at the margins trying to hide my fear and pretend I was having a good time. In my head I would be having never-ending conversations with myself about what was wrong with me, and re-playing (over and over and over again) conversations with friends to work out whether I'd said or done anything that might mean they would, could, should, find fault with me and 'reject' me.

It must have been exhausting even then. By the time I got to about forty it felt like I was trying to balance a tower of acrobatic elephants on a pin in my head. By the time I got to forty-five and beyond it felt like I was lying underneath that tower of elephants struggling to breathe.

But friends, and boyfriends, can be unkind. God I wish I'd known then one iota of what I know now.

Actually, it's wider than friends and boyfriends. It's so many people – teachers, family, so-called therapists, colleagues and employers, and some of the random folk that pass in and out of your life during the course of any day.

I know we all have our own shit going on at any point in time, but we, the human race, for all the posts on social media promoting 'kindness' can be rude, selfish, judgemental, dismissive idiots – but still manage to justify our behaviour to ourselves.

The problem was I could never answer back or stand up for myself. It had been made quite clear that if I wanted to 'be good', to do the right thing, to make other people happy, to make my teachers happy, my parents happy, ... then I had to put up and shut up. I still struggle to completely grasp the scale of the impact of that bitch's few words and her lack of action on my life. Logically I understand it. It's been explained to me what happened and why. And how the layers and layers and layers and layers of need to self-protect became an increasingly complex set of things I needed to do or not do, be or not be, to try and keep myself safe from the threat of something that happened just once and all those years ago. It has been suffocating.

As I said, I have been tall from a young age. Five foot ten at the age of eleven – can you believe it! I was the tallest person at junior school, with the exception of Steven, who came in at the same height. It wasn't easy for someone who physically stood out to make themselves disappear. Somehow making myself smaller inside, not wanting to be seen, to be noticed, worked – no-one ever believed I was as tall as I was. But I couldn't get away from 'being seen'. With a mop of dark brown curly hair and the '80s fast approaching I thought I stood out like a sore thumb. The jokes at my expense started. I don't know how anyone would have known what was going on inside me and I was so ultra-sensitive to all the remarks but each one cut me deep and was further proof of everything that was so wrong with me. Whether it was the innocent comments st school about 'hiding my light under a bushel' or being so tall and having so much hair I I looked like a tree at the back of photos, or the more disturbing comment and 'look' from a friend's uncle when I was there one summer afternoon playing swingball in the garden that 'Tina is pretty. Very pretty' after he'd bought my eleven year old friend an age-inappropriate strappy yellow playsuit and made her try it on, while I say there on the sofa like a spare part in my khaki terry towelling shorts and a t-shirt.

I didn't want any man to notice me. I knew what men could do. I wanted to be invisible. But as my teenage years arrived I wanted a boyfriend – I wanted to be, to feel, normal. It was a fucking nightmare. I had no idea what was going on in my head. But for some reason I just didn't react, feel and behave the same way as any other girl I knew of my age. And I couldn't talk about it because, as we already know, I had (A) been silenced and (B) I knew no-one would be interested in me.

I don't recall the exact route to the beginning of the madness that engulfed my twenties and thirties but looking back I sense the impression that the struggle to fit in, to be like everyone else, was having on me. The more I tried to be 'normal' the harder my mind and body resisted it. Being 'normal' at fourteen, fifteen, sixteen, meant talking to boys, flirting, talking about boys, talking about french-kissing. Nothing that my subconscious would let me do as they all put me in danger of a boy – like him – doing something bad that I didn't want to happen again. I already hated myself, I already knew I was worthless, and this inability to be like 'everyone else' compounded those feelings, that knowledge. I felt increasingly like an outsider.

To an extent I was different. I liked surreal humour, I excelled at Latin, I had discovered a love of Chagall, the painter, and impressionist art thanks to my first trip to the Royal Academy of Arts with my mother, I played classical guitar, I liked French literature, I watched black-and-white French movies from the '60s. I guess if I look back I was – I suppose I still am – intelligent and that I eschewed what I liked for the interests and aspirations of the masses. I denied myself in public the things I loved and that fulfilled me in private.

You get used to sweeping things under the carpet and making crumbs out of them, but I can't tell you the amount of times over the past few years that my psychologist has apologised to me for things that happened and shouldn't have. As I said, people are cruel. I see that now. Back then I expected it and accepted it.

When I was about thirteen or fourteen the school was putting on some end of year show. I don't remember the details. Despite not wanting to do it I was persuaded to perform two pieces of classical music. I didn't want to.

I played guitar for myself. The hours practising on my own in the other room away from the family were not so I could be a concert guitarist, they were because I loved playing, I loved – and still do – the feeling of expressing myself and my emotion through music. The melancholy of music in minor chords was like my soul finding a place where it felt at home, where everything that I was, everything I felt, was recognised.

As with all school halls there was a stage. I asked if I could wear trousers for the performance and was told no. I mentioned this to another teacher who said if the answer was no it was no. I went back and asked the deputy head again – a small woman who lived with the headmistress – and she would not budge. I was to wear my green polyester a-line skirt, regulation navy knickers and natural tan tights.

I played with the guitar between my legs, one foot raised on a rest, the whole audience with a clear view of my underwear. I played beautifully.

I had taken to wearing a trench coat and trilby – it was the '80s - pulled so far down over one eye that I could barely see. After the performance I put my coat and hat on ready to leave. I overheard a husband saying to his wife words to the effect of 'I'd be wearing that too if I'd just sat on stage with my pants on show'.

I was very good at maths. Hate it now – in no small part due to two teachers I had at school. Guidelines to live by (on my list of many which I am gradually reducing as I realise so many of them are no longer needed – in fact never were - but these two stand): have some principles in life – try to be fair and treat all people the same; if you're doing something to make your ego feel better make sure you aren't doing it at the expense of someone else's.

I knew the answer to the question – as usual – so I put my hand up. "Doesn't anyone other than Elle know the answer to this question?". Silence. I went to put my hand down. "Elle, you'll keep your hand up until someone else works out the answer."

In stark contrast to several years later when I was one of the few girls in sixth form maths not cheating by getting her boyfriend from the school up the road to do her homework, and the same teacher made some snarky comment about my having to put some effort in to close the gap.

Humiliated for both being too bright and, subsequently, not as bright as my cheating class-mates.

At infant school, I think the year just before we went on to junior school, I wrote the most epic of fantasy stories across several big white boards. The classrooms weren't so much adjoining as one space flowed into the next in the hexagonal arrangement around the central hall. I had a vivid imagination. I still do. I joke that living in my head is like being in Wonderland – except I'm not Alice on a crazy trip to town, I quite happily live there – and it really is. And when I was a child all that fantasy and creativity was allowed. Somehow, as you get older, you're supposed to become more 'sensible' – whatever the hell that means!

My epic story went down well. I was a brilliant storyteller, it was a fantastic story. Did I want to write another? Well no, not really, I didn't. Why don't you write another? What felt like an ever so slightly shaming 'Go on Elle. Oh yes, I had to be a 'good girl' didn't I and do what other people tell me. I said okay, I'd write another. But I had temporarily exhausted my inspiration. I went to the school library and sat on a little plastic stool and started reading some books. Not long after I went back to the giant whiteboards and began story number two. Except this time it didn't go down so well – I was told off for plagiarising (I don't expect the teacher used the term 'plagiarising' – I wasn't that smart!) a book in the school library. Well – duh!

I was praised for doing something I wanted to do and told off for doing something I didn't want to do. The logic seems perfect but the reality was that the sands beneath my eight year old feet shifted just a little that day – those tiny degrees of uncertainty that slowly caused the foundations to crack and shift so much that a few years ago I was left hanging by one finger from the edge of my existence.

When I was approaching O levels (I was the last vintage year before GCSEs) I wanted to do what I enjoyed doing and what, consequently, I was very good at – needlework, cookery, Latin. Unfortunately, at that age I was also very good at everything else – with the exception of geography which was and remains a mystery to me. I was told that if I did arts subjects there would be no career options for me except teaching (said by a teacher – I'm assuming she saw herself as some sort of failure?) and that it would be a waste of my intelligence.

I don't have kids, I only know what I read and what I hear from friends and colleagues about their experiences with the education system today, but it does sound like things have moved on a bit and there is at least, nowadays, some consideration for what the child wants to do, and children are told they can be or do so much more.

The other problem, which no-one had picked up on (and in fact never did!) was that, when it came to subjects I wasn't really passionate about – such as history and chemistry – I wasn't so much 'so intelligent' as that I had an exceptionally good memory. Any ability you have you assume, until life teaches you otherwise, that everyone else has. Looking back my A+ grades in maths and sciences were not so much, at that age, down to intelligence and understanding, as to my ability to remember what a teacher had said and to re-call visually what she or he had written on a blackboard or what I had seen on the page of a book. If I think back now, I can remember the principles of cutting fabric to a pattern, marking it, tacking it, how to put in a zip – I'm sure they would all come back to me if I had the urge to make my own clothes again – but I can't remember anything about the periodic table, chemical reactions, or history. I didn't enjoy them.

I still have a bizarre ability to hold huge amounts of data in my head, although as I have slowly been through the process of trauma recovery and built strong foundations for my life I have found that I am, again, more selective about what I want to file in the library in my head and what I will just let go.

*

My Great Aunt Mary died when I was about thirty. I always think of Great Aunt Lucy in Paddington Bear when I say her name like that, possibly because she was also a kind, warm, generous presence. I never knew my grandparents – missed out on the wealth of love that comes from your parents' parents as a child. Mary was my mother's mother's sister. I don't really remember much about her from when I was younger – as I don't remember much of anything. She lived in a two-up-two-down terraced house in Westcliff-on-sea somewhere. Does Remus Road ring a bell? Her husband died young. She had a daughter, my Aunt, born Marilyn but called Marion by her husband who thought Marilyn a bit common – each to their own. The house is dark in my memory – dark furniture, dark curtains, dim lights. Maybe everything was dark for me in those days. Or maybe everything just was dark? Do I notice the dark more as, out of necessity, I gravitate towards light, towards seeing clearly? The few memories I have of being in her house are all food related - eating boiled eggs with soldiers at the table, eating jelly and ice cream, a big tin of biscuits being offered around for selection. But I also remember being happy there, and laughter, and feeling cared for. I think some of those memories are from Before – I hadn't realised that. Somehow the warmth of being with her transcended the blackout I suffered from the trauma. How did she manage to do what almost no-one and nothing else could? Was she just far enough removed from the 'don't tell Mummy' for me not to feel threatened by my own fear of telling someone I loved something I wasn't allowed to tell them?

I spent so much time with her as a teenager. By then her daughter had married, had a son and they had moved to Devon and taken Mary with them. They had upped sticks from their new builds round the corner from us to a thatched monstrosity in a little village outside of Peignton. I hated it there. It sounds idyllic. It wasn't. I hated my uncle who would shout at me and my brother to be quiet if were enjoying ourselves. Hated the place which was all dark corners I couldn't see in to. Hated the spiders – great big bastards that watched you from the walls in the bathrooms and crept over the bedcovers at night. Hated the fact my uncle thought he was something special, swanning around in his comfy beige nylon trousers and nylon sports shirt, with his slip on boat shoes, talking loudly, pretending he was some 'big I am' when he was just a puffed up loudmouth who was mean, arrogant, unkind, narcissistic, idiot. Sorry Roger, but you were. And you made my Aunt's life so unhappy. You were so wrapped up in creating and maintaining your little world where you were king that you forgot to see the rest of life, to embrace even a small part of life, even to see what was going on around you as your world crumbled and eventually started to disintegrate. Worse – you reminded me of him.

We would go for two or three weeks every summer. It's one of two places I never want to re-visit. I have such unhappy memories. The light that got me through those trips and the frightfulness of my aunt and uncle was looking forward to seeing Mary. We'd travel down in my father's blue Austin Princess – a shocker of a car. It was a two-day trip back then. No idea where we stopped overnight. But I would travel in the back seat behind my mother with a coat or something over my head, peeping out through a crack at the road-side world as it passed by. I still can't work out why I had this thing about travel. Whenever we went to see my uncle and aunt in Paris I would spend the entire journey under cover. Was it some indirect by-product of the trauma? What was I scared of? As I got older I would explain it away to people by suggesting that I couldn't get my head round the concept of time and travel – how, as the minutes and hours ticked by, was it possible to cover distance and move from A to B? In hindsight that seems like nonsense. Still, there must be a reason for it. Did I feel adrift – unanchored to the familiarity and safety of home - when we were covering long distances in the car? Or did I feel too exposed to the rest of my family, as though, in close proximity for a period of time, they might see through the thick outer layer of camouflage I was growing and see the shame of what had happened to me, of what I had done?

Aunty Mary got very sick. Cancer in the end. She was eighty-three but still, it was too soon for me to lose her. For the past twenty years or so she would come and stay for months ever summer – a constant presence in our home, bringing a love that sometimes, otherwise, felt less accessible. Was it easier to let her in a bit more than my parents because I was more worried about them despising me for what had happened?

In the end my uncle, aunt and Mary moved back round the corner from us. Mary moved into a tiny flat in a block for old people with a reception area and assistance in the event of an emergency. Her grandson stayed behind and moved to Cornwall – jobless, surfing and, as we later found out, getting himself addicted to heroin. She gradually got sick. She went into hospital for an operation. Afterward she told my mother, laughing at herself, how she'd given strict instructions to Marion that she would only remove her false teeth at the last minute before she went off to the theatre and for Marion to put them in the cup in the drawer next to her bed. When my mother told me the only thing I could think was that I'd never known that she had false teeth! To know someone but not to know them. A secret kept.

It became terminal. She was moved into a hospice. By this point I had something horrible called 'a career' which I put all my efforts into as a way of distracting myself, punishing myself and proving a point about how little others – life – valued me. I finally peeled myself away from work to go and see her. I mean – how could I even have entertained the notion of not going to see one of my favourite people in the world on her death bed? What was wrong with me?

It was such a shock. She was tiny. This bird-like, fragile body, under the bedsheets. I left the room, tears in my eyes, and had to compose myself to try again. Finally I said my goodbyes and not that much later she was gone. Had she been holding on for me to come? I hope so. I hope I meant that much to her.

The service was at the crematorium. I wore a straight, black, knee-length skirt from Warehouse, a pair of black knee-high boots and a fuchsia pink roll neck (I was just entering my shopping-addiction phase in my quest to find something that would just damn well make me feel a little better about being alive). My mother possibly thought the pink unsuitable for a funeral – it may have been more a concern as to what my uncle and aunt, who were seemingly too 'proper' and straight for their own good, would think. I don't recall the service. Or the wake. What I do recall is that it was on a Friday and on the Saturday I went out with friends for drinks in town.

When the entirety of your life – all that you are, do, see, say, hear, feel - is experienced through a veil of fear in hindsight it makes the whole of your life so, well, so fucking weird! Forget difficult, difficult is implicit, but some of the behaviours I adopted and developed were so convoluted. I understand now. I understand what I was trying to do, why I was trying to do it, and that 'it' was perfectly normal in the context of having been raped as a child and let down – in the extreme – by the so-called 'responsible adults' who should have helped me. But bloody hell anyone else could certainly think it odd.

I was retreating further behind the wall of the fortress I had been building around me. And with every threat, however big or small, I was adding another brick, another wall, securing my defences. And as I did that I must have seemed less and less. There must have been a point where I became barely perceptible buried in the middle of that fortress, my thoughts and feelings blocked in but at the same time over-flowing like a constantly over-flowing volcano, the only respite sleep. Until that was taken away.

I was, I suppose, a bit lost after Mary's death. Whilst not the first in the family it was the first that I felt so deeply. I drove home after the funeral and, am sure, cried myself to sleep. The next evening I met friends in town. I was quieter than usual. Painfully self-conscious it always took a couple of drinks before I overcame my self-judgement and self-loathing enough to join in but something was on my mind. I desperately wanted to talk to my friends about the funeral, about how sad I was feeling, to share some stories about my aunt.

But I couldn't. They wouldn't be interested in how I felt. No-one was interested in how I felt. Had to keep it to myself. Had to suffer in silence. Had to be 'good'. Even if good was undefinable.

I heard one friend say to another 'Elle is very quiet tonight'. And the other reply 'I think she went to her aunt's funeral yesterday.

And that was it. I said nothing. No-one asked me anything – that night or at any point afterwards. No-one reached out. I know it must have been difficult for anyone to try to break though those walls. I see in hindsight how I was behaving and why, and my heart goes out to that younger version of me for everything I had to keep inside for fear of being abandoned all over again. But what I can't get my head around is how so-called friends never tried. Did they? And I just didn't – couldn't – see it? I've asked myself that so many times, but the answer is always no, they didn't. And I just can't get my head around the inhumanity of that.

But people are cruel. People use other people to make themselves feel better. People pick on other people because it makes them seem more important, more powerful, more in control or whatever more their egos are craving.

At college one of our group was waspish, maybe as he came to terms with his own sexuality, and a couple of the lads were very laddish – nowadays that type of misogyny surely would be shot down by most self-respecting girls on campus. They felt the need to read everyone else all the time. There was a touch of nastiness to the jokes that tipped them over the line. A group of us girls were given songs as our theme tunes. My friend might not have been happy with 'fat bottomed girls' but 'Tragedy' killed me.

The waspish wannabe bi-sexual and I sort of dated for a bit but he strung me along and made fun of me to the boys. Another lad, who, trust me, had no point of reference when he said this, made a throw away comment, supposedly as a joke, one night in the pub about my sexuality and appearance. I can't remember the context. It got such a laugh he said it again. I was sitting next to him. It hurt. It wasn't true. I felt ashamed. Maybe it was true? Maybe that was why men didn't want to date me?

I couldn't do anything. I couldn't tell him the comment was hurtful. I couldn't even pretend to hit him and tell him off for being so rude in a jokey 'If you ever make a joke like that at my expense again I'll tear your balls off' way. I had to sit there and suck it up. No-one was interested in how I felt.

I wish, wish, wish people would take more care with their words.

Yet increasingly we seem to inhabit a world where the opposite is true - thanks to people voicing opinions without facts and generally thinking of themselves when they are being outspoken, judgemental, harsh, to be 'popular', to go along with the crowd as it bays for more, hypnotised by their screens, not spending the time to try to look beyond it, more concerned about the reaction of their 'peers' than people who don't 'like' them.

Instead I think I became a sort of whipping girl and because I needed something to cling to and people's laughter was some sort of sign of acknowledgement and acceptance I began to fake use humour, often at my own expense, as a way of feeling liked and needed.

When I look back I had so many friends where the balance of the relationship was ninety-five percent them five percent me. I never expected more – it simply wasn't my lot. And I was incredibly, insanely, sympathetic, supportive and long-suffering as I never wanted anyone to feel as shit as I felt.

I had friends who almost never asked how I was. I had friends who excluded me.

There were three of us who were best friends at University and we were friendly with three guys who, basically, thought they were too cool for school. Maybe that's how people saw us three? I certainly never felt cool. As if! During one of the holidays Karen and Pippa were invite to stay with Mark, Ben and Jeremy in London. I wasn't. I didn't know about it. The first I heard was from Karen a while later. Apparently I hadn't been invited because I could 'be a bit depressed'. Jesus fucking Christ! And that, apparently, is how the world dealt with people who were depressed back in the day – excluded them, told them why and never thought – not once – to ask if anything was wrong. I wonder if that is still the reality, now that there is so much more awareness of mental health. Would nineteen or twenty year old Karen and Pippa in today's world think to talk to me, to ask me, to persuade the boys to invite me along? Did any one of them stop to wonder if there was a reason I always looked like I was carrying the weight of the world? Because I was!

I often wish I could go back and have some of those moments again. To say what I really felt, to have had the wherewithal to say how hurt I was that they left me out. But I imagine that if I had had the wherewithal to say how hurt I was I would have had the wherewithal to speak up about the rape and ask for help. But it was a different world then. These things were still completely taboo. The very definition of a world gone wrong.

The thing was it didn't happen just the once – it happened again and again. I wasn't invited to a dinner party in my early thirties by a group of very good friends. Apparently, Pete didn't want me there because I could be 'a bit depressing'. Fuck me! Curiously it was the same friend, Karen, who told me. Curious because she seemed quite happy to go along and have a great time and then make sure I knew I'd been left out afterwards. Again! She even told me who had made the remark about me. I took it as read that that was the truth because she was my 'best friend' but maybe, in hindsight, it wasn't. I took it as read that because she was my 'best friend' she was telling me to somehow protect me. In hindsight, maybe she wasn't. That was the first time I walked away from a friendship. I couldn't confront Pete about what Karen had told me for all the usual reasons, silenced as I was by that bitch and her side-kick. And plagued by my self-loathing and self-doubt I was desperately worried about never finding friends that liked me ever again. But a part of me couldn't accept that people who called themselves my friends could talk about me like that. I walked away from the friendship with Pete, his boyfriend, another university friend Alison and her friend, whose name, after all these years, I can't even remember. None of them tried to contact me. None of them called to see if I was okay.

There are so many occasions where this lack of kindness, compassion, concern from people who I believed were good friends, who I had invested time and money in (I was invariably the one to buy the first drink and possibly the last, the one to 'treat' us to another bottle of wine or a bottle of champagne on special occasions, the one to say 'oh go on, I'll pay ...') killed me at some level. I was spending my time with people who fulfilled that very belief that I was worthless and hopeless. I understand now that victims of trauma, people with severe depression will seek out people and situations that support their beliefs about themselves. At the time it fuelled the flames of the inferno of my depression.

By this point I had some sort of persistent depressive disorder that I hid fairly well most of the time. I felt sad, tired, guilty, worthless, ashamed of myself, but every day put on a smile that I hid behind while I pushed myself more and more to somehow 'succeed'. I had what I suppose anyone else would consider a successful career but which served as a mechanism to punish myself more – must work harder, must work longer hours, work more intensely to prove to the 'responsible adults' that I am 'good' and to prove to myself that I deserve nothing less than hard labour.

I hated my job. Hated is a strong word. These days - still doing the same job because I still don't have enough self-belief to jump, because I'm still waiting (almost there now) to defy society's expectations of what it means to 'be good' and do what makes me happy – I say that my job doesn't fulfil me. I try to put a positive spin on it but it's just words. Spending five long days a week, two hundred and twenty odd days a year, doing something that does nothing for me kills a little bit of me slowly each day. These days I do what I can to counter it – I paint, I play guitar, losing myself in something creative, something expressive. My voice – my ability to express all of I am – is getting louder. I want it to be heard. By all the world. I want to shout and scream to everyone 'This is Me!'.

This is My Fucking Life!

As well as a successful career (how much do I hate that word)! I went to the gym regularly, I went out with (so-called) friends at the weekends. From time to time I got drunk and got off with some man I met out. And despite the fact I hated everything about me in hindsight I looked pretty good. Over fifty percent of people who were sexually abused as children develop some sort of chemical dependency, drugs or alcohol. If one in twenty children are abused think what that's doing to the population.

My addiction was shopping. My body wouldn't let me do drink. I could blast my way through copious beers, gins or wine on a night out and end up exceedingly drunk and horribly hungover the next day, but my body would not let me do it again the next night. The vaguest whiff of alcohol when I had a hangover was enough to make me feel sick. And I couldn't bring myself to try drugs – it was hard enough as it was coping with my mind and the million thoughts running around it at warp speed. I had developed my own means of coping with the negative running commentary and anything that might throw that out of whack or make me less able to cope with it was a definite No. So I took to shopping.

Throughout my twenties and most of my thirties almost all my bonuses at work went on clothes. And shoes. I ran up about thirty thousand on credit cards and store cards. One year, when I was around thirty-four, I think I had almost all of that season's collection from Whistles and was buying a pair of shoes or boots or a bag every month from Russell and Bromley. Nuts. Until it reached a point where I'd run out of credit and each month was just about paying off enough to make one purchase before the next statement came in.

I still spend too much on clothes. It has always been a way of trying to make me feel better about myself and of trying to 'fit in'. Back then I had no idea what I was doing - it was an addiction, I did it without thinking. I think there was a point in my late thirties when I became aware that all I was repeatedly doing was finding something 'external' that temporarily made me feel less shit about everything, and that maybe I had to do something to 'fix' things internally.

My parents bought me a sewing machine for my birthday when I was about thirty. It was too late to fulfil that dream of becoming a fashion designer, too late to go back and do Needlework O'level, but it would allow me to do something creative and, in my parents' minds hopefully stop spending so much on clothes.

It backfired!

I found a shop just off the Edgeware Road that sold thousands of fabulous fabrics – some cheap, some expensive, and some the same fabrics as you'd find used for the collections in the shops on Bond Street. Oops.

*

That first flashback that fleetingly made it as far as my consciousness, if only for a split second, was at university in the girls' loos in the campus pub The Village Inn. Anything less like a village inn I've never seen. A brutalist nineteen-seventies concrete cube from the outside with dark brown Formica tables, olive green leatherette benches around the edge, Marston's beermats, a sticky dark carpet with a cut-out one side for a Parquet dance floor. The loos were worse. Inevitably not a sign of any heating which made the old toilets with the black seats and the long metal chains very cold, respectively, to sit on and pull. Freezing water from huge taps above sinks in a row on one wall with mirrors above them. Karen was the one who made the comment about someone at their home in Dubai (her father worked there hence her stint at a well-known public school before university) having exposed himself to her, or something along those lines. Apologies, again, it's so long ago I can't remember the details. But I do remember quite clearly a moment when time froze. An image of that day, of him and me in that pokey room made its way, quite clearly, into my mind. I couldn't do anything with it. I couldn't say anything to anyone – no-one would believe me, everyone would reject me because I hadn't been 'good'. The moment passed. It was gone. I buried it again. Safer that way.

But it wasn't safer that way. As life began to get more and more difficult I desperately wanted a relationship but that was nigh on impossible. Part of me was terrified of intimacy, terrified it would happen again, and part of me truly believed that all men were interested in was sex. Give them that and they'd come back for more. Sometimes I wish I could go back and explain to the men I have met, the men I have slept with, why I was how I was. And that some of them might apologise for the way they behaved too.

So I was stuck in this insane world where I thought I needed to have sex with a man for him to be interested, but dreaded sex because, without me really knowing it at the time, it took me straight back to being raped at seven years old. And because I couldn't get a boyfriend, when all my friends did, because I wasn't able to sit around talking about going out together, spending the night together, what he said, what we did, I thought that something must be wrong with me. And something was wrong with me - but it wasn't my fault. And I really really didn't know what was going on but it hurt. It hurt so much I cried myself to sleep, for years, for decades, until it all blew up.

I had one relationship that lasted longer than a couple of dates and a quick shag. I'm sure boys thought I was easy. Which I hated. I fell in love over sex and hoped they might be the person, the thing, that fixed me, that proved I was 'normal'. that gave me the love I couldn't give myself. They, however, had sex and were gone. In modern terms I would probably be considered quite straight and chaste. But I thought I was awful and sadly that was what counted.

Dave, well, I don't really know how that happened. We ended up dating. Six months later we both found our rental agreements up and we ended moving in with each other. We were at that age when friends were 'settling down' – ironically 'settling' being the most pertinent word. It's an odd concept if you think about it isn't it …. we are sold this story about going to school, getting a job, falling in love, getting married, getting a mortgage, having kids, and so on and on and on. I wish someone had explained to me that there are other ways to live, other stories. I hope that society has moved on now but my generation were very much brought up with the belief that if you didn't follow this very narrowly defined trajectory you were somehow a failure!

I don't know why Dave was with me. Maybe because I went along with his idea of fun – drank a lot, partied hard, had a career. I know exactly why I was with him – because he hadn't rejected me! But slowly, surreptitiously, he did. I told him I loved him – he told me he could never love me. He told me he didn't find me physically attractive, his attraction for me had been my mind. I already hated my body. He told me he never wanted to get married and have children. He criticised me a lot – my mother once counted that he called me stupid over half a dozen times one morning at theirs when we were making scrambled egg and smoked salmon for everyone.

This drawn out form of rejection started to take its toll. Every time he verbally pushed me away I tried harder to please. Every time he told me "No" another piece of me broke. I started to get panic attacks – not that I knew what they were at the time. Once we took a two-week holiday travelling by train around the south coast of France to Barcelona. By this point I had developed a fear of flying. And when I got (and get) nervous instead of becoming very quiet I talked, a lot. I was getting claustrophobic – something that hadn't bothered me too much since I was a child when I couldn't get in a lift with other people in case it broke down, I was stuck with them and one of them assaulted me, and I couldn't get in a lift on my own in case it broke down, I was on my own and this howling sense of abandonment overwhelmed me so completely I actually died. We stayed in a hotel in Lloret de Mar with a swimming pool on its roof and I couldn't sleep as I developed an irrational fear that the ceiling might crack and we'd be killed under the weight of the water. That was the first night I had a full-on panic attack in front of him. Was he sympathetic? I don't know. Logically, maybe, as he explained why it wouldn't happen. But emotionally, psychologically, probably not. What I needed was an arm around me, a hug, a feeling of safety, a feeling of being loved and protected. What I got was the feeling that I was becoming an annoyance.

I hated myself even more for not being able to be the girlfriend he wanted me to be.

In Barcelona it got worse – I decided I couldn't get the flight back. It was in the days before mobile phones. I called my mother from the hotel on reverse charges. I just knew that if I got the plane I would die. Not that the plane would crash, but that my sense of panic and fear and everything else inside me that I couldn't control would be too much to bear. It's like every cell of your body, every organ, every fibre of your being, is screaming and the noise of that scream is raging around inside you, unable to get out, getting louder as it ricochets around, creating a volcano of emotional hell.

I said I would get the train. It meant a day of travel, but the plane was now out of the question. If you'd paid me a million I don't think I could have got on it – unless someone sedated me heavily. I give him his due. Unimpressed and annoyed as he was he said he would come with me. I am grateful to him for that. I'm sure I told him so at the time, sure I repeated it ad infinitum until we were home, but it's worth saying again. Admittedly the Eurostar under the Channel was a shaky moment but it was twenty minutes and I no longer felt quite so trapped. Maybe he did love me as he'd got the train with me …?

We broke up after two years. Amazingly I ended it. He wanted to buy a flat. I thought he was going to suggest he move out and it was over. I pre-empted him splitting up with me by splitting up with him. Turns out that he was intending on buying a flat and asking me to move in with him as I didn't earn as much as he did. But by then it was too late. Bizarrely he expected to sleep in the same bed after we'd split up. I even came home from work one day and for the first time since we had lived together he had done my washing. But it was over. I helped him move out. I still don't know why I did. Driving all his stuff round to his new place. We met up a couple of months later and got very drunk. He said it was "okay for you as you're bound to meet someone new and fall in love again." Oh how little he really knew or understood about me.

Fairly early on after meeting him I told him about what had happened to me when I was seven. I don't really know why. Maybe because he was my first proper, grown-up relationship and I felt he should know. Maybe because I'd had a few drinks, felt safe, and it peeked out from my subconscious and I noticed it there, lurking. Maybe I hoped he would understand. But I knew nothing and understood nothing myself. And he said nothing when I told him. No 'I'm so sorry that happened to you'. No 'how awful'. Not even an 'I can't believe it' or 'are you sure?' which by the way is the worst possible response you can give someone. Nothing. We carried on with the evening, his lack of response underlining some important point my subconscious had already grasped that no-one was interested in what had happened and if I thought it was a big deal I must be inherently wrong.

Because by this point it had crawled out of the dark recesses of my memory and made its way back into my consciousness. I was twenty-three of twenty-four when I decided I would train as a Stress Management Counsellor and Hypnotherapist. Having started light with aromatherapy evening classes, a bit of meditation and crystals this was the beginning of the two decades pf my life when I tried, oh so hard, to FIX MYSELF. I didn't find the course, my mother did it with a view to a new career and somehow, I don't recall, I ended up enrolling in the group after hers. These things weren't yet regulated. I recall so little of so many things now I am starting to wonder what's happened to my memory over the past few years, since everything imploded. I don't even remember where the weekend courses were held. I know the man running the course was from Liverpool but I don't think they were there. And I'm fairly certain they weren't in London. I guess my mind has filed it under 'not important' within the grand scheme of things.

I took out a loan to pay for the course. He was another one of these therapists who had very generously put an arrangement in place with one of the less well known banks so I had to schlep all the way up to London – I was living in Winchester at the time – to find a Clydesdale on Piccadilly circus to commit myself to something I really couldn't afford. I wish to God I had put all this money towards saving for a deposit for a house or flat. I'm sure the outcome of the last twenty or thirty years would have been the same. Perhaps I'd be a bit less knowledgeable about 'the human condition' but at least I might be living somewhere bigger than six hundred and nine square feet and know that I'm not going to be kept awake or woken up by my noisy and inconsiderate neighbours.

The chap who took the course – Guy Butterworth, who I've never managed to find on the internet since it came into existence – was actually quite good. Or maybe I had an affinity for the subject matter of the course. Or maybe it was this overly compassionate heart of mine that thought everyone must be suffering just as I was and wanted to make them, all of them, feel better. We learnt a bit of stuff about how the mind works, how energy works (the start of all things quantum entering the world of all things spirituality), how to use voice and breathing to relax someone, and so on. It all seemed like common sense to me – somehow I'd been doing it to myself for decades. Then at some point he would take us through a guided meditation called The Child Within. This was back in the early nineties so way before Oprah brought this to people's attention. The intention of The Child Within is that it is 'a powerful meditation that allows you to release emotional pain and negativity associated with childhood experiences and to re-connect with the innocence and joy of your childhood'. Again, I don't remember the detail, what I do remember is that with no prior warning I was suddenly back in that room with him. I remember the feeling that I might somehow be overwhelmed by something, unable to cope, so instead of giving in to the emotions that came with the memory I sat on them. And as I sat there, all of my weight, all of my being, focused intently on keeping the lid on that Pandora's box shut as tight as possible, the terror, the horror, of it all proved stronger than me and some of the sadness that I'd buried so deep, and that I hadn't even known was there, escaped.

The secret was out. A whisper of it, the tiniest fragment, echoing round my head 'What? Why? When? How?' and I knew I knew all the answers but my first inclination, as with so many victims of childhood sexual abuse, was to wonder if I'd imagined it.

And I was so ashamed that this had happened to me, and so embarrassed that somehow I had been implicit in it all, that I didn't know where to start telling anyone. If in fact I should tell anyone. Logically I felt I needed to tell someone. Emotionally I had no idea what to do. And psychologically I had absolutely no reference point. But I had been told not to tell anyone. Eventually I bit that bullet and one evening, on the phone to my mother, I told her. Not what had happened when I was seven but what had happened when I did the child within meditation. It was sort of the same thing, but I had found a loophole in the 'don't tell anyone rule'. The first thing she said was 'are you sure?'

I know we know better now. I know the world is better informed, more aware. I know she has explained why that was the first thing she said – because she simply couldn't imagine that something like that could even happen – but …. !

I was so disconnected from my emotions that I don't think I cried. Disconnected not just from the emotions of that forty-five minutes but from every emotion that I had had to bury since because on the one hand I knew how I felt didn't matter and on the other the slightest feelings of vulnerability, fear, being tricked or being lied to felt too much like the emotions I felt on that day and I couldn't cope with them, buried them, ignored them, pretended nothing had happened, for my own survival.

Too much time has passed, too much time dragging the weight of it behind me like an unwanted sack of shit that

I had had to learn to live with, to accept. Something invisible to everyone else but that, ultimately, defined me. I used to remember all these things so vividly. Each and every event that made me feel in the slightest bit threatened or vulnerable I remembered all the details so I could be prepared for the non-existent enemy that had lodged itself inside my mind, body and soul on that day. My memory of things was inextricably linked to how I felt. For every situation, event, occurrence my first memory of it was how I felt. I couldn't tell you what it was about, the story, but I could tell you how I felt when I read a book, or went to see a film

Bizarre how life can change. Now I am free from the fear, now I have dealt with the trauma – as I should have been allowed to do all those years ago – I find I remember places, people, stories, information, not just how I felt. It's a beautiful thing.

Now I remember very little of what happened when I told my mother. I know she told my father, whose reaction, now I look back, seemed far more 'fit for purpose' – he wanted to go up the school and beat the living daylights out of someone. I told my best friend at the time and had a similar initial response to my mother. Perhaps they thought I had made it up? In any event I suppose I thought that the bitch of a headmistress was right – no-one would believe me, no-one was interested in how I felt.

It sort of became a 'non-thing' again.

But it was out the bag, as it were. I had opened that Pandora's box, just a tiny bit, a crack wide enough to let the mists of the past escape, very, very slowly, but small enough that I didn't see what had happened, what was happening. How, for the next twenty years or so of my life. it would get harder and harder to deny that something was 'wrong', harder and harder for me to 'cope' and, sitting in the middle of all the toxicity of the past that, like a cloud of carbon monoxide as the mists pooled around me, harder and harder for me to stay alive.

*

I really did try. So fucking hard. But as my twenties slipped into my thirties and I desperately wanted to be in a relationship - to be loved because I couldn't love myself, to be saved because I felt permanently like I was drowning – and to be 'normal' and get married and have kids, if I look back now I see that I was becoming more and more ill. I was so depressed by my early thirties that I cried myself to sleep every night. Every bloody night. I cried when I got in from work. And sometimes I cried at work, silently, quickly, as I sat on the loo for two minutes. I was deeply ashamed by my depression, by my failure to be a complete and normal human being. By my inability to cope with life the way everyone else did. The only person I spoke to about it was my mother, who had also had depression and, in her early twenties, what was referred to as 'a nervous breakdown' when her mother died. She was always there. Always listened – often to me sobbing down the phone when the worst phase of each depression reached its nadir and my emotions erupted. The storm before the calm the next day, when the worst had passed and I entered a brief numb phase before I started to feel better. And then I started to feel too good and got a bit out of control. Until I couldn't control how I felt and the cycle repeated itself. Over and bloody over.

I wonder if she even knew the extent, the depth, of my depression. I certainly didn't. But because my mother had coped I would cope. Because she had lived with it, put up with it, I would.

For so many reasons I wish she'd never had depression. Because I would never wish that feeling of complete and utter hopelessness on anyone else. And because if she hadn't then perhaps she would have suggested I go to the doctor or talk to someone about it.

But going to the doctor was not an easy thing for me to do. I had two moles right in the middle of my chest, which grew when I hit puberty. One of them was more of a skin tag. I hated them. And the taggy one would sometimes catch on tops, bleed and get inflamed. My mother took me to see a doctor. The nineteen seventies and early eighties were a grim time for décor – it was another dingy room with a rather old doctor who managed to smell dingy as well. I was reluctant to show him the moles but did. He dismissed them as nothing to worry about and, in that gung-ho way of people with no understanding of compassion or emotional intelligence said he could 'shave them off now'. There was no way on earth I was letting this man near my chest and neck with a scalpel. I'd been in a similar position before and the risk was too high. I said No.   We left. My fear of all things medical put down to generally being a nervous nelly – a term I still use to describe myself but shouldn't – rather than someone who has a fear of doctors because she was raped by one when she was seven.

So I kept going, kept getting more depressed, more anxious, and without my knowing it (let alone understanding it) more distrustful of everyone and everything. The feeling of fear that shut me down on that day all those decades ago and kept me stuck in that moment had somehow morphed into a monster of terror that made me hyper-vigilant for any potential threat. The fear surrounding what that one man did in a matter of minutes and the mess of feelings around rejection, failure and worthlessness that the two bitches instilled in me in an equal amount of minutes was, very slowly, killing me. In my late forties I can remember I started saying to my mother that my life would kill me. I told her I didn't mean it figuratively, it was just killing my spirit, my soul. But really I did mean it. The mental and physical exhaustion I felt was killing me. I kept getting ill. If this was death by a thousand cuts I couldn't see how I wouldn't reach a point where I decided enough was enough and I kill myself.

Because I did try to tell people, I did. And every time was like another bullet to my soul.

When I was thirty-two I took a job at a large news / technology company. It was a global role reporting to the Chief Procurement Office where my peer group was a middle-aged white man who played golf on the weekends, had been taken on as a 'consultant' rather than being perm like me and earnt three or four times as much as I did.

I threw myself into it. I had a reasonable-sized team, mostly in the UK, had very generously been given what the middle-aged men referred to a as a 'problem child', had a couple of middle-aged men working for me one of whom didn't like working for a younger and, I guess, attractive woman, particularly not one who was very capable and very delivery-focused.

The CPO was a horror – to me if to no-one else. Despite meeting all my objectives I was marked down at my first performance review because I 'hadn't integrated well enough' with my peers. The example he gave was to ask to me if I could name all of Tony's children. FFS! How was I supposed to 'integrate' with this group of men I had nothing in common with and who had made no attempt to 'integrate' with me. How many of them could tell you whether I was in a relationship or not (I was of course very much single) and what I liked to do with my spare time (at that point in time I went out a lot partying – dancing, drinking and staying out far too late for my own good in an attempt to convince myself I was having fun at the same time as trying to forget the misery that lay inside me)?

I had to travel with the job. Flying. Not being able to show any vulnerability, weakness or to be able to speak up was a fucking nightmare to live with. It stopped me from making any response to the daft reasons presented to me for my poor performance review – instead I felt the hot lava of suppressed words erupting inside me and had to hold it in long enough to get out the room, walk back to my desk in a dignified way, head to the bathroom and then scream silently whilst I sat on the loo with my head in my hands. But it also stopped me speaking up when I was offered this global role. See, I'd gone to the interviews wanting the UK role but they offered that to someone else. And when they offered me the global role my selective mutism kicked in. I would have stayed in the job I was in but the salary was rubbish compared to what I could get elsewhere. Still, if I'd known they were paying the middle-aged men one-thousand-two-hundred pounds a day I might have felt slightly less like I was being offered a dream job at seventy thousand a year.

So I found myself doing a job which involved flying regularly to the US when I had a very obvious fear of flying and working in what became an increasingly toxic environment.

To give you an idea of just how toxic corporate life could be (and in some places still is) there was a woman in the team who frequently didn't get into the office until after nine thirty. They wanted to have a formal word about this with her, but as I often got in 'late' – forget the fact I regularly worked until seven or eight in the evening – they had a word with me first to tell me I had to be in by nine so they could tell Terri she had to be in by nine. Forget the fact that her sister had died recently and she was now guardian for her niece and nephew and as well as dealing with her own and their grief was having to juggle getting two children to school in the mornings before she went in to work, what was more important was some middle-aged man asserting his authority and making it clear who was 'in charge' by clock-watching.

We moved offices and, as the corporate world moved to open plan and the concept of offices based on hierarchy, we were encouraged to sit on a bank of desks with our teams. Fine. Don't have an issue with any of that. Except that one or two of my peers – including Tony whose children's names had let me down oh so badly – didn't like it! They argued the toss and because they were yes-men to our CPO, who valued their loyalty I believe above all else, they were allowed to stay tucked away in their glass boxes, like some rarefied species that might wither and die if exposed to the air the rest of us breathed for too long. I don't think it's unreasonable to expect that colleagues, from time to time, might take a five-minute break from their screens, conference calls, or whatever else they might be doing to have a chat and maybe a laugh. Apparently we were too noisy for dear old Tony. He who sat there with his monstrously high blood pressure thumping his keyboard so loudly when he typed that we could hear it from outside and pushing the office door to when he wanted to call his wife or family had complained that we were making too much noise. From his seat on high he had decreed that the little people were disturbing him and yet again I was called in front of the overlord and told to behave properly.

It was also 'suggested' that I have a word with one of my team who came into work on dress-down Friday with a v necked shirt with no buttons. Someone had taken offence at it. Really – it beggars belief. This despite the fact that a girl called Dina regularly came in in a top short enough that you could see the new ink at the base of her spine. But Dina was a blue-eyed girl and I was, for a reason I cannot totally fathom, considered a bit of a pain in the arse.

I have a feeling I know why. I was and always will be a person of principle. If something is 'wrong' I won't agree to it just because that is the answer someone wants me to give. 'Being good' means doing the right thing – the right thing, morally, for the situation and circumstances – always. Who would I have been, or could I be, without this need to be good at any cost to myself? Might I have followed my own dreams? Might I have said No more? Might I have told these 'corporate monkeys', with their prejudices and fragile egos, to 'go and get a life'? Given them some perspective about what really matters rather than wittering on about 'core hours' and 'dress code'. Twenty years ago it was undoubtedly important to them for some unfathomable reason – today they couldn't get away with it.

In any event I had ended up seeing a therapist, notionally about the fear of flying, but it stirred up my unhappiness. It wasn't the first therapist I'd seen. After qualifying as a stress management counsellor and hypnotherapist I went on to qualify as a reflexologist and a reiki practitioner. I wanted to get out of corporate life, even only a few years after starting out, but I just didn't have any self-belief. I thought I'd be found out. I am told I have healing hands. I am been told the heat that emanates from them when I touch anyone is intense. Maybe that is why the neighbours' cat loves to visit me so much. But no, I didn't have the gumption to do anything. Plus I was so afraid of not being good (insert eye-rolling emoji here) that I got incredibly nervous and on the one occasion when I did give someone a reflexology treatment I forgot a section of about half a dozen movements, finished five minutes early and berated myself so much that I decided I couldn't see anyone again because I obviously wasn't any good.

So I started my journey into therapy with some of the 'alternative' healing kind. It made me feel better, made me feel cared for, calmed me and helped me feel connected to something greater than this version of me that had showed up at this point in time and space – an insignificance in the grand scheme of Time with a human being's propensity to waste that time on thoughts and feelings and petty problems that, ultimately, aren't really important.

There was a point in the nineties when hypnotherapy became 'popular'. Paul McKenna hit the big time, there were TV shows where the public were hypnotised and essentially comedy nights in bars when punters were hypnotised for entertainment. Think along the lines of 'when you hear my fingers click you will think you are a chicken and will squawk and cluck your way around the bar looking for the eggs you laid'. Not terribly high-brow but I have to say it was funny.

Having done nothing further with my own hypnotherapy training because I evidently wouldn't be 'good enough' I sought out the services of one who could help me. This would have been sometime around the age of thirty not long after Dave moved out and at a point when my 'career' had taken off and the stress of the long hours and responsibility was beginning to take its toll.

There have been so many therapists over the decades, and so much intense therapy the past few years, that I seem to have mislaid some of the whys and wherefores. I have one vivid memory of a session with this chap. I can't remember his name, or what I went to see him about. I can remember he wasn't cheap and the room was dark. Every bloody time – why do these therapists think a dingy room in the attic somewhere on or near a Harley Street address, with dark wood furniture and olive-green leather covered chairs is a good idea? I once went to see a woman who sat behind an enormous dark wood desk – the sort of size you'd use in a comedy sketch because it was so ridiculous – whilst she told me how much she cared and how much she could help me. All for two hundred and fifty pounds for fifty minutes! More of her later.

I have a memory of sitting in my olive-green chair diagonally opposite this chap and talking. It was nice to have someone who was, theoretically, interested in me – even if I'd had to pay for the privilege. In retrospect I don't think I shared a great deal with him. I so wanted to give these therapists the right answers to questions that I was almost one step ahead of them the whole time.

On this particular session he asked me to stand in front of a mirror, look at myself and tell the reflection of me that I loved myself. I think there may have been a bit more involved, such as asking me when I looked in the mirror what did I see, could I give myself a compliment, etc etc. But the thing that has stayed with me is the suggestion that I tell myself I love myself. We all know it now. In the words of RuPaul 'If you don't love yourself how in hell are you gonna love anybody else!'. But back in the nineties this concept of loving yourself hadn't yet come of age. The nineties was a time when people in their twenties were still experimenting with the idea of self not chasing memes about self-love, self-worth or self-acceptance.

I couldn't do it. I felt like I was being forced at gunpoint to confront my mortal enemy. I couldn't find anything nice to say about myself – I saw a nose that was too big, eyes that were too deep-set, a face that was too long. I couldn't see myself other than through that veil of self-loathing.

Why do so many therapists get stuck at the point at which you get stuck in their process? I've experienced it several times. Everything is going swimmingly until … until what? Until something gets stuck and they realise they can't fix you? Then they transfer the blame to you rather than looking to themselves for the answer. The concept of transference exists in therapy but typically that the 'patient' develops feelings – of love, of dependence – for the therapist. No one talks about the other side of the coin whereby so many therapists – predominantly those not couched in years of study and practice and who have had to go through a long process of therapy themselves – use their ability to 'heal' their clients as a way of fulfilling their own egoic needs. So many of these people really believe that they are 'special' and have some gift. They use their role as therapist to validate those beliefs. People tell them they feel better after seeing them, that their lives changed. Of course they did. The one thing we human beings need to be able to do is to talk, to feel connected, to not feel alone. But there is so much that we don't feel we are allowed or able to talk to family of friends about, through fear of being judged as a failure, as weak, as mentally ill, that we don't talk. We feel more and more isolated. And of course when we finally have the opportunity to unburden ourselves to someone who we have paid to listen we feel better.

The worst therapists I have come across were those that didn't listen to me. Actually no, the worst were those that pretended to listen and thought that I couldn't see through their pretence. They were so confident in themselves, or so wrapped up in their own self, that they assumed they knew what I was going to say, how I was feeling, and rolled out some formula for what **I** needed to do so **I** 'got better'.

There is no magic formula. Well, except one, which is to feel valued and heard and seen as someone guides you through working out the why, the how, the when, the who and sits beside you every step of the way, caring for you, making sure you have all the support you need, the resources you need, the emergency contact number if it all gets too much. And that isn't a quick fix. That comes with months of working together. There is no quick fix or therapy-nirvana for rape victims. Don't believe anyone that tells you there is. And categorically avoid any therapy which isn't about healing, where you get an hour's 'treatment' and are then told to 'work on yourself at home'. NO! High alert. Exit the premises now. And don't rely on them answering 'yes' to the question 'have you helped people who were sexually abused as children before?'. They may 'help' as you go through the trauma recovery process but after decades of trying to find the answer I can say, with absolute certainty, the only way to fully and completely - and with the utmost care – recover from the trauma of childhood sexual abuse is to talk to someone comprehensively and clinically trained in the psychology of trauma and recovery and childhood sexual abuse. Amen.

Because over the years I reckon I have seen a lot of therapists: the chap who ran the stress management counselling course; the woman who I did Reiki I with; the tutor for my reflexology course; the hypnotherapist who couldn't get me to a point where I could tell myself I loved my reflection; another chap in Kentish Town who I saw for a few months and I think was a cognitive behaviour therapist – he had a very minimalist set-up with two upright chairs in a white room with a few books on a book case and a potted fern – I liked it; a man in a rented office in the City again who I think practiced hypnotherapy and CBT and who did manage to get me on to a plane without completely and utterly freaking out; a team at the Priory in north London where I was referred by the company medical help line for an assessment and attended a one-day group session where I felt a complete fraud; a friend who had trained as a CBT practitioner; a hypnotherapist (apparently 'to celebrities') who I went to see about weight-loss; a woman who did some sort of acupressure on one of those sit up massage chairs at my gym; a hypnotherapist and CBT practitioner – yet another one who rented some poky office on Harley Street so she could charge more – who I ostensibly saw about insomnia but who I then signed up with to 'coach' me for a few months at great expense and with no success; another CBT practitioner in Mayfair (the one with the insanely large desk) who talked about herself for most of the first session and said one of the most potentially damaging things I've ever heard a so-called therapist say; another hypnotherapist for weight loss – who mixed up the timescales for achieving things that we had discussed which is why I may be writing this book five years rather than five months after I saw her; another hypnotherapist; another CBT therapist …. I can't even remember it all. The list is so long. Tens of thousands of pounds. I could be living in a flat twice the size with a garden and have cleared my mortgage by now if just one of them had really seen me. There is no-one in the list above who I feel could get over themselves and their own ego sufficiently to see me, to see that there might be something else that needed addressing. Okay, I'll excuse the woman who did the acupressure – I was seeing her because of my neck and back ache.

The long list of what I tried as part of what started as a 'how to fix myself' journey and ended up as a 'how to stay alive' route march is as follows: acupuncture (at least four different acupuncturists over the years); BodyTalk; reflexology; Reiki; spiritual healing; psychics (a wide selection – I clung desperately to the hope that life would change); tarot; breathwork; yoga; emotional freedom technique tapping; aromatherapy; crystal therapy; meditation; psychotherapy; coaching; ….. mixed results. Some did what they said on the tin – helped with stress, a feeling of balance, restoring calm. Others, where the therapist's egos were so over-inflated they thought they were some sort of messiah who could fix me in one session (and who of course I hoped were right), who did more damage than good.

I've also been on numerous courses around the 'fixing myself' theme (too many to mention) or in the thin hope that I might understand myself better and be able to help myself, including: the Paul McKenna weight loss hypnotherapy workshop at a London hotel one weekend; oh, and once the weight loss plan stopped working I think I went a second time but with less success; massage therapy training - I dropped out just before the theory exams; MindScape introductory course; Reiki II and Reiki Master and Practitioner training (I value and trust Reiki – but it was always going to soothe me rather than 'fix' me); reflexology; …

And attended multiple day or weekend courses with various spiritual 'teachers' and self-proclaimed experts and gurus, mostly around themes of loving yourself (made me feel lighter and more positive for a day or two but ultimately left me wishing I hadn't spent the money as everything just reverted to as it was) or understanding this thing called life (interesting, insightful, the odd philosophical snippet that I still carry with me but were never going to 'fix me').

I can't blame the therapists and 'teachers' who didn't know what had happened to me when I was a child, but I do wonder, if they were truly good at their jobs and this was a vocation, a life-calling to help other people, to illuminate the lives of other people, why not one of the people listed above saw anything else. Was I really that good an actress? Had I become so good at covering it all up, pretending I was alright Jack, that none of them saw in.

For the therapists that I did tell shame on you. SHAME ON YOU.

*

The first time I told anyone, other than what really amounted to no more than the brief chat with my mother and one or two very close friends back in my twenties, was, oddly, at work.

Darren worked for me. It was he who wore the open-necked button-less shirt that so horrified my peers! He'd worked for me for a year or so I guess, after switching jobs as he was 'looking for a new challenge'. We got on well. Liked each other. Were friends outside work, along with a girl called Amy who had worked for me at a previous company and jumped ship when I was recruiting at this one. I thought he was a friend. I trusted him. One morning, after I'd been for a rather challenging session the previous day with one of the

CBT and hypnotherapy people, probably circa 2003, I was struggling. I'm racking my brains to remember what had set me off. I could make something up that feels vaguely right but apart from the fact that 'good girls don't lie' I want this to be the absolute truth, no inconsistencies. So much at that time led back to the man I was working for (this was the job where my peer group was the white middle-aged golfer), the unfairness with which he seemed to treat me, my struggle to fit in as a non-golfing woman twenty years their younger who didn't wear a grey or navy suit to the office; and the fact that no matter how much effort I put in, how much I achieved, he would always find some minor thing that I hadn't covered off. I mean, the guy had it in for me professionally one way or another just because personally he didn't like me. The problem was I did take everything personally. EVERYTHING. I had to be good. There was no scope for anything less than ninety nine point nine percent. Anything less than that was a potential threat to my existence. The possibility that someone might find even the smallest thing 'wrong' in anything I did, said, or was, was not allowed. I had to be GOOD. At everything. To avoid rejection.

More and more it was all getting too much. In his effort to help the therapist had dug close enough to uncover the edges of the box where all my secrets had been buried, hidden away from the world. He had got too close to the truth, taken me with him, and some part of me was scorched, my being held close enough to some flame just long enough to feel the fire. He had got close enough to old wounds, almost touched them, and the pain was too much. Better to keep them hidden, buried under layer after layer after layer.

This happened a lot – whenever a thought or a feeling got closer to the truth it somehow interfered with the energy waves still being emitted from the trauma. There was an overwhelming sensation that I was going to cry, to scream, to breakdown. But the subconscious fear of going there and the fear of not being able to cope stopped me giving in. It was like sitting on that bloody volcano. And like the old stories of the gods, part of me was prodding and poking this one and they didn't like it.

So it was one of those mornings when the gods of my trauma had been stirred and they weren't happy. They wanted to get things going and I just wanted to go home and hide until they'd forgotten about it all again and gone back to sleep. I had been in the bathroom at work having a very short, silent, tear-less cry. It is possible to cry without tears. It isn't terribly attractive but it does stop your make-up running.

For some unknown reason the loos were at the end of the office – a good seventy or eight metre walk from my desk. Another bizarre feat of design layout – if you walked to the end of the office you were either going to the loo or to get a coffee. It was a conspicuous walk especially when you were trying to stop yourself falling to the floor in a heap of unquantifiable despair.

Darren must have clocked I was out of sorts that morning. Head down, not chatty, focusing on work in an attempt to pretend that nothing else was making a bid for my head-space. He suggested we get out of the office for lunch that day – a rarity for me – and I agreed. The concept of nine to five with a lunch-break has always eluded me. I mostly work nine to some time after six – frequently after seven or after eight in the evening – with lunch at my desk as I'm dealing with some new point of lunacy due to people – suppliers, colleagues – not reading things properly, not taking responsibility and letting their egos get in the way of doing the job they should be doing.

We went to a pizza place not far from work. I had the overwhelming urge to tell Darren, to say something, to tell him the secret. I trusted him. We were friends. He was gay, he must understand how difficult it is to live with somehow being different.

If someone shares their deepest secret, or secrets, with you, show some respect for the huge hurdle they have had to clamber over to get to the point where they feel they can do this. Be grateful and graceful about the fact they consider you trustworthy and unjudgmental enough that they have decided to talk to you. Understand how important it is that they feel safe when they are talking about these things and that, for whatever reason, they feel safe with you.

Don't listen with one ear whilst you carrying on chowing down on your pizza and then say '*I don't understand what all the fuss is about with people who say they were abused. It all happened so long ago I don't see why it's still a problem*' or words to that effect.

I was CRUSHED. See, they were right, I shouldn't tell anyone else because NO-ONE was interested in me and no-one would believe me. Yet a small part of me, the tiny part of me that was still left from Before and buried so far deep inside that I hadn't seen or heard it before, was starting to tap on the walls of its prison, wanting to be free, unable to bear the not being, the not living, the weight of it.

I couldn't answer back. My secret silenced me again. I was inert, powerless. I said little more, hoping Darren would realise he had been wrong, and fairly hastily we finished up, settled up and went back to the office.

Every time the volcano, this maelstrom of something, stirred it affected me more and more strongly. Back then it would give me a couple of difficult night's sleep as I got into bed and my mind was whirring, it would launch me into a relatively short depression and I would withdraw, almost imperceptibly, from the world. I would go into the office, function, maybe even go out after work with colleagues or to meet friends, but I was playing a part. 'Nothing to see here'. I existed. I functioned. I rarely if ever talked about myself. I went through the motions of living when I was outside my flat and when I was inside I let those trapped feelings of loss, helplessness, solitude, despair, shame, guilt and whatever else was there have free reign. It was overwhelming. I was perpetually depressed. I hated myself – I couldn't work out was wrong with me. I hated my life – it was so frigging hard. I felt horribly isolated because I couldn't talk to anyone about anything to do with me and was starting, although I didn't realise it, to get compassion fatigue as I spent so much time 'being there' for everyone else. I cried myself to sleep almost every night. I would spend hours in bed, under the covers so no-one else could see (I have no idea who I thought could see!), talking to my make-believe boyfriend about how I felt. It – he – helped me to sleep. It wasn't 'real' but it was real enough in my head that it gave me enough respite to calm down and eventually nod off. He told me how much he loved me. And at that time it felt like the only love I knew. How fucking awful is that – to be sustained by the love of someone you've made up. I was becoming increasingly lost under the vastness of whatever had engulfed me. And the thing was, at the time, I was making no connection between how I felt and what had happened when I was seven. No conscious connection that is. Looking back I see that sub-consciously a little light would flash occasionally sending out the message that it would be useful to 'deal with' the sexual abuse (I couldn't even refer to it as rape then – that came later). But the light was dim, the message only just decipherable, and I forgot (or ignored?) it easily.

But tap tap tap – it was there, and over the next twenty years the knocking slowly, very slowly, got louder.

*

The next time I disclosed what had happened to me was a fair while later, when I was about forty-two. I was a size fourteen and thought I was overweight and that my life would be 'better' if I was thin. To paraphrase something my mother denies saying when I was a teenager 'she won't get a husband at that size'.

Time was most definitely running out to have children – something I thought I wanted – and before I could contemplate that I needed to find a man, someone I actually wanted to have children with. A few years previously I had somehow found myself engaged to someone I definitely didn't want to have children with. I was so so so desperate to have that 'normal' life – that one we're all sold - school, job, marriage, mortgage, kids. I was bridesmaid at a friend's wedding. As usual practically the only single person under forty there. The wedding was at a plush new hotel in Cardiff. I was in the thalassotherapy pool the day before the wedding and the fire alarm went off. Twenty minutes later I was standing outside the hotel wearing a swimming costume and towel and a lawyer from the company I had recently left was in the car park. Justin. He was slightly over-weight and wore a predominance of corduroy and tweed. We'd always got on at work – but the ability to be sarcastic about annoying colleagues does not make someone ideal boyfriend material. He joined us in the bar for drinks that evening. And – again – because I was so horribly desperate to have a boyfriend to prove to the world I was likeable, I was an okay person, that it was perfectly possible that someone might find me attractive, etc etc etc I asked my friend, the bride, if he could come along to the party after the wedding do. And so that is how I found myself dating an alcoholic who liked to use words like micturition instead of pee, who always left for work after me because unbeknown to me he was drinking half a bottle of gin before he went in the office and who, the weekend after his father's death when I had offered to hire a car and drive him to wherever it was in Shropshire, I had to sit next to as I drove a couple of hours up the M1 whilst he drank cheap white wine from a bottle that rattled around the passenger side footwell. It was the weekend that England beat Germany 5-1. I was supposed to be at a bar watching with friends, Instead I sat in this non-descript house in a small village in a place I didn't know with a man who had described, amongst other things, the 'orchard' at the bottom of the garden (three apple trees) and his ensuite (an old 1970s style sink plumbed in the wall of his bedroom in what I believe was called 'claire de lune' blue) and various other features of his family's 'country home' (which was just a 1970s new build with frosted patterned glass in the porch window and a proliferation of parquet flooring). It could probably have been a lovely house with a bit of modernisation (the shower was far from a shower – ancient plumbing that trickled rather than showered) but when someone bills their family seat as a manor house - where he expects the two of you to get married with a marquee on the lawn - to find out it's a four-bedroom semi on a relatively new build estate it's a bit of a let-down. As well as starting to give you an insight into the real measure of the man. We got engaged when he came to New York with me on a work trip. All my wanting a boyfriend in those days was, as I said, to prove to myself and the rest of the world that I wasn't the horrible, ugly, worthless person that a large part of my brain and being told me I was but also to 'make things better' – to help me do the things that I couldn't do on my own, like, having sort of fixed the getting on a plane thing, flying long haul.

Most of that four night trip to NYC I did short days in the office whilst he no doubt was in the hotel bar having drinks or out having drinks or waiting for me somewhere with a drink. We got engaged over dinner in the Russian Tea Rooms. I have an awful photo of me looking like I've just survived a stressful family holiday rather than beaming with joy at being asked to marry the man I purported to love.

It was shortly after this that I discovered he was an alcoholic. He told me that at points in his life he had taken Antabuse (disulfiram). He took some one day when we went up to Shropshire – but only the one day, the next he needed a drink again. I had arranged a meal out with friends some weeks after we got back from New York to celebrate both the engagement and my birthday. Noticeably he had no friends to invite. By this point the survival part of my brain had kicked in and I knew I needed out. It had only been a matter of months but I couldn't cope with the secrecy, the lies, the amount of money spent on bars, pubs and booze. He swindled his work expenses to cover large chunks of the money that was going out and that would surely come up at some point soon as fraud. The meal out was hideous. Mostly because of what I knew was coming. I had a friend staying, Mel, and had told her I was going to say something to Justin about splitting up after she'd gone to bed. I wanted to do it whilst she was there in case he got nasty. It didn't go well but didn't go badly. And the seed had been sown. I told him I didn't want to 'work it out'. It wasn't something I'd said 'after a few drinks'. I wanted him gone from my life.

The next day Mel left and I arranged, with my parents help, a way to tell him it was over, to take his stuff and leave and to avoid him getting abusive. I had a text message pre typed on my mobile – back in the day when all they did was text messages and phone calls. If he started to shout I would press send and my parents, on standby, would call the landline and it would diffuse the situation.

I had two sofas in the main room of the little flat I rented. One too many for a room no more than fourteen feet by twenty feet with a kitchen along one wall and a dining table that seated six! I was sitting on the sofa in the bay window, he on the other. I told him it was 'over over'. I don't think he was really bothered about me but he exploded about the fact that he had just handed in his notice on the flat he was renting to move in with me. Where the hell was he going to live? I'd screwed him over. He temporarily forgot the fact that he had told me he couldn't keep up the rent on the flat on his own. He stood up, walking round the sofa, raised his voice, started shouting at me, calling me names. I hit send on the text message and no more than a minute later the phone rang. He stopped shouting. He left the room. The situation was diffused. I stayed on the phone to my mother long enough for him to start to pack his bag. I don't think there was anything sad about the goodbye. Relief on my part. And I would be second-guessing if I was to suggest what he was feeling. But I'm fairly certain the next thing he did would have involved a drink.

After that I hadn't really been in a relationship for almost a decade. A few dates here and there. A lovely guy from Pinner who I met on holiday in Valencia one summer. He drove a Porsche. Had a lovely home – curtains were a bit flouncy but his mum had chosen them for him. Liked F1. Had good taste in restaurants and bars. Worked out. Had regular reflexology sessions. Looking back he was nice, really nice, probably would have been good for me. But if anyone was too 'nice' it made me wary. Some part of my brain was thinking 'there must be a catch' and 'it's a trap' After all I knew what happened when you put your faith and trust in people who everyone else thought were kind, responsible, human beings – at some point they left you for dead.

So here I was, at about forty-two, off to see another bloody hypnotherapist and CBT practitioner in the hope I could lose two stone, look like a super model, and find a boyfriend – a last ditch hurrah before I gave up entirely on the idea of being a mother. Although the idea of being a mother freaked part of me out.

She'd been in the press recently connected to the weight loss of several 'celebrities' although whether so-called celebrities are well known because they simply wanted to be and do whatever they possibly could to get themselves in the public eye, or because they have actually done something of note or are considered of good repute in the eyes of the world is up for debate these days.

It was another one of those consulting rooms on or around Harley Street. If these therapists were truly philanthropic and felt they had a calling to help the masses wouldn't they rent slightly cheaper premises so they could charge less and help more people? Everything ultimately seems to boil down to money and ego these days.

That said I am sure I was impressed by the receptionist who saw me up, the grandeur of the room, her expensive clothes. I was invited to sit on a chair quite a way from her – it was a big room. Far enough away that it didn't matter whether we were facing each other or in the classic ninety degree seating arrangement that seemed so 'popular'. I did feel very far away though. Quite removed. Detached. Was that conscious on her part? Was it just me?

She started with the admin questions – name, date of birth, yada yada. There was no 'GDPR' – General Data Protection Regulation – back in those days. I wonder what all these people have done with my records. Securely destroyed them all I hope.

I have no idea what anyone's impression of me would have been in those days. I imagine I came across as well-dressed, well-spoken and 'well-off'. Again, I just hate people who make judgements based on what someone looks like. Especially those people that make them and don't then allow themselves to see beyond that first impression.

I don't know why I seem to be able to put an outfit together. I am far from fashionable. Far from cool. But I suppose I see what I wear as a form of art, decoration. I know, that is borderline pretentious. But what I am trying to say is that I don't dress the way I do because I want to impress anyone, I dress the way I do because it's about colour, shape, form, flattery – painting a picture I like to the best of my abilities.

And I can only apologise that I sound 'posh'. Blame my mother's mother! My mother grew up in poverty. My grandmother was a home help, my grandfather's longest held job was head deckchair attendant on Southend beach. The rent collectors would regularly be at the door and my mother, just a child, would be sent to tell them 'Mummy isn't in now'. My grandfather was a gambling man – often what came in went straight out unless my grandmother managed to get hold of it. My mother wanted to go to university – unheard of for someone from her background in those days. In the end she left Sixth Form after one term to get a job so she could bring money in to support her mother and two younger brothers. She worked as a secretary at the Bank of England. Her first suit was made out of the black-out curtains. And she used to the get the milk train up to London at half four in the morning because she couldn't afford the commuter train. I hope her brothers, the second of which did go to university, and both of whom were successful in their own rights, were grateful for the sacrifices she had to make.

The thing was, it was a different era, and if you aspired to be something or someone you were expected to sound a certain way and know stuff. Apparently my grandmother used to tell them 'It costs nothing to educate yourself or to speak well'. And whilst I never met my grandmother it seems to have been passed from one generation to the next and I somehow missed out on speaking with an Essex accent!

My grandfather, well, there's surely a sadness there. Enrolled in the army at the age of fourteen following in the footsteps of his father who joined up aged eleven. What a life. How were you supposed to return from the routine and discipline of the forces, the trauma of war, all the things these young men must have felt and seen and get on with 'normal life'. Much the same as I had I suppose …

At some point the therapist asked me how my relationship was with my parents. Fine I told her. All good. Although in my head I have always wished I had rebelled. Perhaps it would never have been rebellion, just being my true self, my self without being raped at seven, but anything outside of being as 'normal' as I could be and as 'good' as I could be felt like rebellion.

Then she asked me if there was anything from my childhood that she should know about. Oh fuck. Here was that moment again. She seemed kind. She seemed genuinely interested. Should I trust her? Could I trust her?

The answer was no.

I mumbled something about having been abused when I was little. There it was. The slightly raised eyebrower. The moment when she looked into my eyes. I was wrong. I shouldn't tell anyone. It wasn't allowed.

Her next question was the killer. Something along the lines of 'did he have sex with you?'. I immediately felt like I was on trial. That I had done and said something wrong. I was so ashamed. And I didn't even know why I felt so fucking ashamed. She didn't believe me. If she'd just said something sympathetic. Given me a look of support, of concern. Instead she kept her focus on her note-taking and question-asking. That fucking bitch was still right – no one was interested, no one would believe me.

I withdrew into myself and away from the question. I answered No. The hypnotherapist's second and last comment on the subject was to utter something she evidently considered profound, along the lines of 'sometimes it's easier just to think of it as 'being interfered with' – makes it sound less traumatic.'

And that, ladies and gentlemen, was that.

I have, over the years, found the world – the people that inhabit it – to be, in the large part, extremely unsympathetic.

I saw this woman twice. I'm going to guess I paid her somewhere north of two hundred pounds. I lost two pounds (weight) in total – and the two hundred pounds cash. I probably came away from the experience feeling worse than when I went in.

I may have been let down, but, I reckon, somewhere inside me, the very heart of me, the tiny speck of light from Before that hadn't been put out, was gathering a bit of momentum, a bit of strength, from its bravery. It wanted out. The worst, however, was yet to come. Jesus. If I'd known then what I know now I would have done things differently.

*

I always believed I wanted children. But I don't know if I really meant it. Was it another of those 'there's something wrong with you if you don't get married and have kids' things? I desperately didn't want anything to be 'wrong' with me. I wanted to fit in … or rather did I want to <u>feel</u> like I fitted in? Because the reality of it, as I understand now, was that I never would be 'normal'. I hadn't had a 'normal' childhood. I had been the victim of an almost unimaginable crime which wiped my memory of Before and affected my ability to be loved even by my parents After. You know the one thing that would have changed all of this? If the bitches had done the human thing – protected me, cared for me, wrapped me in love, called my mother, taken the bastard to court, let my parents get the appropriate help and support for a seven-year-old to cope with and get over being raped - then the intervening forty-five years would never have happened or might not have been as impactful as they were. Who knows how my life might have turned out – Politics, Philosophy and Economics at Cambridge, acting, writing books and scripts, married to some like-minded man, children, …. In a word 'fulfilment' – or at least my idea of it at various points in my life. The saddest thing sometimes is I still want that, all of it, but some of it I know is too late and the rest I get lost in that old belief that I have no idea how to make it happen so why bother.

Deep down I had been terrified of having a baby. Terrified about having something growing in me. Terrified of having to give birth in front of people in hospital. Terrified I wouldn't be able to look after a baby and it would die. Terrified it wouldn't like me. Terrified I would be a bad mother. Terrified of bringing any human being into the world that might feel as depressed and sad and lonely as I did.

I was terrified of everything in life that I couldn't somehow re-interpret, re-engineer or re-construct so that I was in control.

I had recurrent dreams about either giving birth or forgetting I had a baby. I don't remember them all now, and I'm sure my psychologist would have a field day, but some are vivid enough that they have stayed with me.

I dreamt I went into a library. A very old one. Dark. Wood everywhere. The walls were lined with books and in the middle were rows and rows of wooden filing cabinets. I opened one cabinet and in it was my baby. But I couldn't remember being pregnant, or giving birth. I felt ashamed and alarmed that I couldn't remember. I was worried someone was watching me. The baby was not a baby that you or I would recognise. It was like a rag doll I had made when we lived in Pakistan for some months, when I was nine, out of old tights and newspaper – long, thin, eyes that looked as though they had been drawn on, immobile. I didn't want it to be mine. Didn't want the responsibility. Didn't understand why someone had said it was my child when I couldn't remember having it. That feeling that everyone was pointing at me because they could - because I was vulnerable, because I couldn't put up a fight. I was mute, inert, and they could take advantage of me and tell me I had to do it. I woke up in a horrible turmoil, breathing heavily, as I was trying to walk away from the filing cabinet and pretend nothing had happened.

I think it's quite clear what the sub-text is there!

I often had dreams where I had a baby but couldn't care for it. I would forget to feed it or give it water or give it the sustenance and love a child needs and a mother expects to give. Sometimes I had given birth but often it was just there. And always the same thing – I would come back and find the child weak or dying from my lack of attention and the lack of nourishment. In the dream I would feel such intense terror, hopelessness, failure that the feeling, when I woke up, could stay with me all day, compounding the self-loathing that I was so good at. Maybe the child was me. Maybe it was an expression of the fact I hadn't been able to look after little me when she was seven. Not that I should have been expected to look after myself. But they hadn't. And no-one else could.

For a decade or so, after the age of about forty-two I had to give up on the idea of children. A relationship was beyond my reach and one typically followed the other. I had a friend who decided before she got to forty that she was going to give artificial insemination a go. I am glad for her that she got pregnant and had a little boy who is growing into a young man. But once, when we had been for Christmas afternoon tea. I mentioned that I wished I'd had children. Her response was that if I'd really wanted children I actually 'would have done something about it' like her. It cut like a knife. She messaged me the next day apologising for being a bit direct. I brushed it off. I wish I'd had a voice then to let her know how cruel that was.

For a while into my late forties I thought I might meet a man with kids young enough I could play some part in their life, but it never happened. And now I'm out the other side of fifty I'd rather someone who didn't have the commitment of small children or teenagers. I know, we can't always be that picky, but the moment seems to have passed.

That's not to say I don't occasionally still wonder. Would I have been a good mother? Yes, I think so. Would my children have liked me? Yes, I think so. Would it have been fun? Definitely. Could it have been the making of me? Undoubtedly.

I love children – the way their minds work, the way they see the world, quite literally through a psychedelic kaleidoscope as their brain waves get faster and faster until some semblance of the world we have created comes in to view. I like having daft conversations with them, being very silly, making them laugh. A four-year old, fully dressed, in a paddling pool, could find entertainment in the expression 'I beg your pardon' where the majority of the rest of the world wouldn't. I like being daft generally but find it's not always so well received amongst adults. Whilst adults have a wider vocabulary than children I don't think they explore it as much. Us adults may have a wider vocabulary but do we play with it, or are we too rigid in our use of it? It's not about being clever it's about not filtering a part of yourself. Not filtering the child within.

For me, words and the ability to tell my own fairy tales has been some sort of comfort for all these years. They keep me entertained. All those expressions that peculiarly make my day easier: fuckaduck, fuckadoodledo, holy crap in a handcart, babooooooooon; talking to myself in terrible Spanish or French for my own amusement; making up words. Words allow me to write stories in my head, comedies, great long romances or philosophical treatises that have been decades in the writing and books I go back to and add to again and again for comfort, to understand myself and to feel understood, but, equally, are books that will likely never see the light of day. Words allow me to re-write stories. To re-define my thoughts.

Words are equally a form of art for me. The ability to construct a sentence that appears to tell one story but has layers of subtext if you read it carefully. Whilst not as complex as human behaviour in 3-D the complexity of the human condition <u>can</u> be expressed in language. It feels a dying art form in the age of social media soundbites. Words used to be more tangible, more meaningful, and to have more depth – they existed in books and letters and cards with little notes in that we could touch and feel. Now so much of it is stuck in the cloud in short form. Texts and voice messages and photos. Snippets of conversation, emojis to express sentiment. Send me a poem any day over a kiss emoji. Well, ideally send me both! But the action of writing a letter requires so much more investment and commitment than the ten seconds it takes to send a message saying ' I love you xxx'. Or the two seconds it takes to send that kiss emoji. Or the rushed 'sending lots of love' that so many of us add to the end of our voice messages. We almost do it by rote which undermines its value, its potency.

Actions speak louder than words. And words should come from the head and the heart, not convenience. Convenience is cheap when it comes to words.

*

Some time in the first half of 2017 the whole shit show rose up to the surface of my existence again. A very good friend of mine who is a personal trainer had a friend (or business acquaintance – I can't quite recall which) who was a life coach and MLP practitioner who was promoting a film called Embrace. A film about body positivism before it became quite as fashionable as it is six years later. Incredible how quickly now these things can become part of everyday existence on a global scale.

Life was getting tougher. Work was becoming the be all and end all of my existence – a form of self-flagellation that served no-one. I was perpetually tired, stressed, depressed, fed up, lonely, single and heard myself telling myself more and more frequently that I couldn't cope.

The film was good. The message was important. I remember one thing distinctly. After she took to social media with her story the Australian woman who had written and directed the film started to receive letters from women grateful for the light she had shone on issues around the judgement of and pressure on women to look and be a certain way. She included some excerpts from those letters in the film. In one a woman mentioned how the abuse she had suffered as a child had affected her relationship with her body.

I had that lurch in my chest and stomach, that constriction of my breath, that sudden fleeting and unpleasant sensation that something dark and impending had just blown through my body and mind at speed. My eyes began to water. I tried to hold my breath to stop the sound of sobs from escaping. I sat in the theatre, amongst all these people I didn't know, and cried silently but violently until the end of the film. It was becoming like a pressure cooker that wanted to blow after decades of gentle simmering and stewing, but one I couldn't take off the gas. From this point on it was - almost - out of my control.

A number of us went to a pub over the road after the film. I felt so self-conscious. In that moment I felt like a wreck, a waste of a person. I was judging everything about myself – my clothes, what I said, where I sat, how I sat. I could find no redeeming features. How could anyone be interested in this insignificant and pointless human being. My friend told me afterwards that one of the other girls there had thought I was lovely and wanted to arrange a night out together. This despite the fact I did what I had done so often in my life when the self-judgement in a social situation was overwhelming – I had made my excuses about being tired for work and having meetings the next day and left very early, so I could hang on to my tears on the bus, or tube or in a cab home before falling through the front door and crying until I was drained. What on earth could she possibly have found so interesting and engaging about me?

Fuck me! It's been a fucking miserable and hard life.

My mind is very good at being one step ahead of everyone else, including me. The seed had been sown to contact this 'life coach' and see if, finally, there might be someone who would listen. I found myself getting in to bed at night and imagining the conversations I would have with her about the abuse. I started to get comfortable with the idea. But the more I thought about talking about it the more I began to remember. What had started as the odd flashback - one or two images that had made it on to pages of my consciousness - was developing, like photographs and the images slowly – very slowly - becoming more distinct and taking all my senses back to then.

I called her number and left a message. She called me back later that day. I explained I had been abused when I was a child. She said she could help. I swear she sounded sympathetic. Looking back now perhaps a little matter of fact.

How do so many people in so many so-called caring professions manage to behave in such a detached way? Yes, yes, I get the concept of detachment, but over the years I have so often experienced red flags – are they out of their depth, are they generalising about what they see as stereotypes, are they making inappropriate comments – but the one that seems most common is that they see themselves as the fixer, the 'guru', some sort of saviour for others.

And yet I am probably only alive and well today because of the therapy I have received these last three years.

The difference between one and the other, in my humble opinion – humanity. Compassion. Kindness. In thought and word and deed. That intangible thing that means that even at the end of a laptop screen you can tell that a person is really listening. That they care. That in that moment you are more important than themselves.

In my humble opinion.

So off I trotted one day to somewhere in Mayfair to this woman's office. No doubt rented at great expense. She was sitting at a desk so vast it wouldn't have looked out of place in a parody of bosses that think they are big people but in fact are very small people. Yes, this is her. This is <u>that desk</u>.

I sat on what seemed like a child's chair the other side of the desk. She spent what felt like too much time talking about herself and the events that led her to become a NLP practitioner. I talked a bit about myself and what had happened. I swear she had one eye on the clock. The session was wound up very promptly after fifty minutes. I was two hundred and fifty pounds lighter. I doubt she was much help at all – more of a hindrance in terms of useful therapy. But I hadn't been evicted. She had – sort of – listened. She hadn't told me I had imagined it. I tootled off down the street feeling drained but vaguely positive.

Then some first level of hell was unleashed. Over the days before I went to see her again my subconscious took charge all on its own. I would get into bed at night and find images and memories of being in that room, of being abused, coming back to me more and more clearly. I was rolling downhill and couldn't stop.

Two nights before I was scheduled to see her next I gave in to whatever process my mind was trying to take me on and rather than seeing the memories from outside I decided to go back and be the child, to be me, again, at seven years of age, in that room.

I have no idea how long I lay in bed doing that. Crying. Feeling like I might choke as his hand rested against my throat. Screaming silently. Occasionally allowing myself to sob audibly ... but quietly enough that the neighbours wouldn't hear.

I was drained the next day. I had only got to sleep when it felt there was nothing left. When I had let myself get from the start when I walked in the room to the end when I left their office.

So as I walked into this therapist's room for the next appointment and she started talking about doing some work around going back to the event I told her I had already done it, and didn't want to do it again. It was fucking traumatic going back there – no idea why she seemed to think it was such a good one.

Did she take umbridge at my disagreeing with her?

She looked a bit non-plussed for a moment. I think she then defaulted to asking me to complete a questionnaire. While I was sitting there. I was hoping, as I think back, that it was something she had asked me to do between sessions but am fairly certain I sat in that room and filled in the answers to some questions while the clock counted down and the cost mounted up.

And I can only assume one of the questions was something to do with him because as she sat there one side of her huge desk and I sat there, vulnerable, in my little chair on the other, talking through what I had written down she actually asked me this question 'Do you feel sorry for him?' Or perhaps she said 'You have to feel sorry for him' with an upwards inflection at the end.

Ummm – let me think about this – NO!

NO. Of course I don't feel sorry for him.

I asked why should I?

Her response – because he wakes up every morning and has to live with knowing what he's done for the rest of his life.

What the fuck?

Really?

Why?

Was she so stuck in her own past – one that had led her to cleaning up her act, getting off drugs and becoming an NLP practitioner – that she woke up every morning feeling like she had to live with what she had done and thereby feeling some sympathy must always lie with the protagonist as well as the victim?

Had she forgotten I was in the room?

What the fuck made her think that was an appropriate thing to say, to suggest, to even think!

Talk to a clinical psychologist. I have spoken to two in the past few years. Both of whom apologised when I took them through all the times I'd been let down by so-called responsible, professional, caring therapists. They apologised for something they hadn't done. They apologised because someone had thought these were appropriate things to say to the victim of childhood sexual abuse. They apologised because they were sorry that these 'therapists' I had seen over the years had treated me that way and let me down.

The woman who believed, within about ninety minutes of first meeting me, that I should feel sorry for my rapist and forgive him realised she wasn't going to get me to change my mind and started talking about the reason that she liked working with me was because I was such a strong, inspiring woman. Blah Blah Blah. I suppose what I should have been thinking at that moment was 'yeah, whatever, now just apologise and fuck off'. Instead that foggy mist of anger and impossibility was descending, my thoughts were clouding as too many of them raced too fast around my head and, physically, the volcano was erupting again. I declined, far too politely I'm sure, a follow-on session.

And that was that. Until I received a text message from her some weeks later asking if I'd like to work with her again, repeating the flattery about me being an inspiring woman, etc etc – in the hopes I would cling to that flattery? In hindsight it all feels rather manipulative. I have a feeling I replied asking if this was something she was offering for free - she was evidently so keen to see me again and perhaps she felt bad for the way she had handled things last time. But no … this was her doing a bit of mass marketing. A 'send to all' to drum up a bit of business I assume. Depressing isn't it.

I'd almost forgotten - there was another 'life coach' I went to see some time around 2013. All these decades. All these people I went to for 'help'. It's like someone was playing a very cruel trick on me.

*

It wasn't but it felt that way. It still does. Sometimes. More often than I suspect it should.

Imagine. Something truly terrifying, confusing, unknown, petrifying, alarming, frightening, appalling happens to you. And the person who makes it happen tells you you must not tell anyone. And the next person you meet reinforces that message that you must not tell anyone, not even mummy. Because you must not tell anyone you believe something 'bad' must have happened. Because the people nearest to you when it happened and immediately afterwards seem agitated, you assume that if you tell anyone they will be really annoyed. Your conclusion is YOU must have done something bad, something 'wrong'. And because you have always been a good girl, and all little girls are brought up to believe they should be good, and because you never ever ever want to feel again like you felt then, you decide that you can never do anything wrong again. You spend your life striving for some invisible, unattainable perfection where you are the most 'good' person in the world, because surely then nothing 'bad' will ever happen to you again if you are.

Whenever anyone is annoyed you think you must have done something wrong. Whenver anyone ignores you

you think you must have done something wrong. Whenever anyone is unhappy you wonder if you are to blame. It's exhausting – and IMPOSSIBLE.

And because you are so worried it might ALL be your fault you become horribly, painfully defensive. You have nothing to defend. You are trying to defend something that happened when you were seven when they told you it was your fault. It's not appropriate, not relevant, not now. But you know no better. You need to defend yourself. You have to. You have to fight for your right to exist. Something happens and your head is like an SAS agent – it scans all potential threats to your being beyond reproach. In seconds you have assessed the entire situation – if an invisible aggressor pulled a gun on you now your senses are so heightened you could shoot first. God knows what other people made of this forensic approach to accountability and responsibility. And I would verbalise all the scenarios (well, perhaps not all, but more than enough), all the justifications, a detailed analysis of who said what, to whom, when, how, why with court-room precision. In amongst all of it I would be looking and checking for anything I might vaguely be seen to have said or done 'wrong'.

Again …. FUCK ME.

Shame is so much more than feeling ashamed. It evolves, over a lifetime, into a complex puzzle of words, actions, deeds, aspirations that you have to live by. Really – that you HAVE TO LIVE BY. If the pieces aren't in place it risks your very existence.

And by nature being preternaturally defensive makes you preternaturally subservient.

I first saw this in myself around 2017. I was setting up a Procurement function (yes – that is the so-called 'career' that took me in in the absence of doing anything I wanted to do with my life) at an asset management company in the City. Nice company. Great boss – Glaswegian who called a spade a spade and messaged his Executive Assistant from the train on the way in, to have Alka Seltzer and porridge on stand-by for him when he arrived at his desk if he'd had one too many beers or whiskies the night before. He was honest. And honesty is a quality I prize above most others – for bloody obvious reasons.

His EA was also a genuinely lovely, kind, compassionate human being.

Which makes it so frustrating that he left, she was offered redundancy and I found myself at my desk one day with the newly appointed COO of one the divisions (the company had recently merged) seemingly blaming me for something. A jolt went through me. I explain it that you can know something logically, rationally, but until 'the penny drops' and you know it in your gut, in the core of you, it counts for nothing. In that moment I realised that this woman, the COO, was basically being slopey-shouldered, and in implying the point in question wasn't her responsibility I had assumed the responsibility.

This would have been shortly after the two sessions with the woman who thought I should feel sorry for the old man who raped me. Something inside me had woken up. I hasten to add not because of the therapist.

I thought 'why the fuck does she think this is my responsibility?'. And I did something I don't think I'd ever done before – NEVER! – I pushed back.

In that fleeting moment sitting at a desk in an office between St Pauls Cathedral and Bank tube station the image of the bitches telling me to be good came to the front of the mind. And I became aware of something I had never been aware of before. That it wasn't all my fault, my responsibility.

So I'm surprised I didn't reach this place a few years earlier given my experience with the 'life coach' back in 2013.

*

There were a dozen of us in the meeting room – their account manager, technical lead, lawyers, our project manager, our lawyer, me. I was exhausted. I hadn't been sleeping again. I had called the GP's surgery on the way in to work. They said a doctor would call me back late morning. I prayed that the call would come through during a brief recess from page-turning the contract we were hoping to finalise that day.

My mobile rang just as someone was suggesting a break. I ducked out to the reception, hovering by the window, hoping the women on reception wouldn't be able to hear me. It was becoming a more frequent request – could I have some sleeping pills, just enough to get me back in the pattern of sleep and out of this self-fulfilling prophecy of being so worried about being tired that my anxiety kept me awake. I think they may have given me three or five days' worth – almost pointless. There was nothing more. No concerned questioning about any underlying reasons for the insomnia. A blanket acceptance of my hypothesis that it must be work stress. No doubt some platitudes about trying to get more of a work / life balance. I know these people are generalists, but even then it was starting to feel like I was a crumb they just wanted to flick off the page they were reading.

Before I had reached the point of asking for sleeping pills (with the guilt of a child who had done something wrong – how little I knew about myself at the time) I had tried other ways to help myself 'get better'. I googled 'hypnotherapists for insomnia London' and scrolled through who and what came up. I don't even remember her name. That's how insignificant she is to my life now. But I do remember what she did and said then.

Yet another bloody therapist hiring rooms on Harley Street, charging you for the privilege of the false façade of expertise based on price. It was a tiny room, so in hindsight she was obviously only just starting out. She had trained in hypnotherapy and neuro linguistic programming (NLP) with the great and the good - people that, at that time, I had time for. She had a rather monotone northern accent – not in my view ideal for a hypnotherapist. Somewhere I'll have the recording she made, tucked away in the virtual ether or in a cd or whatever format was used back in the day. I can tell you quite categorically it didn't help one iota. Yet somehow she had moved me from hypnotherapy for insomnia to life coaching to sort my stress levels out and I found myself signed up to a number of sessions for a very large amount of money where I would talk to her about what I really wanted to do with my life and how I could manage things to get there.

I have been consistent all my life in wanting to be a writer – since I was ten or eleven. There was a brief period in my thirties when I wanted to go into footwear design. I have a pair of mules I made on a weekend course and a certificate in footwear design and manufacture from UCLA to prove it. There were, of course, the forays into reiki, reflexology, massage therapy and the like. And around the age of forty-eight I thought I wanted to be an actress. But writing has always been 'it'.

So we sat there and talked about how I could find time to write which really only boiled down to the weekends as my job is cerebral and at the end of the working day my head, to use the technical term, is fried. We talked about friendships, family, relationships, hobbies, and all the usual stuff. And we talked about work. We talked about how I hated my job, hated corporate life, how I could be very good at it, put insane amounts of hours and effort into it, but, ultimately, I found it unfulfilling and HATED IT. I told her about the bastard boss who hadn't even read the business plan (which I had bust my guts to produce) the morning after I emailed it to him and instead came back and told me the page-numbering was wrong. I told her about the CIO who told me to hang on in there doing a job that was such hard work it was making me ill (working for a man who spent half the week in the pub) because the drunk would be going soon and then the Head of Procurement role would be mine. The one who didn't mean it. Him. And his ruse to keep me there and keep me sweet. He used me. They used me. And that feeling I got from being used was almost insufferable. No doubt a remembering of that day however many decades ago when it first happened. When I was used, abused and silenced. I sat there the day that CIO told me there was no job, that wasn't what he had said, feeling that same feeling of threat and impotence.

I told the therapist all of this and more. As usual there was a release and the relief of feeling like I was being listened to – even if I was paying for someone to do it. Then she started trying to take me down the road of forgiving these men and finding a way to enjoy the job. I know what she was trying to do but she was working from rote not reading the person in front of her.

No. I didn't think it was a good idea. I didn't want to go back there and try again. No I didn't want to think about how I might have done things differently. She was pushing me. I was getting ticked off. I'd said No and I wasn't sure why I was having to repeat the No or justify myself. I sat in my little chair, diagonally opposite her (of course), vulnerable, her with her notepad and pen as a first line of defence, and I raised my voice a little, the frustration creeping out.

And then she asked me why I was feeling angry. And I told her. 'I'm angry with you because you keep asking me to do something I don't want to do'.

Silence.

Probably only for a few seconds but nevertheless palpable.

And then she came out with another of the classic therapist lines I have heard over the years.

'Well, perhaps if you're angry we should end the session here'.

What sort of a fucking cop out was that!

It was apparently my fault. I had a quarter of an hour of the session left. She didn't like what I'd said. And instead of doing what she should have done and said - 'Elle, I'm sorry I made you feel that way, …' and then at best giving us a couple of breaths before suggesting we pick up somewhere else or at worst explaining the point she was trying to make before leaving it alone – the implication was that I had behaved inappropriately, I had done something wrong, it was my fault.

I really really really hope that there are better people out there these days. I don't feel confident in that hope but what can I do. Therapists and courses need more regulation. It is not appropriate to put someone who's done a two week course in NLP or hypnotherapy or CBT or whatever, and who has had no clinical training, in front of another human being and dig into their psyche without having the depth and breadth of understanding of the human condition to be able to properly care for everyone that crosses their door.

There is surely a reason why the people who helped me out of the infernal hole I was in three years ago trained for so long.

*

The itch was getting itchier and the scratching scratchier. My whole being was starting to creak with the weight of carrying the secret for so many years, this secret that got heavier with the passing of time as I built my prison around me, trying to protect me.

Physically my body was struggling. I developed a rash that wouldn't go. It spread all over my body except my face. My skin was on fire. I lay in bed at night with frozen peas on my back to take the heat out. I scratched so hard I bruised myself. No one could see how bad it was because it wasn't visible – hidden under my clothes – the story of my life.

I developed spots inside one eye lid. My psoriasis got worse. Patches of it all over my legs, spreading up my arms, over my torso. People at the gym stared more when I got undressed. People on the tube stared harder at my legs. And the dry skin flaking off making it look like my legs had dandruff.

I started to get sick every couple of months. A twenty-four hour fever that wiped me out. Another cold. Headaches like I had never had in my life.

The consultant that I eventually saw for my rash gave me a tonne of steroid and anti-fungal creams and decided that she wanted to remove a mole on my arm. No one came to the hospital with me for the minor operation – no-one, except my parents who lived two hours away, offered. She was unsympathetic. As she started to cut there was no pain but it was as if part of me had floated off to the side and I could exactly see what she was doing. I said I felt very faint and dizzy. The nurse took the pillow out from under my head and tried to calm me down. Afterwards the consultant, a goth in her sixties, said 'it's obvious you've never had children' somehow managing, it felt, to both belittle me for being nervous and for not being a mother.

I went to the Royal Free Hospital every six to nine months for someone to have a look at my psoriasis. Every time I filled out this same long form asking to what extent my condition interfered with my daily life - going to the shops, doing my job, what I wore, my sex life. Every time, given I had lived with psoriasis since I was a teenager, I would answer each question 'not much' because I had learned to live with the judgements of others and learned to put up with hating my body. The questions they should have asked are 'does it affect how accepting you are of your body?' and 'do people stare at your psoriasis and how does that make you feel?'. Every time they prescribed dovonox, emollients, the works. I gave up using them. It could take thirty minutes or more each morning just to try and dab a spot of dovonex on the dozens of patches on my legs and on my elbows which frequently looked like someone has dragged me across gravel. Once I told the consultant that if I used dovonex for over a month I started to feel depressed. And I definitely did not need to be doing or taking anything that made me feel more depressed. There is no link apparently. Well, chemically perhaps not, but psychologically he may have missed the point. I stopped using them. It was pointless. It always came back.

I started to be a regular at the GP's surgery. Could it be the menopause? One of the doctor's at my surgery wrote weekly in a national newspaper. The previous year she'd written a long article on the menopause and how she, as a doctor, could help. I went to see her expecting some understanding and support. I told her that once a month I was so tired you could kick me and I still wouldn't complain. I got headaches, I ached, weirdly even my gums hurt. Basically I was feeling like shit a lot of the time. She asked if I still had periods. I said yes. She told me there was nothing that the NHS could do until I hadn't had a bleed for a year. Remind me – what was it you wrote in your article?

When I had the hideous fiery rash I gave up sugar. Because of the psoriasis I gave up gluten.

I was trying to do anything and everything I could do simply to keep going. All pleasure began to disappear from life and the chorus I heard myself repeating and repeating was 'I can't cope'.

*

Who can really say when something began and when it ended. Isn't there always something that pre-dates the thing that we thought pre-dated the thing that we thought was the beginning? And isn't what seems like the end just the beginning of something else?

In 2011 I walked one hundred miles of the Camino de Santiago. It's a whole other story but it truly felt like the beginning of something. The Camino is a pilgrim route. I walked it as a pilgrimage – not a religious one – but it held a significance greater than it just being a long walk as I was walking with a prayer for some God, the universe, the powers that be, in my head and my heart. I was walking because I wanted a boyfriend. But because that sounded shallow I told myself – and anyone that asked – that I was walking for LOVE.

I apologise now to God, the universe and those powers that be (and myself!) for not being specific enough and for the hard work that followed over the next six, seven, maybe more years of excruciating emotional and psychological effort to get me to a place where I understood LOVE, where I loved myself and started to allow myself to feel a more 'loving' connection to others.

From the first night I arrived in Leon my subconscious was doing all it could to sabotage my Camino experience. After two nights I called the emergency line for the travel company that had arranged flights and accommodation and said I needed to get out. In reality I was a bus or taxi ride from civilisation but felt like I was lost in a land I didn't know. I hadn't done anything like this before – because I didn't think I could. I was the person that friend's excluded from meals out to restaurants with spicy cuisine because they thought it would be too adventurous for me. I was the person that was mocked on a camping weekend because I'd bought a pair of flat gold mules with me – gold sandals somehow implying that I was unfit for and therefore incapable of partaking in camping life? I was nervous about a lot of things. I had suffered from claustrophobia since I was a child. I know I was something of a closed book, perpetually scared I would be judged and rejected, but no-one ever asked, no-one extended that sympathy. No-one ever touched my arm, looked me in the eyes and said 'are you ok?'. NO-ONE.

Well, not that I remember.

Was I that impermeable?

To cut a very long story short I made the one hundred miles and, with a lovely woman from Wales who had been my walking partner most of the way, we arrived at the Cathedral in the middle of a service, the incense swinging in a vast censer up and across the nave. The feeling of the achievement, of having done something for myself, of having kept a promise to God, of having discovered I wasn't entirely worthless, useless and un-lovable … it was overwhelming. We made our way around the back of St James and I gave him a hug of deep gratitude. Then down to the sacristy. There was a narrow wooden prie-dieu with a deep red velvet arm rest on top. Room for two. It faced a window behind which … I don't even remember because I knelt down and I cried. I don't know what I cried for, but I cried, head in hands, unafraid (in that moment) of being seen, knowing that if nothing else God loved me. I don't mean a religious God. I mean God in the sense that there is something greater than us, some energy that makes our brief human lives so insignificant, and in that moment, knowing what I had achieved, knowing why I had done it, I felt that magnitude, that sense of being part of something much bigger than the mundanity of daily life, I felt connected.

But they say whatever you ask for on your pilgrimage you will get. I wondered what on earth was going on for the next maybe six, twelve months, possible a bit longer, when the boyfriend didn't materialise. And then I realised the rookie mistake I'd made. I'd asked for LOVE. And love is vast. Understanding, knowing, being and feeling, love is on a grand scale. There followed a very difficult period of time as I started to dismantle the first bricks in the wall I'd built up around myself over the previous decades – at the same time as having to erect some temporary defences as I delved further into the experience of what most people would call a 'normal' life' and found myself feeling, constantly, under some sort of threat.

Not too many years later I enrolled myself in acting classes at The Central School of Speech and Drama. I had this almost violent need to be seen. Something kicking and screaming inside of me with no way out as I had no voice and had spent my life trying to be invisible, to go un-noticed, for fear of a recrimination that never was and never would be. And this perpetual fear of being rejected all over again. I rejected myself so no-one could do it for me. Of course, physically I was present. I existed in some human form. But emotionally, psychologically, spiritually, I was absent.

And I wonder, still, if anyone noticed.

I wonder what, in fact, people did see.

People have always made the same sort of judgements about me – somehow I give the impression of a privileged childhood, wealthy parents, a life of luxury (whatever that might constitute). Oh how far from the truth all of that is. And on what basis do they make that judgement – my clothes, the accent (or lack of one), how I choose to spend my hard-earned money?

Well I'm sorry to disappoint, but I am very much working class. At a push first generation middle-class (I fucking hate these ridiculous generalisations and the need to pigeonhole people – to decide whether they merit your empathy and compassion or not).

So my mother was born and brought up in the old-fashioned sort of poverty. A little girl sent to the door to tell the bailiffs 'Mummy isn't home at the moment'. A fire lit in her bedroom only when she was ill in bed with the flu. Little money coming in. No financial support, no scholarships, no opportunities other than sheer determination and desire. She wanted to go to university to defy the expectations of her forebears and her upbringing but instead had to leave school in the first year of her A Levels to bring in money to help her mother pay the rent and feed her younger brothers. She took a job as a trainee secretary at the Bank of England. Her first work suit was made from the old blackout curtains. She used to get up early enough to catch the milk-train into London as it was cheaper.

My father grew up in Waterworks house, which his father managed. The family lived in. He was sent away to the countryside during the second world war and whilst the family took to his older brother and twin sister they didn't take to him – surely through no fault of his own. Just a little boy they would lock him in the cupboard under the stairs, opening the door occasionally to the throw boots in at him. He did his national service up in Liverpool and went on to do an apprentice in electrical engineering, eventually qualifying as an aeronautical engineer.

I am so proud of my parents. So proud that they survived their own difficult childhoods. So proud of what they achieved to give me and my brother a family home, holidays, presents, and a sense that we could choose where we wanted to get to in life but on the understanding, unless you were a very lucky sod, you had to put the effort in.

So why don't people believe me when I tell them I come from working class stock, when I tell them that my parents, in their dotage, are not financially 'well-off' (even though they still consider themselves 'fortunate')?

Is it really because of the way I speak, the way I dress, my education (at school and in life)?

It drives me nuts. My life has been far from easy, far from privileged. Don't make your judgements about me based on your first impression and then leave them hanging there without even getting to know me. Don't call me 'lucky'!

Drama school was at once terrifying and life-affirming. We were a right old mix! The teacher, Lena, was divine – and equally life-affirming. At that first class we played lots of games. And I love a game. I like competition. I like to win. It makes me think I must be 'good' at some thing. Or at least it used to.

Being present, filling the moment, keeping everything moving. It all seemed to be designed around those requirements. I was self-conscious, yes, but I felt safe. Yes there were people here who had made that judgement about me without knowing my truth, but there were also enough people who saw beyond that, possibly even a couple of people who saw beyond the fortified outer walls.

I left after three hours to get the bus home. Except something was fizzing inside me and instead I walked home in tears. Why was I crying? Frustration I think. I was frustrated about how uncomfortable I felt in my own skin, frustrated about how difficult I found it to express myself, frustrated about the fact that deep down in me I could feel this other person who frantically wanted to get out but was trapped.

Of course that's not what I actually thought as I walked home. I may have had some vague concept of it deep in my subconscious that momentarily passed across my consciousness, but I didn't really know it. I felt it. But couldn't put words around it. I wasn't even connecting the dots and understanding that this feeling of not being myself was linked to what happened when I was seven.

That was yet to come.

I loved the classes. I started to wonder if I could become an actress. Television or film, not the theatre. It was too much to think I'd be able to learn, at my age, to cope with the nerves that must come from walking out, live, in front of hundreds of people. Having them see me, judge me, tell me whether I'd been good or bad. The risk of being a failure, of not being 'good' was too high.

That was the most terrifying part of the acting classes – the homework, or our little thirty second improvisations in front of the rest of the group. That feeling of complete exposure. Each time I was fighting the thing I'd run away from for decades. The first homework we had was to pretend we were an animal. To study the mannerisms and behaviour of an animal and do it in class. I was, literally, petrified. Yet at the same time wanted someone to see me and tell me how great my panda impression was. It can't have been too bad as I was one of the first up and it was guessed within two seconds. Far from feeling chuffed at my evident ability to mimic a panda I felt cheated that I had had so little 'floor time' given the immense psychological effort that had gone into coping with my fear of and feelings of being vulnerable. I wanted to be seen, I had been seen, but not for long enough for anyone to see the girl that was trapped inside the woman in front of them.

We were to put on an end of term show. In pairs we were to act out short scenes from Chekhov's The Three Sisters. I wanted to be one of the sisters. I was cast as Andrei Prozorov. A man. At the age of ten I had had all my dark curly hair cut off because the other children at junior school used to make fun of it (why?) and having had it all cut off was repeatedly mistaken for a boy. When I was at college me and two girlfriends went to a fancy dress party in hideous 1960s dresses, cheap wigs and awful make-up. I walked past several people during the evening commenting that I must be a man in drag because I was so tall. I get sick to death of people working out of call centres calling me Mr because I have a deep voice. All my life I had avoided embracing my womanliness, my curves, what I assume is some inherent sexiness, because of what happened to me, because I wanted to avoid men wanting sex with me and nothing more. And yet I wanted so much to be seen and to be seen as someone attractive – something which I assumed I wasn't as no-one ever asked me out, I rarely dated, I had never been married, I didn't have children – as an attractive woman, even as a beautiful, graceful, seductive, woman.

It was nothing to do with not being attractive. And if I look back now I see I was beautiful when I was younger. I think I scrub up okay now. But I had this wall around me and no-one could come in. A beautiful woman stuck in some hell of believing everything about her is ugly. Trying to prove her worth by competing intellectually.

So no - I wasn't happy that I was cast as a bloody man! Not happy at all.

Life can be so ironic. I was cast with Jo, another woman I'm guessing a few years older than me. We were to act the scene where Andrei is talking to Ferapont, another male part. As we sat in our pairs and were given our scripts I was talking to Jo about how I didn't want to play a man, telling her about school, about being the tallest person in junior school until Steven caught up with me, about being mistaken for a boy so many times, ... Once, after we had all become friends and there were the occasional social drinks, I met up with Jo and she told me that she had transitioned to being a woman over twenty years previously. How brave. And how curious that neither of us, in very different ways, had wanted to be men, but found ourselves acting out these male roles in front of the class. Maybe it was something we had both had to do during our lives, for very different reasons.

In any event, she just listened, she didn't say anything. She only suggested that our teacher must have some reason for it. Which I eventually asked her. And which she confirmed. Without telling me why.

I have no idea how much anyone else in the class became obsessed with getting it just right but I reached the point where I wasn't getting to sleep because I got in to bed and ran through the few pages of dialogue over and over until the image of the performance in my mind's eye was perfect. God, it was stressful. And all for what would amount to no more than five minutes in front of a group of people I hadn't known three months earlier in a warehouse of a room in a building in Swiss Cottage.

I hadn't known it was possible for every organ in your body to be shaking with fear and yet to still somehow be able to sit quite still, in a chair, and open your mouth and structured, considered, acted words come out. I think now of another context – silenced by fear at seven and managing to act through it forty years later. Even when we don't recognise or understand what is going on around us or happening to us there is a part of us that does somehow pick up on the 'rightness' or 'wrongness' of a situation, the 'rightness' or 'wrongness' of the intent of others …

Our teacher announced to everyone afterwards that I had given 'a masterclass in stillness'.

Stillness. Something I rarely gave myself over to other than in the confines of my home or out and about on my own. Always distracting myself, distracting everyone around me, always a conversation to make, to be had. Never a moment of complete silence, stillness, when I let the absence of words and actions reveal how I felt or the emotion I was holding back, giving myself (and given) enough space to then let that emotion flow.

At home I was invariably still. Lying on the sofa. Lying in bed. I'd give myself permission to feel all my character could and should feel given the events of her past, the need to reveal herself, the doubt, the rethinking again and again.

So acting – tick. I could.

But I couldn't. The more I connected with these emotions, the more I showed myself to the world – this tiny subset of human beings in whose orbit I existed – the more unbearable the weight of something became.

In the years after the Camino I lost my way spiritually. I'd always believed in that sort of 'Godness', an energy of existence that embodied something positive that gave us a reason to live and to aspire to live. I lost that sense of faith in life. I lost the ability to find a reason to get up every day and carry on walking. I struggled, psychologically, to put one foot in front of the other and yet my head only seemed to clear enough for me to lose the feeling of suffocation if I walked.

I walked everywhere. Into town, round the park, across town to meet friends, to Waterloo station, home from work. I walked and walked and walked and bloody walked. I walked to clear my head, to fill the time, to distract me from being at home and acknowledging how I felt, what was going on, what had been punching and kicking all these years and was getting nearer and nearer to breaking out.

I was ill on and off for six months but still, seemingly, functioning. I had no concept of self-care. I signed up to the next term of acting class. Another group of lovely people, a few who had been on the first course with me. That feeling of non-judgement again. But the teacher – no, not this time. I'm sure this new teacher had made a judgement about me – and perhaps I had about him – and that played out every week I was there. I skipped a couple of classes – I was so frigging tired. Some days the alarm went off and I don't know how I hauled myself into the office and sat there over-performing day after day. I was putting on weight. Who knows – the menopause, depression, the recurrent bursts of insomnia and the related increased consumption of Disaronno? Was this extra fat another layer of protection as I started to feel more exposed? And did the teacher take umbridge at my absence? Think I wasn't taking it seriously? Think I was just some middle-aged posh woman finding another hobby to indulge herself in the evenings? Think I didn't have an appetite to learn, to do something different, to change her life?

We were all asked to prepare a monologue that we would do in front of the class. One or two of us each week. Because I knew no better, and because my research extended no further than Google, I chose Shylock's monologue from Act three Scene one of the Merchant of Venice.

I may have been imagining it but I always seemed to be this teacher's last choice for everything. And yet anything I did he was complimentary about. One week he said, after class, that we would do my monologue the next week. I went into meltdown.

Shylock's words spoke to me – a man as equal as the next but judged different, through no fault of his own 'laughed at … mocked at … cooled by my friends … have I not hands, organs, dimensions, senses, …. Healed by the same means, warmed and cooled by the same winter and summer, … if you prick me do I not bleed? If you poison me do I not die? …. Revenge. The villainy you teach me I will execute it and I shall go hard but I will better the instruction.'

Wasn't I the same as everyone else? Why should I feel different, have been treated differently, have been judged for nothing that is my fault? The words boiled inside me as I learnt them and lay in bed for hours seething inside as I recited and recited feeling the weight of every observation and accusation and … for the first time in my life the feeling of the desire for revenge.

I even messaged Lena to ask her what was going on with me. Was this 'normal'? I was starting to freak out about the extent to which speaking these words with real emotion in front of twenty other human beings felt more like I would be standing naked in front of a camera broadcasting my darkest secrets to the four corners of the world.

I turned up at the next class ready, if not raring, to give myself over. We had some students in from another class who were studying production and spent the evening at their bidding, exploring the actor / producer relationship of what, when, how, why. I was expecting, at the end of the class, to be asked to perform my monologue as that had been the format of previous weeks. The clock ticked on and the big hand got close to ine. Nothing. The class ended. No monologue. No me. Overlooked, as usual.

I don't know if there would have been another opportunity. I have a feeling I didn't go to the next class. I know he had no idea what acting meant to me – but that was because he never asked. I know he didn't know how much it hurt to have the pattern of my life repeated yet again and not to be given the same chance, the same time, the same space as everyone else, but that doesn't mean it doesn't matter that he didn't.

Inclusivity. The voice of those that don't speak up is as equally valid to the voice of those that do. Sadly social media is skewing what we read and hear – at one end of the spectrum of the 'voices' are those with the uber confidence and self-belief to 'show' themselves because they believe so categorically in themselves and their right to be seen, and at the other end those who hide in the darkness but spew out vile judgement and criticisms because they believe in their opinions and their rights to express them so categorically. And what of the silent majority?

But with Shylock's speech had come the unlocking of that rage inside me that had never had a voice, the unlocking of a belief in my voice's rights and a right to be seen or heard.

*

I took some time out in 2017-2018 to write.

The past was seeping into the present. Everything was an act of trying to find a way to get rid of this feeling, this thick black cloud of nothing and everything that I breathed in every day, that followed me everywhere, weighing me down, reminding me how completely and utterly shit everything about my life felt and therefore must be.

I had an idea of what I wanted to write. I don't have the foggiest idea now what it was but I had it all mapped out – structure, purpose and so on. Then I went to see a play above a pub, somewhere near Tooting Broadway. One of my friends from acting classes was in a re-imagining of the relationship between Lewis Carol and Alice and four of us went along to see the performance.

She was good. Except there was something about the play, the way it portrayed Alice, as being somehow promiscuous, somehow knowing 'what she wanted', somehow 'playing' Lewis for her own conscious gains, that didn't sit well with me. As I sat there I felt the quiet anger I had carried around for so many decades starting to shake inside me, as it did so often now. It's not the little girl's fault, I thought. It never is. She doesn't understand the complexities of what's 'right' and 'wrong' at that age, she doesn't understand manipulation, she doesn't understand why she has to keep 'it' secret other than she has been taught that you're supposed to be a good little girl, and knowing that if you annoy the grown-ups then treats, toys, fun will all be in short supply.

Regardless of whether the story was one young writer's view of the world and attempt to write and produce something 'shocking' did the writer realise that he was, subconsciously, perpetuating that very judgemental, gender-stereotyped view that it must somehow be the woman's fault?

We got a drink at the bar downstairs afterwards as we waited to see Siobhan fresh from her performance. One of us made some comment about the play. I must have been feeling safe with this group, un-judged, able to be a little bit more me, confident with their mixed backgrounds and lifestyles that they would get it, so I found myself making a comment about the play's stereotypes, about its very male-orientated perspective and that so few representations of rape on television or on stage really truly show what really truly happens when you are the victim of sexual assault, when there are no circumstances or behaviours that could lead anyone to think even for a split second that it was your fault, and really truly capture the violent and immediate impact this has on every cell of your being, how it shatters everything – ABSOLUTELY EVERYTHING.

I didn't express it quite like that. But I made the point.

I was waiting for someone to say something back. To understand that maybe I knew because I knew. To say something, anything. Even to bloody disagree so I could argue, could tell them about me, tell them how no-one knew anything and everyone was fucking wrong.

But nothing.

Nothing. Nothing. NOTHING.

The same nothingness that I'd been met with every time I thought it was safe, thought it was time.

So I went to bed that night thinking I would be sat at my writing desk at half nine the next day to start the new book and woke up knowing that there was another book I had to write. I would write a fictional account of my own story. I could be seen without being seen. I could give my voice to someone else who wouldn't meet the resistance I had met, who could find the support I had failed to find.

I wrote almost every morning for ten weeks. Every morning I cried. Every sentence was tears. Every word felt, as I remembered. I wrote the book. I was exhausted. I was depressed, but didn't know it. I felt better for allowing myself what had always seemed the indulgence of feeling my feelings.

That feeling barely lasted.

I took a trip to Rome and Florence. As well as having saved up enough money to give me eight or nine months freedom from work I had taken out some additional borrowing on my mortgage and I blew a chunk of it on business flights and nice hotels. I didn't sleep well in Rome. I paid eleven euros for a thimble of coffee one morning in Piazza del Poppolo when the rain came down and I had no umbrella. The waiter didn't even thank me. I visited a Palazzo somewhere not too far from the

Vittorio Emanuele II and was so overwhelmed by the feeling of some memory that I sat on a chair at the edge of the room, pulled my sunglasses over my eyes and cried.

After three nights I took the train to Florence. It was a short walk from the station to the hotel, the Firenze Porta Rossa. I had a 'superior room' booked for four nights. I checked in, was given a key card and pointed in the direction of the lift. The room was poky and the building's air-conditioning unit was outside my window. I was exhausted from not sleeping well the past few nights in Rome. I was exhausted because I was letting whatever had been buried deep, almost dead, for all those decades come back to life and the rage I had been carrying that little me had never been seen or cared for or considered, was gathering force and pace and potency. And I just couldn't cope any more. The inability to cope had become my mantra. The struggle of getting through each day was increasingly difficult. I lay on the bed desperate for some sleep, some respite from life. An anger started to spill over – how dare they put me in the cheap room just because I am travelling on my own, how dare they not see me, how dare they not treat me the way they would treat the next guest. I howled, silently.

I called reception to complain about the noise of the air-conditioning and she came up to the room. I opened the door, red eyed and puffy faced. She said there was only one other room available but it was small. We went to see it and it was so small there was just a single bed wedged between the window and an internal wall. I was trying, unsuccessfully, not to cry. A noisy hotel room had tipped me over the edge. It may have seemed ridiculous but it wasn't, not to me, not at the time. I think I may have exaggerated the truth of some aspect of my exhaustion to her as I held back the tears. Fifteen minutes later she called up to the room and said they had managed to work something out. I moved to a room that was light and spacious and quiet – one that, curiously, looked just like the room in the photos when I made the booking!

The sun was out and I changed into a dress to go and find somewhere to eat and then see the sights, my fear of not sleeping temporarily put to one side.

I don't know what happened next or why. I tried not to cry but I couldn't stop it. I wandered around and around the same few streets to walk the tears away but they wouldn't stop. I was a mess but I was hungry. There was one table left outside a restaurant near the Uffizi and I took it. My big black sunglasses didn't leave my face. I cried my way through a litre of sparkling water, some bread and a salad. I imagined everyone else was staring, wondering what was wrong with me - as I had done all my life. I paid. I left. I walked around Florence under an increasingly cloudy sky until it felt time enough to go back to the hotel.

My brain was wired. Creatively it was so on fire I couldn't keep up with all the ideas - books, stories, plays, images that came and went before I could commit them to memory or write them down. I couldn't switch myself off. I did the only thing that was within my means at that time and went out for dinner and to drink some wine. Someone out there will be telling me I should have been lying quietly in the room, phone off, no distractions, practising breathing techniques and mindfulness. Well fuck that. It doesn't work. I know. Up to a point maybe, but when you are out the other side of that point and the anxiety level has switched up from 'average' to 'chronic and consistently debilitating' the one thing, other than drugs, that switches my mind down a gear, slows down the insane pace of my thoughts, is a glass or two of wine. Three or four if I'm looking to spin my thinking out completely before bedtime. Five, six or more if I want to forget. Then I live with the regret and shame the next day.

I got back to the room sometime, I imagine, around eleven. Probably three glasses of wine down. I no doubt did what I always did before bed – un-dressed, took my make up off and washed and moisturised my face, brushed and flossed my teeth, got into bed and read a few pages of a book. I drank some water, put some lip balm on, turned the light off, lay there for a few minutes on my back reflecting on life, the universe, everything, put my eye mask on and turned over.

The last time I checked the time it was approaching five in the morning. I could not get to sleep. COULD NOT. Fuck me. Those bloody thoughts and feelings had crept up on me as I lay there, stealthily encroaching on my dream space, until they were whirring round my head, in the air around me, liked crazed tormentors. Then that moment of implosion and explosion and the calm after the storm – but more like the realisation there has been a collision after the impact. Shocked but alive, the mind and body calm and sleep comes. They don't calm by themselves. I have to find a route in, a distraction that holds enough interest, strikes the right chord, to properly take me away from it all.

*

I was lost. Completely and utterly LOST in this dense fog of thoughts and feelings that I couldn't see, couldn't describe, couldn't put a name to and yet was stuck in the middle of with no way out. The emotions were consistently overwhelming and suppressing them all day until I got back to the safety of home was exhausting.

Logically I knew something was up but I couldn't, logically, put a finger on what. Some part of me knew it was something to do with the assault but there seemed to be so much of 'it' that I couldn't find a way in, a road to follow that would lead me somewhere, take me out of this heavy darkness.

Sometime in early 2019, maybe even over Christmas and New Year, when I had some space to sleep in, go to the gym, to relax, to get away from work, I read an article in a Sunday magasine written by a someone who always came across as rather cynical and curmudgeonly about having attended a 'transformational workshop' and had their socks knocked off by the experience.

I googled. I was drawn in to the idea that this might be some sort of nirvana to resolving what remained unresolved. There was a similar workshop at a yoga centre near me in a few weeks so I booked. And a few weeks later I found myself lying on yoga blankets on the floor with thirty or so other people, mostly women, in a heavily incensed yoga studio. Music was playing. I had taken a spot right at the edge of the room – never one for centre stage. The chap running the afternoon talked a bit about himself, talked a bit about what to expect, talked about the role of his assistants who would come around the room and spend some time with each of us as we experienced our 'transformation'. And then off we went. Eyes closed, mouth open, deep breathing in and deep exhales – the room was not quiet. The theory was that this experience, and the giving over of ourselves to it, somehow enabled the mind and body to access and let go of emotion, feeling, trauma that was trapped. As the time passed and we all got further into this rather hypnotic state of being and breathing I heard the sound of people crying quietly around the room. And then the woman next to me – some glamorous type in skinny leggings and top, hair perfectly coiffed, the sort that commands attention just by their presence and who knows it – the absolute fucking opposite of how I felt about myself or how I imagine anyone might perceive me – started to cry. But not just quietly. She was howling. One of the assistants came to her. I remember that no-one had, yet, come to me. Why her? Why not me? Just because I wasn't making a show of my emotions did they assume – do you assume – that I am alright? Do I have to scream and shout and wave my hands in the air for someone to ask if I am okay?

My rage at 'why her, not me?' was starting to bubble up. In my head I was shouting 'ME … ME … ME … ME.' All my life it had never been me. I had never been allowed to be seen or heard. I wanted to be let out. I wanted it to be okay to be seen. I gave in to myself, just a little, and let myself cry, quietly. But they were big fat tears. My body convulsed as I cried and as I tried to contain the noise of the emotions erupting inside me.

An assistant came over. She was kind, caring. She let me know physically she was present by putting her hand on my arm. Part of the process was to use acupressure to press on areas of the body that have been (supposedly) mapped to emotions, states of being, and to repeat affirmations about yourself. A cynic would say this practice grew out of the post-criminalisation of hallucinogenic drugs in the US in the 1960s and the search for a legal 'high'. I am ambivalent.

What I'm not ambivalent about is how the rest of my year panned out.

The assistant guided me – she pressed under my breast bone and repeated phrases in the first person which I supposedly took on as my own. I don't really remember anything she said but I do remember that feeling of someone caring about me. The problem was the bloody floodgates. They had been opened and there was such a torrent inside me I could only fake closing them as she moved on and circulated around the room.

And there was the problem. I had decades of hurt that I had been burying inside me. It was never enough, and never would be enough, to take the odd couple of hours out to 'process it'. I didn't understand this at the time but it would take weeks, months, possibly even years, to work through, accept and learn to live with the enormity of what had happened and how it had shaped me, and then to re-become the person I was born to be.

But that workshop had given me an idea – perhaps this was the tool I could use to get over the trauma. Writing the book hadn't worked. Talking to that bloody therapist hadn't worked. Talking to friends was obviously a non-starter as no-one had really shown any concern or interest. Family was too complicated. And generally everyone seemed to want to find a way to 'fix' things – as did I – rather than caring for me – which I had never been any good at.

So I spent the next year lost but keeping my head above water as I hung on to my latest life raft of transformational workshops and teaching. I booked into an all-day workshop somewhere Shoreditch way. I even chatted with some of the other people on the workshop over lunch rather than doing my usual thing of either leaving the building and going for a smoke, or sitting on my own. I have a feeling people often thought me aloof – in reality I was incredibly self-conscious, thought I had nothing interesting to say, naturally assumed everyone else was 'better' than me, and at some level resented the fact that no one ever seemed to see 'me', the real me that was stuck somewhere at the end of a very long path into the darkest forest, like the final, almost impossible level of the world's hardest video game (not that I have played video games). It often felt as though I only truly existed as the tiniest version of myself inside this body I inhabited, like the Hightopps in Alice Through the Looking Glass. That miniature me waving away furiously, deep inside me, hoping, just hoping, someone would spy me out of the corner of their eye.

I was following the 'guru' who ran the workshops I'd been to on Instagram. He announced that he was running a training course for small groups of people to become practitioners. Two thoughts ran swiftly across my consciousness – this could be the route to eviscerating the past and this could be the route out of corporate life.

A third thought loitered around the back of my consciousness not wanting to draw attention to itself – that perpetual hope, whether friend, boyfriend, other, that someone would come along to save me. Looking back the only person who could – and did – save me was me. Even when I was on retreat at Plum Village in France in 2019 (therein lies a whole other story I had momentarily forgotten) and had the realisation that 'I had always been me', even when I knew that the only person who could fix me was me, I still had this feeling of needing someone to save me, of wanting someone to come along and save me the effort and the complexity of having to save myself. I just didn't want to have to cope – on my own – with being me any longer.

Actually, Plum Village was such a bizarre experience perhaps I should stop off there for a couple of minutes for some light relief! Where to start …. I guess with the fact that after wanting to go on retreat for years but not going predominantly because I was worried I wouldn't be able to sleep in the very basic accommodation and worried about sharing a room with people I didn't know, I decided I was in the sort of place where I could in fact cope with it for a week. Oh how wrong, in hindsight, I was!

I flew into Bordeaux one afternoon. It was around Easter time. Nice hotel in the centre of town. Had to move room – just the once this time - because they had evidently hoped that I wouldn't mind the noise from the lift shafts next door despite my request for a quiet room – if there were emojis in books I would insert the eye-rolling emoji here. Got myself some dinner somewhere, couple of glasses of wine, reasonable night's sleep. Woke up a bit on the early side the next day and went for a wander around Bordeaux. Final pit stop for coffee, a croissant and a last smoke before I got the train to somewhere where I had to change for the bus ride to somewhere where I picked up a taxi to Plum Village.

Train was fine. Had another last smoke as I waited for the bus which was bloody uncomfortable. No leg room. Too crowded. Of course, I assumed, these were visitors off to vineyards as well as us retreaters. The bus thinned out and when we got to my stop only a handful of people got off and no-one else joined me in heading out to Plum Village. I had a final last smoke waiting for a taxi.

I arrived a little earlier than they said they would be open for guests. It was very peaceful. I took a photo of the Plum Village welcome sign and promptly posted it on Instagram – look at me everyone. LOOK AT ME. Look what none of you thought I could do but I did! Without realising what I was actually thinking was 'look what I didn't think I could do but I did'.

I checked in, a nun was assigned to show me to my accommodation and show me around. I had booked one up from the dormitories where I might be sharing with a whole group of people and was in a double bedroom with shared bathroom. I hadn't realised I'd be in what amounted to a treehouse for adults. We walked the couple of hundred metres from the main buildings along a gravelled path to a two-story wooden building, me dragging my suitcase on wheels noisily behind me. I was in a room on the first floor up a tiny, very narrow spiral staircase – the sort that could kill you if you missed your footing. The nun didn't offer to carry my suitcase. I'm not sure I had expected her to but I thought she might offer and I would refuse. But she did manage to ask why I had brought so much stuff with me. I explained to her that I had spent the previous night in Bordeaux and was spending two nights there after the retreat so I had enough clothes for nine days and nights. She rather pointedly told me I didn't need that many things. I was a bit stunned she had got so judgemental on me quite so quickly. And surprised that she had made that judgement without knowing anything about me. Without knowing that I had a fear of sleeping in places I didn't know, that one of the things that helped me was bringing a bit of home with me – Hercules the travel bear, a mug, Rooibos tea bags, books to read, snacks. And without knowing that one of the things that made me feel better about myself was wearing colour, dressing up a bit and feeling like I looked nice because sometimes feeling like I looked nice was fucking hard work – and so no, a pair of joggers and a couple of sweatshirts for a week wouldn't work. She made a judgement about me, because of the way she had chosen to live her life, without asking me one question or knowing one single thing about me.

After I'd dumped the suitcase in a room that I really didn't want to have to think about too much we left the giant wooden wendy house so she could show me around the grounds. We walked around the mindfulness bell and she explained it would be rung before morning meditation (which was going to be very early for someone who had a fear of not getting to sleep and being too tired to function the next day), she pointed out contemplation areas around the pond and we set off down the path to where they grew vegetables and the land stretched out into the distance. As we approached the slightly smaller wooden structure where the village cats lived the path was quite muddy. It's mud. It washes off. I don't care. I'm not materialistic I just like shiny, colourful things. She asked if I wanted to go back because my trainers would get dirty (they were sparkly with black and silver stars – made my feet happy and made me happy when I looked down and saw them). Was that a sneer? Was she judging me again? I didn't get the impression she was asking me out of concern rather because she was laughing at what she perceived as my attachment to material things.   Was this a part of Buddhism I had missed?

There was so much time to kill before the first group meditation session. I love meditation. I started in my early twenties. Giving the mind all that space and freedom. Taking a step away from the material, tangible world. Bliss. I went back to my room to wait for my room-mate to arrive. The bed needed making and as I pulled out the iron frame I noticed waves of dust accumulated across the floor. I mountaineered down the spiral staircase to get a dustpan and brush and tidy up. I sat on the newly made bed and looked out the window. To wake up in the morning and be so close to nature would be beautiful. The bits of material wedged around the window frame to stop the draft coming in were slightly more of a concern. In fact the whole structure seemed a little like something my father might have built in the back garden if we'd had the space and he'd had the time. Probably safe but not somewhere my mother would have been very keen on me and my brother spending the night unsupervised.

I unpacked. I had so much stuff!   And nowhere to put it. The travel kettle, tea bags, alarm, books, hand cream, lip salve, notebook, pen, rescue remedy, tissues, eye mask, glasses, hairbrush went on the table next to the bed. The clothes I arranged back in my suitcase in an order which I hoped would make it easier to get dressed at six in the morning rather than rootling around for something I might want to wear – there was no cupboard or drawers. And my vast toiletries bag sat on the end of the bed waiting for the point at which I had to head down to the communal bathroom to take my make-up off and brush my teeth.

Eventually my room-mate arrived. A German woman, in her late twenties. A doctor who was in need of some time out and who's friend had suggested Plum Village. She had one small rucksack with her. I laughed at the contrast at the same time wondering, as usual, if something was wrong with me.

It was time for our first meditation. We went across to one of the communal rooms, took our shoes off and chose a spot. Unfortunately, the microphone wasn't working properly – the nun guiding the session would surely have been better off without it – so rather than the peace and calm and relaxation I had been hoping for it felt a bit like I was listening to vinyl on a record player with the needle jumping.

The session finished and it was time to eat. No meat of course. But I can't eat pasta – gluten intolerant unless I put some real effort in to push past the symptoms and don't mind what it does to my skin – so I didn't feel terribly satisfied once I'd finished everything on my plate. But equally didn't want to seem greedy and go back for more.

We ate in silence. We took our plates and cutlery and washed them in the many bowls to get rid of any trace of fairy liquid or whatever was the French equivalent. The time was approaching nine o'clock and we had previously been 'invited' to be in our rooms by nine for an hour's silent contemplation, reading or similar before lights out at ten. I took my toiletries down to the bathroom wearing my M&S cropped jimjams with lemons on them, my white waffley dressing gown and my pink flip flops with orange hearts on them. I hadn't really thought about sleep too much but it was starting to peer around the door between my subconscious and conscious.

At ten we put the lights out. My room-mate was chilly and asked if I minded if we left the little heater on, despite her wearing leggings and a sweatshirt. Because I still didn't know how to say no I said it was fine. I was plenty warm enough. I lay there, feeling rather proud of myself, wondering how the next six days would pan out, and feeling tired after the day's travels and all the newness.

Except I couldn't bloody sleep. It got so far into the night that my stomach was rumbling and I worried it would wake my neighbour. I very slowly and very quietly dug out what felt like a chocolate bar from my suitcase under the bed and nibbled it as quietly as I could. Maybe a satisfied tummy would let me sleep.

But no. I was getting more and more anxious about not sleeping. I had no idea what time it was as checking the time when I couldn't sleep made me even more anxious. I started to talk to whoever my god might be, pondering what it is all about. I had moments of calm, but couldn't get lost enough in them that my brain switched off and I nodded off. At some point I did something terrible and I apologise now, profusely, to the nuns. I crept down the tiny staircase and stood outside smoking a cigarette. I made sure the butt was out and put it back in the packet before I crept back up the tiny stairs hoping a ciggie would have worked its magic and calm me down.

Nope. I had another word with whoever my god is. I was contemplating life, the universe and everything. I felt my body detaching from myself. I became just the energy that I am without this constructed physical form. It's a beautiful state to be in, to find yourself in. I've been here so many times before in meditation, or when I'm letting myself, my thoughts, drift off. Then I experienced something I'd not experienced before – a light show in front of my eyes. And the phrase repeating itself in my head 'I was always me, I was always me, I was always me'. I realised I was trying to prove something about myself that I didn't need to prove by being here at Plum Village. I was wearing a hair shirt that I didn't need to wear. I was trying to fix myself when there was nothing wrong with 'me'.

I decided I would leave. I didn't need a week of 'quiet contemplation' – I spent large chunks of my life in contemplation. I didn't need to connect with 'god' – in truth the only times I found peace were when I meditated, when I was walking in nature, when I was lying next to the sea, with a clear view and space for my mind to drift and see what is truly important in this life and this world. What I needed was to understand, at the deepest level, that there was nothing wrong with me. That I was free to live 'my' life.

Except of course I wasn't. Yes, I needed to understand all of that, but until I was free from the past it would be impossible. Something I wouldn't get my head around until my world almost ended a couple of years after that sojourn in Bordeaux.

I think I had about an hour's sleep. My room-mate got up. Before she went for a walk I said I was going to leave. She said she was thinking about it. Sometimes what you don't need when you have a busy, stressful job and lots going on at home is a week in a camp bed on basic rations, however beautiful the experience at a soul level. Sometimes what you need is simply to have time to spend in nature, a bed no less comfortable than the one you sleep in at home, a bathroom no less functional than the one you have at home, someone to cook for you, someone to clean for you and to know that for a week or two you haven't got to think about work, the bills, and everything on the long to do list that you keep running. Sometimes we all just need someone to help look after us rather than having to look after ourselves the whole time.

I packed. It was still so early. I checked I could move my BA flight. I went for breakfast. I went back to the wendy house, got my mobile and walked just beyond the edge of the property where I called the hotel I'd booked in Bordeaux and asked them, whilst I smoked a cigarette, if I could bring my booking forward. I was doing nothing wrong. In fact I was doing what felt right for me – I was extracting myself from a situation I didn't want to be in (and which no-one had forced me to book in the first place) to look after myself for a week.

I checked the bus timetable and called the taxi firm that had driven me to the retreat to book a return. As soon as the office was open I went in and explained that something had come up that meant I needed to leave. No, don't worry, I wasn't expecting a refund of any of the five hundred euros I'd paid for the week.

I skipped out the office, overheard two nuns talking about the fact I had stepped off the property to have a smoke – as if I had somehow committed a wholly unacceptable and sinful act? – collected my suitcase which I trundled, noisily, back along the gravel path and waited for my taxi at the side of the road. I had another smoke as a last act of defiance – though what I was defying I don't know. The judgement of others?

The journey back to the hotel was made longer by the fact I was knackered. I was almost dead on my feet waiting the forty minutes for the bus but as soon as I was sitting in my seat, my knees wedged tight against the seat in front of me because they weren't expecting anyone over five foot seven to travel by bus, I fell into a deep sleep.

My forty-five minute nap took the edge off, and by the time I'd had another half an hour's shut-eye on the train I wasn't feeling quite so ill. I decided to treat myself to a cab from the station rather than the long walk or the tram. Well that was a mistake. A demonstration lead by environmental activists was slowly dispersing after a gathering in the centre of the city and the traffic was gnarled up and roads had been closed. I had never seen so much rubbish as there was left in the wake of these people – plastic bottles, food containers, flyers, beer cans, left everywhere, on the pavement, in the road, in the fountains. The hypocrisy, I thought as I sat in the back of the car, of so much in life. All those people in the 'do as I say not as I do' camp of 'how not to live'.

My request to the hotel to put me in a quiet room had been taken far too seriously for a change. I was in an annexed building at the back of the property. Chilly as it evidently hadn't been used since the end of the last season, the water in the jug thing at the back of the Nespresso machine was calcified it had been there so long, and with ceilings so low I couldn't stand up straight in the bath to use the shower! I ate the complimentary biccies and had a nap.

After a rather drawn out couple of days in Bordeaux - which is beautiful but two days is more than enough time to walk the city, sample the food and see the sights – I flew home.

The only people who knew I was home early were my parents. I managed to craft clever replies to texts asking how I was without lying (because, remember, good girls don't lie) by answering that the week wasn't what I had expected but I was enjoying myself. No-one needed to know I was home. I had four days to myself. It was bliss. I spent ages at Regents Park and Hampstead Heath, walking, having coffee, watching the ducks and the trees and the pigeons and the water. I went to the gym. I had a bit of a spring clean. All the things from which we derive little pleasure when we are working all day every day but yet, when we have the luxury of time, can give us great pleasure and fulfilment.

All this was great.　But.　BUT.

BUT. BUT. BLOODY BUT!

To paraphrase a well-known saying – everything had changed but nothing had changed.

Life carried on much as it always had after my brief respite from it all.

And things were about to get a whole lot worse.

*

So when I spotted that Mike, the 'transform your life' guy, was running a training course my brain went into overdrive.　I was convinced (yet again) that not only was this a way for me to 'deal with' my trauma and help me lose some weight (I had managed to put on another stone and my clothes either didn't fit or were splitting at the seams)　but also to get out of corporate life which still felt like a leech sucking the life blood out of me.

I called him up.　　Somewhere north of five thousand pounds!　First thought was 'no fucking way' – I can't even vaguely afford or justify that.　Second thought was 'oh he must be really good if he can charge that much'.

I wish I had stuck with the first thought and not been there to find out if the second were true or not …

How much self-belief (and possibly self-delusion) do you have to have to charge thirty grand for about nine days of your time!

Somehow, between that call, my initial disappointment at not being able to afford it and getting into bed that evening I convinced myself I could find the money and make this happen.

I could and would be free. I'd be the skinny one, wearing some boho yoga outfit, sitting in front of a group of people telling them my story, letting them know anything was possible, helping them to be free of whatever was holding *them* back. I'd like myself. People would like me. Life would be okay. Life would be better than okay.

A zoom call was scheduled – a sort of 'interview' with Mike. I had rehearsed a few lines, noted down a few thoughts on a piece of paper next to me, in case he asked me about my spiritual path, my beliefs, my intentions. I chose the spot I would sit carefully so there was some light and texture behind me instead of a blank wall. I thought about what I wore, my make-up. Was I so worried about rejection it became a full-blown theatrical production?

I shouldn't have worried or bothered! When he finally dialled in, some ten minutes or so late, he told me he had his camera turned off as he had some technical issues. If this had been a date that would (should) have been my first red flag!

We talked for maybe twenty minutes. He mostly talked about himself, although he did ask me why I wanted to do the course. He suggested I come and have a one on one session with him. He, or his PA, would be in touch. He had one more space on the course but he had one more person to talk to.

I should have remembered from his introduction at the first workshop I went to that this guy used to be in sales.

But none of that crossed my mind. What I wanted more than anything was for the cool kid in school to ask me to join their gang (even if I was paying a premium for it) and to hang out with all the other cool kids. I wanted to be accepted. I wanted this feeling of being on the outside and of disliking myself so much to go away.

And I was accepted! Hoorah! Maybe there was hope. I could pay in three instalments. There would be five days at his retreat in Mykonos at the start of the course and six months later another five days when we would have to take some sort of practical test. Once a month we would have an hour's check in with Mike on zoom and another hour's call when we'd all come to together to talk about what we'd be doing and how we'd been feeling. I would not only have to pay for the course but find the money to fly to Mykonos, and stay in a hotel the night before as we were under strict instructions to be there by early afternoon on the first day of the course.

But I had been accepted. There was hope for me yet.

*

I'd had just the one one-to-one session with Mike before I started the course. I'd rushed out the office to get to Marylebone station and sprinted about twenty-five minutes up the road to find his London apartment, then paid him around one hundred and fifty pounds for an hour of his time.

My mind drifted so far off into the outer reaches of the universe during that session and it was so blissful, such a relief to leave the tangibility of the physical world behind, that I didn't think I'd be able – or want – to come back.

But I didn't really go anywhere near the trauma. Why? Why did I miss that? Was it some implicit fear that he'd think I was making a fuss over nothing, drawing attention to myself. Would he decide he didn't actually want to spend any time with me as I dragged the mood down?

Did I simply not want to go down that road when there was a feeling of hope?

I can still cry rivers of tears for the me that could never tell anyone that anything was wrong for fear of rejection and for fear of it being 'wrong'. I look back and think of all the times I pretended I was okay, pretended I didn't mind, pretended not to care, and hid my tears, for the odd five minutes, tucked away where no-one could see me, or when I was behind the safety of my own front door.

*

We all 'met' on a zoom call before the first week. There were five of us. Me, of course. A woman I didn't initially take to and took up a lot of the conversation – I've always tried to do the opposite and take less than my allotted share of air-time, for fear people thought I wasn't at all interesting and were already bored with what I had to say, for that old fear that no-one wanted to know anything about what I felt or what I thought – nothing new there! A chap in his early twenties who had been diagnosed with chronic fatigue syndrome, left his job in recruitment and lived at home with his parents. And a couple - which in hindsight seemed an odd thing to do with such a small group of us - who were very much into their journey to spiritual enlightenment. Robert and Nadine.

The 'highlights' of that first few days of the course in Mykonos (if I can even bring myself to refer to them as that) were many and varied …

We had been told we needed to be at the villa by early or mid-afternoon on the first day. Fine if you can cope with the charter airlines and flights at silly o'clock in the morning but as someone recovering from a fear of flying (which stemmed from a fear of enclosed spaces, which stemmed from a fear of not being able to get out – go figure!) this would be my first 'medium haul' flight in some while and I couldn't cope with a five in the morning start on top of that. I'd flown out the night before and stayed at a very middle of the road place (recommended by our host as one of the best spots nearby). Except I really hadn't slept very well.

Things were on my mind. For me this course was all about getting rid of the trauma associated with the rape and the cover-up and (that other obsession) losing the weight that I increasingly believed I carried around as some sort of protection. The closer it had got to day one of the course the more all those thoughts were coming to the forefront of my consciousness. Psychologically I had already primed myself for diving deep into the maelstrom of fear and loathing I'd carried around all these years. By the time I got to the villa I was poised and ready to fly out the starting blocks.

But no-one was there. The PA dropped me off, showed me where the kitchen was and not long after left to collect two other 'students' from the airport. I sat there, with no distractions, as everything continued to bubble and boil its way to the surface.

When we booked the course we were told we would all have our own rooms. Caroline arrived and I was told that, because Mike had decided to take Robert and his girlfriend as a couple Caroline and I would have to share. She wasn't happy and I definitely wasn't happy. People … a bit of expectation management goes a long way. If you promise someone something and the parameters change don't cross your fingers. Be mature, open, honest, collaborative and trustworthy and let them know. Apologise. Ask them if they mind, if they'll be okay. Give them the option. Don't tell them they'll have their own room and then when they turn up have to hide your annoyance that they aren't happy at your proposal that they will in fact have to share.

The rigmarole ensued of the PA trying to put some sort of large folding room divider in place, and showing what the sofa bed would look like with pillows and a duvet on it.   Trying to sell something neither of us wanted to buy.

Caroline and I sat there, having only just met, and, thank god, were in agreement that we weren't happy. Especially given the huge amount of money we had shelled out for the course.

Separately to that Mike finally turned up. By this time I was already over-sharing with Caroline about my on and off insomnia and the reason for it as we sat on a couple of loungers near the drive way.   There was some food available at some point – sadly we were going vegetarian for a few days and a pseudo detox was planned. This concept of deep-cleansing of the body was like a form of torture on top of the deep-cleansing of the mind and soul we would already be doing as we meditated, breathed, tapped. shared and generally felt our way through the next few days.

I remember distinctly that it was a good couple of hours after the time we had been told to be there that the couple arrived.

Not sure what bought them this special dispensation, but again, if this had been offered as an option it would have saved me the cost of the hotel the previous night.

At some point Mike came over to talk about the accommodation, realising Caroline and I weren't going to capitluate. He was trying to get access to a small studio flat five minutes' walk away. Somehow we got onto me. Was Caroline still sitting there when we had this conversation? I don't recall. But at some point not too much later he announced he was going to do a one-on-one session for me as he hadn't seen me before. As we walked to the room at the back of the villa that he used for running the course and giving treatments I tried to explain that I had already seen him once but it either fell on deaf ears or he cut across me. That was to become a pattern for the next six months.

It was a fairly heavy and traumatic fifty minutes. What's interesting about this 'transformational process' but which I didn't find out until I was wearing an ECG monitor for twenty-four hours six months later is that it puts your body into a state where it mirrors how it would be if you were panicking and your mind into a state relaxed enough to access the subsconscious.

I was letting the feelings of the trauma, the terror, the fear, come to the surface. I cried, I wailed, I tried to let go. But Mike was confusing me, trying to get me to come back to the here and now every time I wanted to give in to the feelings I'd buried for decades. A sort of 'you can go there' followed by 'oops, I didn't really mean it'. In hindsight it feels cruel.

After fifty minutes I felt cried out and spent. Mike suggested I lie there for five minutes and 'come back into my body slowly'. I said I needed to talk about it. He wasn't one for advocating talking to his clients after a session. His approach was to give it a few minutes then pack them off with some advice to drink plenty of water and get plenty of rest as they may find themselves with a headache and feeling de-hydrated. Do you know how many therapists I've been to over the years who have said the same? And yet what are two of the most clear and obvious signs of a state of anxiety – dehydration and a headache. I wish I'd found this out sooner. It took a whole lot more shit and fourteen months until anyone explained panic attacks to me.

But I did get it all out – a tumble of words about being 'sexually abused' (it still felt more polite to refer to it by this more socially acceptable definition than to say 'rape' – even if rape is what it was) and being told not to tell anyone if I wanted to be a 'good girl'.

I got my words out. But I rushed as he evidently didn't want to hear it. There was nothing back. No suggestion that in fact this might not be the thing for me given what had come up in the previous hour. No suggestion that I might see a psychologist or someone who was used to working through complex childhood trauma with their patients. Nothing in fact. A big old 'Nada'. My problem not his.

What was it – a belief that he could heal anyone regardless? Money over humanity? Lack of experience? Lack of understanding? Disinterest? I know he never set himself out as clinically trained and asked us all to sign a (fairly comprehensive) disclaimer (which I never did) but he still set himself up as offering some sort of therapy that could, amongst other things, heal trauma. Much the same as so many of these other bloody therapists I've seen over the years. I'm sure ego plays a part. But if you are on the path to spiritual enlightenment shouldn't you be aware of when your ego is getting the way? Or is the right thing to do to sit and hold court over dinner and tell everyone about the time you met Jesus Christ in a past life? I kid you not.

Life isn't a competition people! It isn't a race. Your judgements about yourself or others needn't be an invitation to big yourself up or belittle someone else. The news, social media, the stories and opinions of others needn't be an invitation to be angry, to agree, to disagree or to feel you need to show up and show off or talk about someone behind their back. It really is ok to just mooch along in your own reality, being loving, kind, compassionate and respectful.

But I did feel some temporary relief after the one-on-one session. That sense of optimism that everything was going to be okay. That here was a group of people (surely?) that were going to support me as I worked through everything. People who would be loving, kind, compassionate and respectful. But if I look back I can see that even on that first day some deeper concern was tapping away inside me. I mis-read the signals. I should have got out there and then. Instead I thought that the feeling of apprehension that I was experiencing - the feeling that something about my interaction with Mike just wasn't right – was to do with what was wrong with me, what I'd been trying to fix all along. Not a warning sign that this wasn't for me, or that, perhaps, someone else needed to take a good hard look at themselves.

What was to follow over the next twelve months or so was the full unravelling of a life. To the point where I did not know how I was going to manage to put the kettle on in the morning let alone get through the day.

*

Some weird stuff happened in that first week in Mykonos. Admittedly not as frightening as what happened the week we went back six months' later but weird none the less.

At our first group session the six of us were squeezed into that little therapy room at the back of the villa full of mattresses, cushions and blankets, the air thick with the aroma of palo santo. I was, unknowingly, suppressing what was by now a tsunami of emotions around the trauma. I had always buried them. But before it had been so deep I wasn't consciously aware they were they. Now Pandora's box was open and all the evilness that I'd buried decades before was being released. Except now I was just a passenger. I seemed to have relinquished any control over what was going on in my head, my heart, even my body, when I'd decided I needed to be rid of whatever it was that had been making my life so bloody difficult, so unbearable, for all these years. I had no idea what the hell I was going through or how to help myself. As I had always done I was simply doing the next thing that had come along that I thought might 'fix' me.

I don't know how long we'd all been lying there, doing our thing and drifting off into wherever the space took us, when the emotion welling up inside me became too much. Emotionally I was right back in the horror of it all – the anger, the rage, the hatred for what the two bitches did to me. I couldn't lie there any longer. I couldn't. I wanted to scream. I didn't feel safe. I didn't trust these people – why should I given the way I'd been treated. My brain was whirring – I should stay but I needed to go. I should stay but it didn't feel safe to stay. I didn't feel safe. But this time I could go. This time I could escape from the feelings and find sanctuary instead of being abused and used the way they did. Finally, I felt safe enough to run.

I stood up. Mike tried to persuade me to stay. I said I needed to leave for five minutes. He said something about it being important we experience everything as a group. I just couldn't. Didn't the man see what was going on, the state I was in. Hadn't he heard everything I'd told him after our session the previous day?

I crept over whoever was lying next to me and out the door. My bedroom was nearby. I went in, shut the door, sat on the bed and howled. Great rivers of tears running down my face, through my nose, pooling on my feet and the floor as they fell through the gap between my legs.

I wondered if anyone would come. No-one had come then. And no-one had come since. Here I was spending over five thousand pounds to heal myself wondering if for that money anyone would come.

After a few minutes there was a knock at the door. Mike. He came in. He wanted me to come back. It was important we were all together. I shouted at him. The words and the emotion came out of nowhere with no warning.

'Don't tell me what to do!'

'I'm sick to death of doing what everyone tells me to do!'

My body and voice shook. I sat back on the edge of the bed and sobbed loudly. Mike sat next to me, but just far enough away for me to notice the distance. It would apparently be really good if I could go back and join everyone else.

I would think about it.

He left. I still to this day don't understand how anyone, whatever their relationship to the person suffering, could not reach out and let them know they are there for them. It needn't be a hug or any massive physical show of affection or support. But to have someone connect with you when you are feeling so vulnerable, so scared, so distraught – the contact of a hand on an arm or a shoulder, lightly rested there long enough for you to know that they see you, they see your suffering, your sadness, that they are there for you. Not to try to fix you, to cure you, to tell you what to do to make things 'better', to talk about themselves and what they did when 'bad stuff' happened to them, to compare their suffering to yours, but instead to show a tiny bit of compassion, of tenderness, of human warmth. To let you know they are there, they are present.

At a later date, on one of our monthly check-in calls when he offered his pearls of wisdom on my psychology he accused me of running away from people and things. Said I needed to stop doing it. He alluded to that time when I had left the room. I should have known then to stop and get off the ride. Didn't he realise that had been a moment of deep catharsis? Didn't he realise, when we were sat in a circle after the session (I did go back in) and sharing what had come up for us and I told them that I had been abused at seven, that I needed more than Mike's transformational 'how-to' and to read a couple of books on 'working with your shadow self' to find my way through the trauma of being raped as a child, the trauma of being silenced, and to recover from the decades of living this imposed life of fear? He really thought I was running away from something? Even when I'd told him one of my reasons for doing the course was to run headlong at it and try to smash it to pieces?

And why did he expect me to trust these five people I hadn't met or started to get to know until twenty-four hours earlier, himself included, with details of my life that I had hardly ever shared with anyone up to now? When I had been ignored. Rejected all over again.

I wish to God someone had had the wherewithal to suggest what I needed to do was get some properly qualified help, and then, if I still felt like it, to come back to the course. I like to think it's what I would have done. If I'd seen me. But did anyone ever really see me? When I didn't, consciously, want to look at myself?

I'm sure at some level, in similar circumstances, my ego would be waving its hand saying 'no, really, I've got this'. But if you are to be of any value when you profess to being in a profession that involves the care of other people, if any part of what you do you deem to be 'therapy' then you have to be able to see when the ego has got even a bit over-excited, put it back in its box, look at the person in front of you or at the end of a phone or screen and ask yourself 'what is the best thing for them at this moment?' And if your intuition tells you they need something you can't provide – not that you think you might be able to provide but that you know, in your heart, in all honesty, you shouldn't be doing – then let them know. If you know the direction to point them in do that. And do it sooner rather than later. If you don't then either find out, or tell them they need to find out and that you will support them. And even if you have to step away don't forget to let them know that you are still there, that you still see them, to rest your hand gently on their arm, even if they flinch, with care and love and compassion and respect for what they are going through, for just long enough – which may be no more than a few seconds – for them to feel that connection.

What you don't do is tell them you have arranged, included in the course for free, a naked massage with some Greek guy. And then tell you that you have briefed the masseuse so he will tailor the massage and the experience to support whatever you need most as part of your 'transformational journey'. Because either one of the two of them was a sadist, or knew nothing about the human psyche, or in fact, no such 'briefing' happened.

I was really not comfortable with a man giving me a massage. My only previous experience was when I briefly lived in Bath (what a mistake that was) and I got a massage at a sports centre somewhere nearby. I believe I was going through a period of insomnia and the doctor had prescribed me some Valium. Not too many days later I was in the midst of a full-blown nervous breakdown. I think the only people who ever knew about that were my parents. I mean how is it even possible to be so mentally ill that you can find yourself sitting on the floor behind the sofa crying your eyes out and no-one ever knows. Or wonders if you are ok. Or asks if you are ok? Really ok. Not the 'how are you?' and 'I'm fine', but 'are you sure?', 'It must be tough being somewhere new on your own and having lost your job a few weeks after you moved in and finding out that guy you thought you were dating has a girlfriend twelve years younger than you.'

The masseuse in Bath was an arsehole. What's the first rule of any therapy session – turn your mobile off. I am going to guess we were about twenty minutes in, I was lying on the massage table, nothing on but underwear and a towel, and his phone rang. He excused himself, answered it, asked if I mind if he stepped out the room for a bit. I (of course) said no because I never wanted to cause any trouble and because (of course) I had absolutely no rights as a human being having been relieved of them at seven years old. And he left me there, feeling incredibly vulnerable, for what was probably a good five minutes. Arsehole.

I should have complained – but (of course) didn't.

The experience in Mykonos was worse. Infinitely worse. All that man needed to have said at any point during the first five minutes was 'if this is too much for you we can stop'. But no. He persevered. And at times I swear he found my constant tears and the need to blow my nose an irritation.

It started when I walked in. I'd already explained to the more sympathetic of my fellow students – at that time just Caroline – that I wasn't comfortable with being naked given what I was trying to work through. Caroline and I assured ourselves Mike would have said something and that I would simply explain to this guy that I wanted to keep my underwear on.

It was an odd arrangement to get to this room. There was a small outdoor staircase that led to a a flat roof and then you had to climb through a window to get in the room itself.

I waited outside the window until the person before me clambered out. The Greek guy said 'Hi', waved me in the room, told me to get ready and lie face down on the massage table and he'd be back. When he came back I had to explain about keeping my underwear on.

I didn't realise this was what was happening at the time – and what had happened so so many times over my life – but that feeling of vulnerability lying there was triggering the memory of the feeling of vulnerability when I was seven. I was already stuck in the fear of the memory, the fear that it was happening again, now, because every bloody 'transformational session' brought it back, quite literally, to the forefront of my brain. So I lay on the massage table and started to cry. Great convulsing sobs. What did that man think – that somehow his 'healing hands' were bringing the trauma out? That he was a magician and this would all make me feel better, be a better person, help me on some supposed journey to spiritual enlightenment? Did he not think, once, to ask me if I was okay, to say 'shall we stop?', 'would it be useful to just sit and talk instead?'.

What the fuck was wrong with these fucking therapists?

And I couldn't move. And I couldn't speak. I was paralysed by fear. So often I look back on events or conversations in my life when things could have been and felt so different and the memory of them not continue to haunt me as it does, and think 'why didn't I say something'? Why couldn't I say No? Why couldn't I say how I felt? Why couldn't I answer back? I have berated myself for it. Been angry about it. Been furious about it. Been sad. Cried. Hated the other people. Hated life. Hated the unfairness of it all.

But all I could do and all I could say was nothing.

So I lay there, hardly able to breathe through the snot. Used tissues littering the floor around the massage table. And that man just carried on. And I, stuck in my seven year old self's fear, unable to say anything because I was not just paralysed but also wanted to be a 'good girl', lay there and sobbed and sobbed and wished it was over.

His lack of empathy was so strong, his conviction that he was somehow fulfilling some higher purpose so certain, that when he asked me to turn over, despite my saying I wanted to keep my underwear on and he was not to go near my chest, he flung my bra to one side. I jumped and said no, you need to put it back, and he rested it there. And it was as if I was being violated all over again.

I don't recall exactly what happened at the end, I was in such a state of exhaustion, but he must have passed me some cotton sheet or throw or something similar because I remember sitting up at one end of the bed, and watching as, in a very casual but demeaning way, he threw the neat pile of my clothes, that I had left on the side, on to the end of the massage table and said, like a pimp talking to a whore, 'get dressed'.

Scientifically, logically, emotionally I understand now why I couldn't say anything, couldn't do anything, but there is no part of me that understands how any human being could watch as another shook and cried with fear the way I did and not even ask if they were ok …. Could then walk away from them without a backwards glance or a gentle smile.

Ego over humanity? Money over humanity? It all boils down to the same thing.

I survived the rest of the week and spent the next five months trying to build up my case studies to share with our esteemed teacher, and (not) looking forward to the regular monthly check ins with Mike both as an individual and as a group. He had advised us to read two books. I suppose they will be somewhere on my bookshelves but I don't recall the names or the authors. Or did I want rid and took them to the local charity shop knowing I had read, and would read, many, many better books?

One of them in particular he was fixated on – the one about the need to unveil our 'dark side' and 'work on it'. I had read and re-read the book and it was making no sense to me. I had an epiphany moment – I lived on the dark side, what I needed to find was my light. I saw only the badness in me, the inability to reach the unquantifiable perfection I had always aimed for, the awfulness of who I was, the awfulness of my life and my very existence. The failure that everything was.

I don't think he bought it. He'd had the audacity to accuse me of running away from my anger issues which threw me completely. What anger issues? He took me back again to that first group session in Mykonos when I left the room and then shouted at him. I explained to him (AGAIN) that I hadn't been running away, that in fact that was a moment of deep release. I explained I had never run away from anything in my life. I always – ALWAYS – stayed (frozen) and sucked up whatever was going on, feeling responsible somehow for the situation, the outcome, everyone else's feelings.

You see, I understand these things. No I'm not qualified. No I'm not clinically experienced. But I have spent a life time studying myself, trying to understand, trying to fix, to heal, acutely aware of my interactions with the rest of the world and observing the rest of the world's interactions with me.

At the time I didn't understand the neurobiology of it. I didn't know about how trauma affects a person. I didn't know about the recovery process. The need to talk. The need to feel safe. But I certainly bloody knew about how people react to things. And I knew how to care for people – because I cared for others in a way I couldn't care for myself. Because I never wanted anyone to feel how I felt. Because I thought if I cared for them they might care for me back. Because I was a 'good girl'.

Maybe he didn't like the fact that I answered back, that I had some awareness and understanding that maybe he didn't, that, God forbid, I knew more than him. Maybe he had some unresolved issue with women. Maybe I made him feel insecure. Maybe he felt guilty. In any event he kept pushing. It was October 2019 and we were heading back to Mykonos again for the last few days of the course.

Some part of me really didn't want to be there.

If I had trusted my intuition I would have backed out as soon as I got to the island.

But I couldn't.

I was STUCK.

*

I realise that some part of me has always been stuck as that beautiful little seven year old girl sitting there, terrified, desperately hoping someone – anyone – will reach out and help her. Save her.

Every time something has triggered that feeling of fear my clever old brain has gone 'Uh oh, I felt like this once before. It wasn't good. Alert. Alert. ALERT' and fired off a giant dose of cortisol, switched all my senses to High and gone into its SAS commando mode looking for and trying to protect me from a threat that doesn't, in that moment, exist … until I realise I was in fact looking for someone to protect that child. My child. Little Me.

I have spent my life in fear waiting for someone to save me.

Why did no one ever come? I understand that no-one knew about the past, the trauma, but why did no-one ever see the distress, hear the quiet calls for help. Was no-one listening – not properly? Were they all far too wrapped up in themselves? Because I was such a victim did this give their egos a reason to indulge themselves, to feel they were 'better' than me?

I don't know. But I do know this – a lot of people ignored me.

Why?

*

The return trip to Mykonos wasn't something I was looking forward to. I flew out the day before again and stayed at the same hotel. Caroline had done the same thing. We went out for some tapas at the ticky-tacky row of bars over the road from the hotel. I had a few glasses of wine, smoked a few ciggies. We went to bed. I didn't get much sleep. Looking back now I see a part of me was preparing for what it knew would be a tough few days. I got up. We had breakfast. Caroline had hired a car so we weren't stuck in Mike's villa every night with feck all to do. She suggested we drive out somewhere as we had time, get a bite to eat. We sat, under the grey skies, watching the ocean, talking about I don't know what. She ordered wine I ordered a decaf cappuccino. She left the table to take a call. I was starting to feel edgy, twitchy, uncomfortable. I wanted to be at home. I wanted my mother to put her arms around me and tell me everything would be okay.

We arrived at the villa to find 'the couple' wouldn't be there until the next day – one rule for some another rule for others. I don't really remember the first night other than I didn't sleep terribly well and a couple of times walked out of the drive and loitered in the main road smoking.

The second night, once we were sure the couple had left the premises to go to the other villa and everyone was tucked up in bed, I went over to Caroline's and she opened a bottle of wine she had in the fridge. Naughty. But oh so nice and oh so needed. We put some music on. I have a feeling we had a giggle at the others' expense and made the observation we'd made so many times before about the course not being great value for money, about the fact we were really just paying a shed load to Mike so we could piggy back off whatever reputation he'd created for himself. I smoked a couple of ciggies out her window working on the basis the drive way was two floors below and it was windy. I did my Ace of Spades head-banging party piece as it's always good for a laugh. I went to bed and went to sleep.

I woke up very early and couldn't get back to sleep. A sense of foreboding.

We were talking as a group after or over a mid-morning herbal tea (yawn) in the conservatory area off the kitchen. I don't remember what we were talking about. I made an innocuous comment about some people having more money than sense and thinking they could spend enough on vitamins and supplements to 'fix' or 'heal' themselves but that sometimes you had to look at your life and fix or heal that instead. It was a passing comment, the same as other passing comments made by the group - and by people since the beginning of time.

We went back into the mattress-covered room for another group session. Lots of noise, wailing, crying, all hallmarks, we had been told ,of great progress as my 'new friends' were accessing and releasing their traumas.

Not I. I was going off into a state of meditative bliss. My sessions were becoming all about imagining a positive future, seeing myself in a more positive light, manifesting my hopes and dreams. I don't think Mike liked it. He said I wasn't grounded enough. Fuck grounded. I was a victim of rape and had been living with, coping with, that trauma for decades. Which he knew. Fuck him and his fucking need to lean more deeply into my transformation and connect more with my base chakras. I lived in my head because it was too painful to live in the grounding of fear. Going to the fear was overwhelming. Utterly utterly overwhelming. A feeling like I would drown in it and not come out alive. Did this man know nothing about trauma despite his professing his methodology was a great way to heal from it?

After the session the usual questions and sharing around 'what came up' for each of us .

For Robert the anger that had come up because of the judgement I'd made about him was apparently really painful.

What judgement?

I hadn't said a word about him.

Oh no – apparently I had.

Apparently I had said (and I paraphrase) that he was a bit of a muppet for spending lots of money on vitamins and supplements and all the other things that he spent money on. I'm sorry mate. I said nothing about you, it was a passing comment. I went to say something but Mike very abruptly shut me up and told me to let Robert have his say - his golden boy. There followed ten minutes of how Robert had felt, how he felt about me, and I sat there silent but sitting on such a volcano of pressure my insides were shaking. After he had finished I went to say my piece, expecting my opportunity to address how what Robert had said had made me feel, but was cut short. It was lunchtime. Silenced yet again.

I was fucking fuming. No-one had managed to see past the end of their noses when it came to the trauma I must be dealing with, but Robert's 'trauma' around an opinion someone had shared in passing was worthy of being discussed and shared in the group and Mike showing a degree of tenderness and concern he had singularly failed to show to me. Had he developed a crush on the man? Was he somehow infatuated?

I was beyond furious at lunch. I know I needed to say something to Robert before I imploded. I stopped him as he was walking past me. Shaking with the fear of speaking up I said I thought he owed me an apology. He agreed. No idea why he couldn't have said that in front of everyone else. He then said 'let me do this properly'. He thought for a moment, looked up, made eye contact with me and said 'I'm sorry …. blah blah blah.' I don't remember what he told me he was sorry about – it was the least sincere apology I think I have ever heard anyone deliver.

One evening Caroline, the youngster and I drove up to some bar and restaurant in the mountains. After a walk around Caroline and I polished off a bottle of wine and I smoked a few smokes. It was hardly the detox that Mike had tried to inflict on us but you have to do what you have to do to get by in any moment. Don't you?

Another night, or maybe it was the same one, Caroline drove the five of us out to a local beach. I didn't want to be with these people. Everyone felt so fake to me. I asked if she could pit-stop at a mini-mart on the way back. I picked up chocolate, crisps, and a couple of cans of lager – I felt it was all I could inconspicuously conceal in my bag – that and the fact there wasn't a screw-top bottle of wine to be found.

Everyone had gone to their rooms by about ten. I was not in a good place. I needed some company, to talk, to be at home, for that someone to metaphorically scoop me up and tell me it would be ok. I needed to be anywhere except stuck in this bloody villa doing this bloody course being re-traumatised again and again and again.

I messaged the youngster to ask if he was still up saying I needed to talk. No reply. I messaged a couple of friends back in the UK saying I was having a really tough time and going crazy. No reply. And then, out the blue, my mobile started buzzing. Darren. I haven't seen Darren for a few years but in that moment it felt like he had saved my life.

We talked. I felt better. I got back into bed. Nothing. My mind was in overdrive, whizzing around like Roger Moore on that centrifugal force thing in the Bond movie. I lay there. I could feel Mike in every corner of the room. Every part of me felt threatened by him. I couldn't breathe properly. My heart was skipping beats. One, two, three, four, five, six, … eight, nine, ten, eleven, … thirteen, fourteen.

I gave up on trying to be 'good'. I was going insane with whatever was happening. I chain smoked sitting on the chair outside my room, hoping the Mykonos night and breeze might blow the ash away. My heart wouldn't stop, wouldn't slow down. Was I having a heart attack? Was I going to die? I couldn't calm down. I couldn't sleep. It was, up until that point in my life, truly the worst night of my life.

At about two or three in the morning I wandered over to Caroline's door in my jimjams and dressing gown and stood there crying silently wondering how much she'd hate me if I woke her up.

After my fingers had finally tapped on her door and she'd seen the state of me she told me to come in. A physiotherapist, she had me lie on the bed, and very gently, over the course of the next hour, managed to relax my head and neck, talking to me all the while, until I calmed down.

I am grateful for what she did for me that evening, and for her support over the entire course. Although I would like to hope it was mutual. She showed me kindness and compassion. Something that, in my experience, had been sorely missing the rest of the previous six months.

*

I must have had about an hour and a half's sleep. I felt like shit. But off we went again

I explained to Mike that I had a banging headache and hadn't slept well. His answer to everything – another session.

Lunch time came. I ate something then told the group I needed to go and lie down as I felt so awful.

I went to my room. Apart from feeling tired I felt horribly nauseous. Dizzy even. Dehydrated. I didn't move. No-one came in to see if I was okay. At some point the youngster stuck his head around the door and said they were starting the afternoon session. I told him I felt too ill. He disappeared.

I lay there for about forty-five minutes. No-one came. No-one checked on me. Why was that? Eventually I got up, put on some dark glasses as the light was making me feel worse, and headed out to the conservatory to join the group. As I sat down no-one said a thing. No-one even turned to look at me, let alone smiled or asked if I was feeling better. Mike ignored me completely.

He said we'd be taking a short break and then working on each other again. How the hell was I meant to run a session for anyone in this state. It wasn't right. Even though I knew these people surely I shouldn't be treating one of them when I was feeling so crap?

I stopped him for a quick word. I explained I felt dreadful. I told him about the headache, the nausea, the dizziness. His response? 'Elle, you need to participate, if you don't I'll have to fail you.'

Fuck me.

I mean, what the actual fuck?

How could anyone – anyone - have that little respect or compassion for another human being in that moment, in that situation?

I told him I didn't want to fail but that I felt so sick.

He said to me 'the alternative is that you come back on another course and do the last week again.'

I absolutely DID NOT WANT TO HAVE TO COME BACK and spend any more time in what for me had become some sort of living hell.

To demonstrate his extreme generosity he 'let' me pair up with Caroline for the next session.

Bastard, I thought.

I won't apologise for toxifying his sacred retreat with my cigarette ash. I won't apologise for drinking alcohol on the premises. And I won't be waiting for any apology from him because I know it will never come.

The next day was 'exam day'. I asked if I could go first. If I didn't get another good night's sleep and had to wait until the afternoon I would be comatose. He did at least agree to that.

And then, after lots of waiting around, we were handed our certificates. I have no idea where mine is. I was proud of having survived, proud of the association with this self-styled guru, for, oh, about one week.

*

I had booked myself into a nice hotel along the coast for one night to get some sun before I flew home. I was exhausted by the time I checked in. I'd asked for a quiet room with a double bed. I got to the room and it was two singles. I don't think they were happy but they sent someone up to sort it out.

I tried to sleep for a bit but couldn't. I went for dinner. I went to the terrace bar afterwards and had two too many Disaronnos. I went back to my room. Smoked on the balcony. Walked into the patio door by mistake and laughed at myself. And eventually crashed out.

The sun was shining the next day and my flight wasn't until the evening. I swam. I lay in the sun. I read. I looked at the sky. All the time aware that my heart was racing and skipping beats. I spent the day counting, counting again, and counting again and again.

It would be better when I was home. I'd feel safe in the sanctity of my little flat.

It was miserable weather. We boarded the flight. I put my head phones on and tried to regulate my heartbeat. We sat at the gate for ages until the pilot announced that because of the heavy rain we were too heavy to take off so we would be off-loading some fuel, flying to Faro, pit-stopping to take on more fuel and then heading home. I watched as other planes sped down the runway and up into the air, wondering what sort of trial the universe was trying to inflict on me.

We sat for almost another hour – counting, breathing, anxious as to what it all meant – before the pilot came back on the tannoy and announced there was a window when the rain wasn't so heavy so we could re-fuel, get in the air and fly direct back to the UK.

I tried to laugh with the woman next to me all the time trying not to cry.

I got home some time after one in the morning. I was exhausted. I opened my suitcase, made a pass at sorting my clothes into washing piles then got into bed.

But I couldn't fucking sleep! All I could do was count my heart, listening to it rushing and jumping.

I knew I wouldn't – and couldn't – sleep. I was worried I was going to have a heart attack. There was nothing for it. I threw on some jeans and a sweater, got in the car and drove to the Royal Free A&E. I howled in the car on the way there. Howled like a terrified animal. About everything. About how shit everything felt, how shit I felt, how 'wrong' everything seemed to always turn out.

I calmed myself down, dried my eyes and registered myself at the desk. I sat and waited. Full ECG and a blood test later I was sent home. I wasn't having a heart attack. I wasn't about to die.

I lay in my bed wondering what it would take to distract myself from listening to my heart and lying there with my right thumb on the inside of my left wrist counting. At some point I must have been suitably engrossed in whatever story I was telling myself that I'd fall asleep.

It was still there in the morning – that skippy jumpy disturbing heartbeat. I couldn't get away from the damn thing now. I booked an appointment with my GP who referred me for a twenty-four hour ECG. I was told it could be months before I was offered one so asked for a referral to go privately. Two days later I was wired up and good to go.

I'd asked for the results to be sent to the same NHS doctor that I had seen. He called me one afternoon as I was walking home from work. It was indeed nothing to worry about. He explained to me how the nervous system can get out of balance, become unable to regulate itself and how stress can lead to a state of hyperarousal – which could be causing my increased pulse rate and the palpitations.

I felt re-assured momentarily but the constant feeling that my heart was thudding around in my chest, completely out of control, meant that feeling of re-assurance went out the window very quickly.

I had no idea what to do. It was like a one thousand piece jigsaw of nothing but blue sky – I was lost in not knowing where or how to start!

I made some semblance of normality out of my life for those few weeks, but the monster from the past was catching up with me.

And then he caught me. The night of October 31st 2019. I was a week away from my first appointment with a psychologist at the PsychoDermatology department at the hospital. Subconsciously I knew it was going to come out. In my head I had already been rehearsing how I would say 'I was sexually abused as a child' to be sure I would be able to get the words out. Would anyone even believe me? Would anyone be interested? Or would I be fobbed off as so many times in the past?

But the monster caught me before I was in safe hands. It surrounded me, suffocating me, feeling completely and utterly unbearable.

And that was when I called the surgery. And the emergency doctor told me I needed an emergency appointment. And I went in and disclosed what happened when I was seven years old to someone I'd never met before and would never meet again.

*

When things have never gone your way it's difficult to imagine why you believe and hope that they might next time. But I always did. I was the eternal optimist. Maybe too optimistic. So optimistic that I was unrealistic. Un-measured. No sense of balance or perspective.

The GP said his referral to the Tavistock Centre for Trauma Recovery services should take no more than eight weeks. In the meantime I booked an appointment to check in with him in a couple of weeks and explained I also had the PsychoDermatology appointments to support me.

So much from that initial disclosure to a GP stays with me. Did he realise how difficult this was for me given it was a doctor who had raped me. The blank face of a second medical student in the room – they surely hadn't expected this when they arrived that morning for their work experience. The suggestion that I should talk to friends, family, and make sure I was supported. That stumped me. Past friends hadn't listened. And how was I supposed to do this – drop then a text message saying 'oh by the way …'? It felt like throwing myself out of a plane with no parachute.

A year or so later, as I applied for Criminal Injuries Compensation and obtained a copy of my medical records to forward on, I was stunned to see, for all my talk and tears and the time I spent with them – just those few perfunctory notes. It made me sad and angry to think someone could reduce everything I had said, the tears I'd shed, the courage it had taken, to that. No emotion. No sympathy. No notes on how traumatised I was or the support I needed for the next person to be aware of in the event I turned up at their door.

*

The psychodermatology appointment had been booked for some weeks. Had I known this release was coming? Could I not hang on the extra days? Was my subconscious one step ahead of the rest of me as usual?

I approached the appointment with fear and hope in equal measure. Fear that I wouldn't be believed, I'd be told I was making a fuss, that I'd be expected to 'cope' on my own, that the weight of my feelings would be too much. Hope that I might finally be free of whatever it was I had been carrying around for decades – the black tar that clung to me, inside and out.

I think it had been at least two years prior, maybe longer, that I had had the referral assessment. Did my psoriasis affect my image of myself? 'Yes'. The appointment for the assessment was made. There was a link between psoriasis and childhood trauma. 'Oh, I had a traumatic experience when I was seven'. I was referred.

And so I found myself sitting in the corridor of clinic 6 at the Royal Free.

Her name was Theresa and she was lovely. The room was small, no window. I sat on an old-fashioned olive green leatherette chair in a corner. There was a tiny desk, a mirror on the wall and that was about it. After some admin she started to talk around the connection that had been identified between skin and mind. The focus of the sessions was, I'm sure, predominantly to come to terms with and perhaps to get to a point of acceptance of your psoriasis, to not be so critical and hating of yourself because of the way your skin looks, to not let your life be determined by how you see and feel about your psoriasis.

I was so many steps ahead of her. I needed to talk. I needed help. About twenty minutes in (there was a clock on the wall and its hands always moved too fast) I broke cover and started to talk. About going to the doctor. About the disclosure.

I did my best to hold back the tears. Never show any emotion. Don't make yourself vulnerable Ellie.

My eyes watered and the water gathered, waiting, until it began to drip in a slow almost controlled way down my cheeks.

There was a box of tissues on the little table next to me and I reached for one.

Over the course of the next eleven weeks I saw her almost weekly. It was a lifeline I'd never known I'd needed. I had homework which I did religiously. I was a model patient (of course)!

I recall several key things from my therapy with Theresa.

I must have been talking about how I felt this darkness that enveloped me. She asked me to draw something, some shapes, colour, I don't remember the specifics. I drew a rudimentary squiggly bean shaped thing and shaded it black – all except a little section somewhere off centre. She asked me what that was. I couldn't speak. That feeling as some powerful emotion seems to travel from the base of your spine to your heart telling you to let go, and at the same time your brain remembers - something from the past - and sends a message to shout it out but you are so scared of speaking any of your truth that it sticks in your throat and no matter how safe the space, no matter that logically you see no threat, some part of you is so terrified of this feeling that your voice is paralysed.

I still do it. Something brings that wave of emotion over me and instead of fully letting go I temper the tears and hold the words back until I have some degree of control over what happens next.

That little un-shaded circle on the page in front of me was a light. The light of little Elle that was there before her life was stolen. But it was there. Trapped. Lost. Not knowing how to get out. But I had always known it was there. That there was something inside of me that needed to be set free.

We did a lot of work around what big Elle would say to little Elle As homework one week I wrote a letter to little Elle. I still have it. I don't read it so often these days but it still breaks my heart. I wrote it one day between meetings, working from home, as I had left it late and my next appointment with Theresa was the next day. It took me forty-five minutes. I sobbed and sobbed. And half an hour later I was on a work call. No-one would have guessed a thing.

Somewhere at the beginning of February 2020 I finally got an appointment from the Tavistock for my referral assessment. Some medical centre I'd never been to before in Kilburn on the High Road. I had no idea what to expect. I assumed I'd go in, someone would ask some questions, I'd come out and wait a few more months for the first trauma recovery session. Jesus! If I'd known what the next forty minutes would hold would I ever had set foot in the door?

It was about a twenty minute walk. A sunny day. I got there five minutes early and was seen on time. The woman I saw was young, in her thirties. Nice enough. Kind I thought. Then the questions started. She took me right back to that day, in that room, with him. I was all over the place. I felt assaulted. Under attack. She took notes. The time was up. I asked how long and she said it would be within the next six months. I told her I had been seeing a psychologist at the Royal Free but I had almost come to the end of my allocated sessions. She made a note.

And I walked out the consulting room, out the building and into the sunshine and noise of any other day. Except it wasn't any other day. My head was splitting. I was thirsty beyond measure. I bought a bottle of water and drank it down. I got home and I truly felt like shit. What the fuck had just happened? Was I ill?

The next time I saw Theresa she told me my last session would be the week after next, they wouldn't be able to offer the full complement of sessions as originally advised. I was worried that between my sessions with her ending and the long wait for the Tavistock I wouldn't be able to cope. She had written to the woman I'd seen from the Tavistock for the assessment, but she wasn't able to commit to offering me any sort of touchpoint. My last check in with the GP had been the previous week. I could be strong. I could cope. I'd waited all my life I could wait a few more months.

But something was afoot.

My last appointment with Theresa I took her a bunch of flowers. Gratitude. But I wasn't feeling great, like I was going down with something.

It was the 5th of March 2020.

Covid had come to get us.

My life was about to become pure, unadulterated hell.

*

I left that last appointment with Theresa feeling both a sense of anticipation and deflated. Whilst we assured ourselves that Covid was 'just flu' in hindsight it was clear the NHS was clearing appointments, refocusing and readying itself for what it (but not yet us) knew was about to come.

I worked from home on the Friday. I emailed my boss and told her I was feeling shattered – which wasn't unusual given the amount I perpetually had on my plate. Friday night I felt a bit odd but nothing I could put my finger on. Saturday I drove out to Berkshire to see my brother for lunch. I had a dry cough which I blamed on the two cigarettes I'd smoked before I left. On the drive home I developed this very odd sensation like indigestion and belched my way along the M4 and round the north circular. Delightful. I went to bed but woke up some time after two feeling rough. Shivery. I was going down with flu. Sunday I felt rougher. I schlepped to the supermarket to stock up in case I was too poorly to go out for a few days. I collected my dry cleaning. I came home and messaged a few people to say I had 'some bug'.

I spent the next four days feeling rough as fuck. I sat down to log on for work on the Monday at nine fifteen and at nine thirty-five I had to go and lie down. I mentioned to people at work that I wasn't feeling great but the phone rang and my inbox filled up as people expected me to fix some problem that was apparently more urgent than my health. And I didn't say No (of course I didn't day No!). I carried on, feeling sorrier and sorrier for myself. After all, that's what I did, I had to get on with life regardless of how I was feeling.

By the end of the week some politician was interviewed in the news talking through the symptoms of Covid. It was exactly what I'd had, and still had. I felt vindicated having spent the past few days with people telling me it was 'just a cold' and not the dreaded virus. What were they scared of? That agreeing I might have 'it' was an admission that 'it' did exist? Ignorance was bliss? I didn't really get the impression they were denying it to make *me* less anxious.

The shivering finally stopped but then the headache came, like my head was being crushed in a vice, and a fatigue so heavy I could barely scrape myself out of bed or off the sofa. But still I tried to work, to deliver, to meet this expectation I believed everyone had of me to be somehow invincible.

And the fear started to kick in. What if my lungs couldn't cope. I took to doing five minutes deep breathing exercises every hour to aerate them. My subconscious woke me in the night to remind me to breathe.

A couple of weeks later I had started to feel more human, more like myself, more able to cope. But the panic was setting in at a national and global level.

At the same time I started to get vivid, regular flashbacks to being seven and being in that room, with him.

But there was so much rushing around my head so fast that I couldn't see or feel anything clearly. I had no vocabulary to explain myself. I had no precedent.

I simply fell.

A very long way.

Right to the bottom.

As lockdown became a reality and the countdown clock started ticking I was still feeling washed out but I made a tour of the local shops to pick up shampoo, conditioner, all sorts of store cupboard 'staples' that were flying off the shelves as the people of the world prepared for the apocalypse.

God knows how but I managed to get my parents a regular milk, bread and eggs delivery before the website crashed. I arranged for them to have their papers delivered.

And I did my best to ignore whatever the fuck was going on with me.

Most of my life I had managed to find a way to quieten my thoughts, to suppress them even if they then showed up as long-standing depression. But there was an uncontrollability, an unpredictability, to how I was feeling and what was running around my mind that was making that almost impossible.

I felt so out of control I couldn't bear the thought of being at home on my own. The safety and isolation of home had always felt like a refuge but now it felt un-safe. I needed to know someone else was there. I needed to know I wasn't alone. I was scared of myself.

On the day before lockdown would officially begin I packed my suitcase and a couple of bags and drove to stay at my brother's as he was the only one amongst family and friends who had a spare room.

I arrived. I unpacked. We went for a walk. We no doubt had dinner and possibly we watched a movie.

I was okay(ish) for a few days. Then I started to wake up in the middle of the night and couldn't get back to sleep. Then I started not to be able to get off to sleep in the first place.

I had brought a few sleeping pills with me. I had spoken to the GP I'd disclosed the abuse to a couple of days beforehand to ask for some sleeping pills. I think he had (oh so) generously given me five. He'd asked what I wanted them for (!) and I'd told him I was feeling anxious and was having difficulty sleeping. He asked what I was anxious about. What … apart from the fact I was sexually abused at seven, waiting for trauma recovery therapy and there was a global pandemic?

For fuck's sake.

After I'd eked out these last few pills out I called him again from my brother's. He didn't want to prescribe any more sleeping pills. He said he could prescribe antihistamines. They wouldn't even touch the sides. He suggested I could try Kalms. And eventually he told me I would just have to 'ride it out'. What had been an emergency just five and a half months earlier was now something I apparently had to suffer in silence and isolation. Everything felt like a body blow, being thrown across the room from one person to the next as they failed to see me, hear me or help me, wrapped up in their own wants, needs and fears.

*

The temptation to rush. To not bother with the details. In part because there is some pain in making myself go there again. In part because I've always believed no-one is interested in me. I have spent a lifetime skimming over everything that hurts me most, convinced it's the best thing to do to avoid being rejected again and again.

*

All my days were becoming a strange internal dialogue between different parts of myself. The rational, logical me that was used to exercising rigid control over everything in order to 'cope' in order to function, was losing the battle. It frantically searched online or through the repertoire of the past decades, for 'things that might help'. I went for long walks with my brother – a distraction for my logical mind I hoped, with the added benefits of endorphins from exercise, vitamin D from the sun and being in nature. Nothing changed. I took any and every alternative medicine that was listed as having any therapeutic benefit with respect to sleep. I glugged Rescue Remedy Night. I doused the bedlinen in lavender oil. I took Kalms all day. And still nothing changed. I would take off in the car and drive around in circles, chain-smoking out the window – terrified the Covid police would stop me yet hoping they would and an intuitive and kind officer would look at me, know something was wrong, and ask me if I was okay. I could tell him 'No' and they would somehow save me from this hell. Nothing changed. I started, secretly, to pour myself a large drink before bed to get my head to switch off, my thoughts to shut up. I would slap myself on the front of the head hoping I could physically dislodge something that was stuck. I played bat and ball in the garden for hours, counting, always counting, because counting meant my head couldn't go anywhere else.

I stopped talking to friends. While everyone went online I was retreating from the world. The thought of reaching out to anyone and telling them how I really felt was terrifying. Paralysing. I couldn't summon the tiniest bit of energy to pretend it was okay any more. And the world was worried about Covid. Everyone else had their own problems. No-one was interested in mine. I spoke with my GP again and asked if they could do anything to accelerate getting access to the trauma recovery services and he told me, categorically and without hesitation, No.

I was trapped in my head. Which was trapped in time. At almost every moment of every day I was sitting in the room outside her office. Feeling terrified, vulnerable, ashamed, un-loved, unimportant. I couldn't move on. I had no idea what was going on. I was putting so much effort into keeping up some semblance of a normal life during the day, and not descending into a despair like I'd ever known during the night, that there wasn't an ounce of physical, emotional or mental strength left for anything else.

And I was trapped in Covid time. Nowhere to go. No one to see. None of the usual distractions. No shops to spend money in to treat myself. No cinema. No café at the park. No friends to meet for a drink. No gym. No doctor to go and see. No acupuncture. No Reiki. No massages. No facials. No therapists to talk to. None of the things that I had relied on in the past when I had needed to re-set, re-balance. Even at work I had been shafted. I contract. Often treated like a second-class citizen despite all the years and effort I had given them. Someone permanent was coming in to do the role I'd been doing for the last year. I was going to take another role – they were getting rid of another contractor who had not, by general consensus, been delivering. But with Covid they decided it would be unfair to him to give him notice. So instead they 'gave me notice' and made up some role filling the gaps on projects no-one else had wanted to pick up. I lost my little team, I lost management support, I lost the connections at work that might have held some part of me together. I lost the one thing that had been the biggest distraction over the past almost-thirty years. Something I could throw myself into that made me feel useful even if, by working all the hours God sends, it also played to my need to feel un-appreciated, and to be, to feel, like a martyr.

I knew who I was. And every knock. Every blow. Every rejection. Every little thing that didn't go my way just proved the point about how little the world cared for me or valued me. And how little I expected.

But I couldn't do this on my own.

And I didn't really know how to ask for help. Asking for help I became that seven year girl sitting in that room. Powerless. Silenced. Fearful. And sent away.

What do I remember most from that time? The feeling of being increasingly out of control in a world that was out of control. Everything was tinged with some feeling of madness. And there were no stabilising factors, no routine I could immerse myself in to create some impression of normalcy.

My brother lives opposite a forest. In the first few days we would do a full circuit together, somewhere around an hour's walk. Everything was so quiet. No planes. So few cars passing on the roads nearby. People speaking in quiet voices as we passed them. Nothing to drown out the noise in my head.

I started to walk on my own. Mostly because I couldn't sit still. If I sat still I sat there with my thoughts, my feelings. Partly, I'm sure, because I knew my brother wanted some time to himself.

Friends from the past came out the woodwork. People started contacting people that they hadn't been in touch with for years as we all feared the end of our world.

I walked. I smoked when there was no-one else around. I even ran a few mornings, early, to try and run off this excess of thinking and feeling. To try and create those endorphins. To distract myself.

Nothing worked. We could go for an hour and a half, two hour, walks and nothing but nothing took me out of myself for more than a second.

I took to heading off in the car more frequently and would drive around several times a day, ciggie in hand, playing loud music, until I realised it was futile and there was nowhere to run.

One night I went to bed and was overwhelmed by everything. I couldn't order my thoughts, I couldn't collect my emotions. I had no idea, at the time, what was happening to me. I went downstairs in my jimjams and dressing gown and stood shaking and crying in the entrance to the lounge, my brother, around the corner, sat at a screen in the kitchen. He didn't look round. I was scared. I cried and he didn't say anything, didn't move from what he was doing. I was living the nightmare of the past on repeat in the present.

My brother told me I needed 'professional help'. But there was none to get. The GP had told me to 'ride it out'. I'd emailed Theresa at the Royal Free but not heard back. The Tavistock was probably inundated and it was still a long way off the end of their revised estimate of an eight month wait.

I called the Samaritans one afternoon after I hadn't stopped crying for hours. He was sympathetic. I cried a lot. It was inconclusive. I could talk, he could listen. But it wasn't the help I needed - because that wasn't available - because of Covid.

It was driving me insane.

I had spent hours worrying about getting my parents, both in their eighties, a food order, making sure they were okay, ordering deliveries to try and cheer them up or when it was a ten day wait for the next supermarket slot.

One day I told my mother, as I choked on my tears, that if I had the courage to drive my car into a wall to end it I would. I'm sure she was horrified. I felt guilty and selfish for having said it. Was I trying to shock? I don't think so. I actually, truthfully had the idea, the image, in my head. It felt like no-one was trying to help me? But how could they? What I wanted was for someone to come and get me, to save me, from myself, from the world, from everything, to take me away, put me to bed and look after me until I was better. But we were all stuck at home, on our own. Anything and everything that I might have used as a support mechanism previously had gone and I was left staring into the eyes of this monster that had emerged from the depths of my past and was terrorising me.

I tried to talk to my brother but for whatever reason it's not the sort of conversation we ever had or, in all truth, are likely to ever have. We weren't a family that discussed how we felt or that made ourselves vulnerable. That familial love was implicit, inherent, but wasn't characterised by displays of love and affection or the emotional (rather than logical) expression of love and fear.

I didn't want to burden my parents more – telling my mother I wanted to drive into a wall was the least of it.

I spoke to a small number of friends but did what I had done all my life and ended everything with a joke. Someone told me that I can tell a sad story about myself, be on the verge of tears, but somehow turn the end of the sentence into a reluctant comical smile, somehow, apparently, signalling that it's okay for the other person to duck out of being interested, of caring. Because I don't expect them to want to care. I signal 'it's okay, I'm laughing, no need to take anything I've just said even vaguely seriously'.

*

Sometimes I can't comprehend how I got from so lost to where I am now. But of course I know. Of course I remember everything I've been through. It just hurts. And remembering, now, makes me feel it all over again, although each time it recedes further into the past until, one day, I hope, it will be so far away it will, I am sure, have no place in the present.

*

Andy. Thank goodness for Andy. At that point in time he helped me decide what seemed like the only way out. I couldn't stay at my brothers – I was going mad. I thought it was because of him, because he couldn't help me, wouldn't help me. But now I realise I actually was going mad.

In any event I decided to go home. I packed my bags. I left. It was a few days before my brother's birthday and I felt such guilt. But Andy was right, I couldn't stay. And there was only one place to go.

I bought my brother a lot of presents instead.

The roads were deserted. I drove slowly, carefully, not wanting to attract attention to myself in case 'they' sent me back. Rehearsing, reciting, repeating what I would say if I was pulled over. This level of fear of breaching covid restrictions on top of the all-consuming fear that had taken root in every cell of me …. I was terrified. Terrified of simply being alive.

I got home, unpacked and for a very brief moment of time there was some sort of relief. It didn't last. The only thing that lasted was the anxiety, the insomnia, the not knowing what to do with myself.

I was still working – hanging on to some routine like the last passenger hanging on to the last life raft in the middle of a cruel ocean.

I got more sleeping pills. A different doctor. No mention of 'how are you?'. No asking how I was coping with the recently disclosed trauma in the midst of this lockdown.

I worked. I disclosed too much to colleagues telling people I'd only ever known in the office and had never spoken to about anything personal that I had been sexually abused as a child. Which made me feel worse. But I couldn't help myself.

I would chain smoke three or four cigarettes and throw the rest of the packet away – stick them under the tap so I couldn't fish them out the bin later when I was desperate. I sat down to eat around six thirty or seven in the evening but could barely manage more than a couple of mouthfuls. I walked, hoping that allotted one hour of exercise would somehow clear my head.

One evening, about six, I went out for the second (or third) time that day. There was a rage inside me I couldn't calm. Everyone I walked past felt like a taunt. How were they all coping with this. I was so angry. Everyone else was baking bloody banana bread, doing home work-outs, watching Netflix, on group chats, and I was this wreck of a human being chasing myself. I got to the end of the road. So many people out in the sunshine, queueing for the supermarket, walking, with family, loved ones. I had never felt so isolated. Furious. Crazy. I began to cry. I marched up Finchley Road, tears streaming down my face, begging the universe to make one person notice me. I needed so badly to be seen. I had always needed to be seen. To be heard. But there was never anyone. Ever. I had been stuck in that fucking room all my life screaming inside. A police van went by. 'Stop me' …. please. Arrest me for having gone out more than once in a day. I don't care. I just can't be on my own in this world any more. I can't be left alone. All the way to the top of West End Lane. Zigzagging down the side streets to make it last longer, to save me from going home and being faced with four walls that provided no safety, instead reflecting the fear, the memory, the horror, everything, back to me.

I don't know how it's possible. For a grown woman to walk the streets crying for fifty minutes, to pass so many people and not one of them notice her, ask her if she was okay. Were they afraid? Of me? Of themselves? Of covid?

As I turned the corner into my road there were two traffic wardens sitting at the bus stop. I looked at them and they acknowledged me. But I didn't know what to say. I had no vocabulary. I made some inane comment about the weather. They replied. I wanted to string it out so I didn't have to go indoors and sit there with myself, but there wasn't much more to say.

One sunny evening I climbed out the bedroom window to smoke and see if a gin and tonic would help. Drink had become something I couldn't face. If I drank enough it might stop my thoughts whizzing round sufficiently for me to get to sleep, but it wouldn't keep me asleep more than a few hours, and I'd wake up at some stupid time in the morning tired and hungover and even more depressed. My neighbour was on the roof outside his flat having a smoke and a drink as well. We introduced ourselves and chatted for a while. He was calm, collected, normal, which just shone a light on how worked up, stressed and out of control I felt.

I talked to the GP, the one who I had disclosed to, about going to stay with my parents as I couldn't cope. He cautioned against the risks. I spoke to my parents about going to stay with them. I imagine they were worried about me but I was petrified I would be carrying some fucking covid germs around and could kill them.

I had been to visit them once already. On the pretence of taking a food delivery. I drove around the north circular at a snail's pace with two large bags of M&S shopping on the seat next to me. It was a fairly chilly day and I sat a few metres from them whist they sat outside the patio doors. My father was as stoical – or possibly blasé – about covid as you can imagine. He steadfastly refused to wash his hands more than usual and would have quite happily had me sit inside with them – even if it was by then a 'criminal offence'!

I stayed outside. I peed in a bucket in my parents shed and washed my hands in a bowl of soapy water my mother had put there for me.

All I needed, all I wanted, on that quick trip out to Essex, was to be held. For someone to put an arm round me. To be seen. But we couldn't because of covid. And I couldn't because I was trying to put on a brave face for my parents.

But I was getting too desperate. It was decided. I would pack my bags again and go and stay with them for 'as long as I needed'.

*

The deciding factor in needing to go 'home' was a very early morning call to 111. I wish I could say that all of this happened over the space of weeks and that I was broadly managing to act out some semblance of existence, but I had been back from my brother's a matter of days.

I couldn't sleep – again. Caught up in a storm of anxiety I howled like a banshee (desperate for someone to come and help me) but quietly enough not to draw attention to myself from the people upstairs. My heart was racing – again. Skipping and jumping and speeding along like a mad frog on too much cocaine. I understand now – if only I had then – that one of the symptoms of having a panic attack is that you believe you're going to have a heart attack. I didn't even know that I was having a panic attack, but the heart attack felt like a distinct possibility.

At four in the morning I called 111. The usual questions. Someone would call me back. I waited. They called. Could I get myself to A&E? I could. At six in the morning I drove like a crazy woman back to the Royal Free. How many times had I been there in the last year? A virus at the start of 2019 that floored me until an ambulance came. I sat in the back repeatedly asking if the vehicle was moving everything was spinning so much. One ECG later, a full suite of blood tests, a comprehensive visual examination and I was sent home to bed. Unilateral tinnitus in 2018. The GP referred me for an urgent scan in case it was cancer - which was fucking frightening. One evening I was convinced I had a tumour and off to A&E I went again. Full bloods, a visual examination, told not to worry and sent home. Had my body been struggling, the more time that passed, with containing the stress of the trauma? Like one of those stress toys – you squeezed in one place and another popped out, but nothing ever broke the surface?

But it was lockdown – where the hell could I park? I took a punt that the traffic wardens wouldn't be scanning the residential streets of Hampstead so early in the morning, parked up and walked the five minutes to the make-shift A&E entrance. Covid fear gripped me. That and a massive question mark that hung round me asking me what on earth I was doing. My body was resisting breaching the entrance despite a masked security officer smiling as he told me everything was okay. It clearly wasn't.

I'd never thought about it before but hospitals filled me with a quiet fear and I always felt like I had to be on my best behaviour. Was that 'normal' or had I never put two and two together before and understood that he had been a doctor, that I had to be a good girl?

Even if I try really hard I don't remember what happened for the next hour or so. I'm fairly certain I waited a while. I know I had another ECG. Why wouldn't I believe that my heart was okay? Because physically, medically, it was fine, but emotionally it had been broken for most of my life?

I repeated what I had repeated so many times in the past two months – about the abuse, the disclosure, waiting for trauma recovery therapy. I cried. I told the nurse or doctor or whoever saw me that I couldn't cope. I felt and looked a wreck.

There was very little they could do.

They would however refer me to the Mental Health Crisis service near Euston.

She suggested I go now.

Now?

It was sometime after nine in the morning. I was so tired, hungry. I wanted to go home. I just wanted to be wrapped up in the care and compassion my mind and body craved and tell someone I believed in who could tell me it would all be okay. Instead I picked up a chocolate bar at the hospital shop and drove to Euston.

Oh holy crap. It was frightening. An old Victorian building. Security like they expected trouble. I got past the initial reception and was directed to the end of a corridor. Another reception. Another security guard. I was told to sit and wait.

I sat and waited, listening to a woman in a room around the corner moaning and shouting.

I didn't understand why I was there. Was I that ill too? I just wanted someone to listen to me, to look after me, to talk to me, to believe me, to tell me it would be okay. How had it reached the point where I needed to be here? Nothing made sense. Nothing. My entire world had gone. Everything I thought I'd known I didn't know any more.

Someone came and took my blood pressure. An insane reading – one hundred and eighty over one hundred and thirty – no wonder I felt like I was going to blow up.

I waited some more. I was told to go and wait at the reception back at the front of the building. I did as I was told, stopping en route to go to the loo and scrub my hands.

Then they came to get me. Neither of them looked older than thirty but of course I couldn't see their faces behind their masks. We sat in a large room a long way away from each other and they asked me the same questions I'd now been asked so many times, and I gave the same answers, and each time went back to then, feeling myself in the room, his hands on me, and then watching the two of them through the crack in her door as they whispered about me like I wasn't there.

Every time the relief of talking about it contrasting with the horror of emotions it took me back to and that kept their hold on me long after I'd stopped talking.

Yes, I understood the NHS mental health services must be overwhelmed at the moment. Yes, I understood it was difficult to offer me any treatment. What they would do was to recommend someone from some mental health service call me, some sort of over the phone therapy. I should expect someone to contact me in the next day or so.

I'd been in the room with them almost an hour. My time was up. They no doubt had other things to do. Probably people more in need than me I thought to myself.

I drove home. I let my manager know, who I'd texted earlier that morning to say I was at the hospital, and said I would log on later.

It was just too too much. Someone once, rather unhelpfully, told me, when I said to her that I couldn't cope with it all, that the fact I was sitting in front of her was proof I could cope. But coping at what cost and what effort?

The thing is I wasn't coping. I had even developed some weird phobia about my new kettle and toaster. It made me uneasy every time I wanted a cup of tea. I was definitely not coping.

*

I reflect on those few months now and know that I was doing my utmost best to make it all okay.

I arrived at my parents' frightened to get close to them, wondering if I should wear a mask around the house, concerned I'd brought some deadly germs with me in my luggage, in the car, in the very air that clung to my skin.

My parents were far more pragmatic. We agreed no close contact for a few days, to be 'safe' - whatever 'safe' meant at that time.

My stoic of a father gave up his bed for me. An eighty-five year old man who I loved decided to sleep on a sofa bed. Were they worried about me? I assume so. But I was so horribly lost in myself I don't think I would have seen a raging rhinoceros running towards me with a bunch of flowers and outstretched arms.

I took a zopiclone and slept for a couple of hours. Other times I could take a zopiclone and not sleep for more than sixty minutes. I needed something strong enough to fell that rhino to send me off to sleep for a whole night.

There was a semblance of normality. We did our online food orders. I walked for miles back and forth along the seafront. I messaged an increasingly smaller number of friends who I still trusted with my emotions and ramblings. I signed up for an online dating app on the advice of one friend who suggested it would be a distraction. It was, briefly, but wasn't an answer.

I worked intermittently. I gardened, something I'd never been keen on, but hoping it would both focus and divert my thoughts. I bought a bicycle and the wind whistling past me brought some relief. But the saddle was so bloody uncomfortable. Served me right for buying cheap.

The psychologist at the Royal Free eventually replied, having been granted dispensation by her manager to reply to someone who was no longer under her care. She recommended a friend of hers who was a psychotherapist.

I got another prescription of zopiclone. I told this particular GP that I was often so anxious by bedtime that they didn't have much of an effect. She suggested a glass of wine with dinner might help with the anxiety and then to take a sleeping pill before bed.

Really???

I took to pilfering my parents drinks cupboard. If they noticed they didn't say. One night I drank a bottle of wine after eleven o'clock to get off to sleep. One glass took the edge off, two began to calm me, three started to stop my racing mind and anything after that switched my brain off so completely that I passed out.

A bottle of sweet sherry went a similar way over the course of a week.

In my defence I had little choice. I needed to stretch each prescription of sleeping pills out so my reticent GPs wouldn't need to lecture me and perpetuate the already turbulent belief that I was 'a bad person'.

I had to tell my parents that I smoked when I was stressed. In truth I had always smoked. It was a cover for so much – lack of confidence, fitting in, calming my nerves – quite literally smoke and mirrors. I would get in the car, drive along the front and chain smoke for half an hour. I would creep down to the end of the garden, hoping I was out of view and have a quick ciggie. Sales of mints in the area soared.

The psychotherapist seemed to make things worse. Instead of talking about the trauma she asked about my relationship with my parents, particularly my father. One night she left me feeling so abject about what was apparently some absence of love that she wanted me to believe in that I was awake until five in the morning, generating a long list of times when I felt he had let me down. In truth he hadn't. He had been a parent, living his life, doing the best he could.

But if you look too hard for something you will find it - why are some of these therapists so fucking cruel?

I cried, quietly. I heard my mother get up to use the bathroom and willed her with all my might to knock on the door and come to me. She didn't. She couldn't I assume. Equally as lost in my despair and downward spiral.

I reported the rape online to the police. I thought maybe that would bring some closure. I recall finishing a conversation with the detective who was my case officer that had left me in tears – a normal state of being by this point – drying my eyes and joining a work call to negotiate the schedules to a contract. I sometimes wonder if I was doing my best or if I would have been better taking more time out of work. But I had already had a couple of weeks signed off with PTSD and I needed the money. I was a little surprised the GP was so matter of fact asking me what I wanted her to put down as the reason on my sick note without really following up on how I was doing.

I started the menopause. Talk about adding insult to bloody injury. Might it have explained the anxiety, the insomnia, the night sweats, the foggy head … I doubt it. It may have exacerbated it but there was no standard prescription of HRT that was going to stop the avalanche now the trauma had surfaced like a raging bull and had me in its grip throwing me about like the world's largest lion toying with the world's smallest mouse.

The referral finally came through from the mental health crisis centre. They couldn't offer any one on one sessions any more as they were inundated. Instead they offered me some online service. There was apparently someone at the end of the chat when I logged on at the allotted time but it may as well have been automated. The same opening question that I heard so many times over that period but phrased differently – did I think I was a danger to myself? Did I think I was going to do anything to harm myself? Was I thinking about harming myself? Did I have a support network?

No, no and no I replied. I told them I didn't think I was going to harm myself. But, in truth, I was worried I might. I just didn't want to admit it. Couldn't let anyone know I was that weak, that vulnerable. And yes I had a support network but I couldn't talk to them. Everyone was dealing with shit given the pandemic, the lockdown, and no-one wanted my shit on top of their shit. I was down to just two friends I had any contact with. I stopped looking at social media. Couldn't cope with all the photos of 'ordinary people' who were apparently coping.

I stopped with the psychotherapist. I had three sessions at over one hundred quid a go but they were leaving me feeling worse than before I started.

I carried on working. If I didn't work I didn't get paid.

I was put in contact with someone from Southend Rape Crisis Centre. It was the first time I spoke to someone who I felt understood how I felt.

And then I googled 'rape trauma recovery' and some part of my brain that absolutely, fundamentally, was doing its best, took some sort of control, however much I felt like I was spiralling more rapidly into complete and utter insanity.

*

It's exhausting remembering. Was it wise to tell this story? To make myself go back? Or is it an act of healing? Yes, this story has a happy ending (eventually). Yes, I am no longer in active therapy for trauma recovery. Yes, even after the trauma recovery therapy I have found the need to go back over so much of a life that wasn't led as it could have been – should have been – if I hadn't been raped as a child and told to be a good girl and not tell anyone, not even mummy. Life is infinitely better, freer, fulfilling. But is telling this story really some act of full and final evisceration of everything?

I very much hope so. I would even go so far as to say I expect so. Ally, my psychotherapist, would say the same. Feeling the emotions helps my brain to process them. And each time the past moves further away. Never gone. Never forgotten. But without its hold on me. Without its potency.

It's just that every time I take the time to write another word I remember – I feel – how I felt then. The absolute and utter despair of being adrift on a tiny island of terror, and yet here I am, writing and choosing to take myself there.

And why? Because this story has to be told. Because it didn't happen so long ago that I'm just making a fuss over nothing. Because these things – however quickly they might have happened – create a hold over everything you are, do, say, believe and think that stays with you for life. Because I'm not making it up. Because because because …

Because this happens too too often. And I want people to know. To be shocked. Horrified even. To know that this may be happening in the house next door, at the school up the road or that this may have happened to someone you know who was never made to feel like they were allowed to speak about it and for years, decades, has kept quiet because they feel the misplaced sense of shame that comes with being abused or because they were told not to tell anyone, or simply because this isn't talked about enough or they don't know where to start, who to approach, or because they are so frightened for themselves at the prospect of telling any living soul.

I'm so tired now. I was so tired then. Tired beyond any tiredness I can even begin to explain. Nothing feels right. I have to remind myself this isn't happening now. I remember how I felt. I felt sad and angry I had to feel that way. I can still feel that sadness, the anger, the grief, the despair, the feeling of utter loneliness. But it isn't happening now.

Not much further to go and I am there, in hospital. Terrified, but relieved to have taken myself out of the equation as it were. Not much more of this until I reach the point when I began, with the help of Dr H, Edward and Ally, the journey to freedom.

It sounds such a fucking cliché … but it's not. Allow me this one moment, in the midst of all this despair, to take some strength and peace from the memory and the reality of these past few years.

*

Somewhere, in my on-line research into trauma recovery, and left to my own devices with the absence of any seemingly useful help from anywhere else, I had read that it can be useful to revisit the trauma but safely, in a way that will help to soothe and put the cork back in the bottle after it has been shaken and exploded. I don't believe I knew consciously what I was doing, because at that time I couldn't order my thoughts sufficiently to even cook a meal, but my subconscious was, to some extent, keeping me as safe as it could in the circumstances.

One night, about half one in the morning, I was in bed, crying, as usual. The anger, the grief, the hurting, they flooded out of me at any – all – times of the day and night. My mother, eighty years old, must have seen the light on as she went to the bathroom, and tapped at the door.

Something instinctual took over. We sat there, side by side, with her arm on my back, and for the first time ever I told her what had happened. I told her as that child of seven and she asked me questions as if I was her seven-year old daughter. Her hand on my back. The care I should have got at the time from those two bitches. The empathy. Nothing was solved but there was a space to talk, for empathy, for healing, that opened up. I cried, great dripping tears and streams of saliva. Into a scarf as I was still so petrified I might infect her.

My emotions, the panic attacks that I didn't even know were panic attacks came in waves. Sometimes rolling sometimes crashing. I might be quiet, still, lying on the sofa in some void for an hour and then I would be overwhelmed, sitting down to eat a meal and the contrasting normality between a meal with family and my internal anguish causing me to cry so much I had to leave the table and lie on the bed sobbing for an hour.

I would find my mother watching me. Just watching. Looking at me. My primary need at the time seemed to be for someone to be there for me, to reach out to me, to help me. I would talk about how I was feeling for a few minutes as we sat there in the lounge and she would simply look at me, saying nothing. I was so trapped in the re-living of that traumatic experience I felt this as some form of rejection – of what had happened, of me, of my right to feel the way I was feeling. And yet what was she supposed to do or say? She was surely as lost as me – no understanding of what was happening, no point of reference, no possible distraction outside the walls of their home due to lockdown. I am sure she wanted to help but didn't have the means. And everything was compounded by her own childhood, always caught between her parents' arguments, and her own feeling that she was somehow responsible for whatever had happened, that she was at fault.

But, of course, she wasn't.

I had one place to go that felt like an escape – Andy's. Andy is a celebrant, a reiki master, a healer. A gay older man he had worked in a homeless shelter, as a foster parent. He was, and still of course is, a kind man. And yet one who doesn't mince his words.

I don't know what the lockdown rules were at that time but I drove round to his. I parked and went down the side alley to the garden gate. He had set two chairs up, five metres apart. The sun was out. He offered me a glass of red wine. I took it. I don't know how many times I went round during the month I was at my parents, maybe half a dozen, but I include him in the list of people that helped save my life. He listened to me talking about the trauma, talking about living with my parents. We talked about having some sort of business together in the future. I might move to Southend. I would have enough money left over from the sale of my flat to rent a space. I couldn't face London, couldn't face corporate life. I didn't think I would be able to live my 'old' life ever again. I couldn't go back. The concept of going forward hadn't even entered my awareness.

I still feel guilty because I haven't done any of those things. We said we'd go to cabaret night at The Cliff when the drag queens were in. I keep saying I'll let him know when I'm in Southend next so we can go for coffee or a drink, but everything is always such a rush, and I haven't seen him as much as I should.

I need him to know how important he was to me at that time. That I will forever be grateful.

*

In one of what seemed like an infinite number of rambling conversations with a colleague she mentioned she had once been to stay at The Priory – for depression amongst other things. It was an unsubtle hint. I took it. I told my parents I needed to call them, I couldn't think of anything else to do. My parents were probably shocked, disbelieving that it had come to this, thinking surely there was some other option. They didn't seem supportive, but then no one and nothing felt like they could support me by now, my fear and anxiety had become impenetrable. I screamed in tears that I might as well kill myself if this was all there was for me. I know! Disturbing, inconsiderate, selfish. I thought I knew how I sounded but I've no idea what they heard or how helpless they felt.

I called The Priory. They could fit me in at the North London location. I had been once before, on that day visit that made me feel so ridiculously out of place. I said I would think about it. I spoke with Andy. It was so much money. Was it the right thing to do? In the absence of anything else I didn't know what could be wrong with it.

When I had been there before, around 2002, had they known something I hadn't? I had a job that involved lots of long haul travel and I couldn't get on a plane. After a conversation with the company employee assistance line I was referred for a day assessment at The Priory. It was the days of being offered Prozac if you went to your GP and said you had a rash , were stressed at work and couldn't sleep. I know because that's what they once suggested to me. An aged locum with a pale pink crocheted tie offered me Prozac and told me to wear lightweight pyjamas. You couldn't make it up!

I headed off that day somewhere round the north circular and parked up. After letting reception know I was there I went to a small room in the attic with someone who I assumed was a counsellor, filled out a questionnaire whilst she was out of the room and afterwards we talked. Three things stick with me from that day. The first was trying not to answer honestly a question about how much I wanted to live. The second was thinking to myself I didn't belong there as I walked past the room of a patient who was crying and shouting. And the third was the shame I felt as I joined a group therapy session in the afternoon.

I didn't want to stand in front of these people and talk about myself. Having heard about their addictions, anorexia and all the trauma of their lives I felt a fool telling them I was there because of a fear of flying – which is what I did. I said 'I'm not sure why I'm here' to a sea of blank faces.

I was asked if I wanted to go back but said no. How could this possibly help? I was a fraud.

But I still do wonder what they saw that I didn't.

Instead something else happened. I had started talking to a chap on Hinge, or Bumble, or one of those dating apps that every single person in the world took to during lockdown. We quickly moved from messaging to phone calls. Then to WhatsApp video calls. He was apparently (I was later to find out otherwise!) in marketing, having worked as a buyer and seller of vintage paintings (whatever a 'vintage' painting is). But he was creative, interested in the arts – hurrah! And - some sort of icing on some sort of cake - he worked as a life coach and mentor.

Oh how vulnerable and gullible I was. But all roads were leading me to the same destination.

He was named after a character in a 1960s children's television programme. He was tall. I found him attractive. He looked and sounded genuine.

He had been sexually abused as a child.

It was like fate intervened. He could and would understand. I knew it – some things are surely meant to be?

And I was desperate to get back to London. I just needed something to make me feel safe whilst I was in my flat on my own. Did I know then that a plan was formulating at the back of my mind?

I decided to go back to London for one night, to see how I fared. My parents must be sick of me. I couldn't find what I needed with them – but in hindsight there was only one place that I was ever going to find what I needed.

So in the interests of my sanity I paid no heed to the request to the populace not to travel, got in the car, and drove back to London. We were to have a zoom call that evening. I dressed up (there was fuck all else to do and it was a diversion). I bought some nice food and a decent bottle of vino.

We spoke. For almost two hours. 'God bless Zoom' I thought.

There was something about the way he looked at me that I read as kindness, as compassion. How easy it is to see what we want to see.

He asked me to take him on a tour of my flat which I duly did – taking all of five minutes to show him the three rooms and a bathroom. Did he in fact have a plan too?

I was drunk and went out like a light. True to form I woke at about five in the morning. Really? Even the prospect of 'love' wasn't enough to override this sleep-insanity?

I messaged him. He had said something the night before … 'if only it wasn't lockdown' he 'could come and visit and we could go out and get to know each other' … the seed had been planted. Why didn't he come and stay for a while, a few days, maybe longer, if he was comfortable getting the train into London? We could hole up together for lockdown and see what happened. And yes, he was right, so right, we had some profound connection, maybe we were soulmates and it had taken lockdown for us to find each other?

Again – how vulnerable and gullible I was.

Knackered, but by now very used to being knackered, I drove slowly and carefully back round the north circular and along the A127 to Southend.

I announced to my parents that Hector (let's call him that) was going to come and stay with me in London.

Did my mother have a bad feeling about it? No. Did she think it was crazy? It was lockdown, what constituted crazy in that world?

I drove back to London the day before he arrived. Went to the supermarket. Cleared a couple of drawers and made a little space in a cupboard - and didn't sleep well.

It would take me fifteen minutes to drive to Kings Cross. I was so comically nervous – here I was, in the middle of lockdown, struggling to stay afloat and welcoming a man I really didn't know into my home. What on earth could go wrong eh?

I set off far too early. My thoughts a whirlwind. I was so early that I pulled over the south side of Regents Park to waste time. My heart was beating out of my chest, more rapidly than it had been even when I was in Mykonos having the mother of all panic attacks.

I parked outside the east side of Kings Cross wondering if there would be armed police interrogating anyone who was out and about when they shouldn't be.

Finally he arrived. In a shirt, jacket and jeans. With an enormous suitcase and two holdalls. I didn't even stop to wonder how long he thought he was staying for. Hadn't we said a couple of weeks?

We were polite. I did my best to appear calm and normal. I had pulled it off all my life so why should now be any different.

And I drove back to mine. Ostensibly in a new 'bubble'. Probably in a new relationship. Surely out of my mind. But nothing seemed more ordinary and expected than what we were doing in that moment.

The benefit of hindsight is an admirable thing. The reality of the situation was I was a woman drowning under the weight of past sexual abuse who was about to hook up with a man who had been sexually abused by his mother's partner over the course of years and who he professed to have loved and loved still.

What can I say? Where do I even start with the events of the next five and a half weeks?

In one way or another I was using lockdown to give myself permission to behave in a way I would never normally behave but that was a fallout from where my mental health was at the time. We had had sex. He initiated it. Oh, how many warning signs I missed. I had hoped he would be someone we could sit and have a laugh over a couple of bottles of wine and he would bring the fun that had been missing for the past few months. Rather he was nigh on teetotal and, to be excruciatingly honest, a bit too bloody serious for his own good.

I had told him, when we first started talking on the phone, I was working my way through recovery from disclosing childhood sexual abuse. God, it sounds so factual, so clinical, when I say it like that. He told me he mentored men who had been sexually abused as children having worked through his own issues. How anyone who had 'worked through their own issues' could think the man who raped him as a teenager was a benevolent older man who he remembered for treating him to ice-cream when they were out, and was therefore to be thought of kindly, beggars belief. I know 'we are all different' but whilst it may have seemed 'normal' to him surely it was quite the opposite?

He had only bought himself. No gift. We had to pop to the supermarket up the road and he rather cloyingly said 'let me buy you some chocolates and a bottle of prosecco 'as a thank you'. At the time I honestly thought 'how sweet'.

I simply don't know how to sum up that time in words. There was something entirely farcical about it. I can categorically say that none of what happened could ever happen the way it happened ever again. It simply isn't in my beliefs about who I am, how I should be, what I should say, what I should do or what is acceptable in any – ANY – circumstances … other than if someone were to find themselves in the exact – EXACT - same circumstances I found myself in at the time.

Momentarily I found it charming that he wanted to read to me, hug trees on Hampstead Heath (now that we were allowed out more than our supposed one hour a day), look for shapes in the clouds and generally while the days away in some sort of pseudo-romantic Room With A View way.

But I needed to dance wildly round the lounge to Personal Jesus and let all this pent-up emotion and tension out – which I did, very very quietly one night when he decided to go to bed early.

We were the ultimate 'new couple in love'. For two weeks. Or so I thought. Then the cracks began to show.

He would ask me what I wanted in life. I would tell him I wanted to be with him, start some sort of business together, to move out of London and buy a house together. He insisted we had a shared spirituality in common. Then he disagreed on where to move to despite the fact it was my house and my money.

And then he slipped up and told me that he wanted to be with 'someone' who fulfilled him – and I don't remember what else he said because an alarm bell rang, almost inaudibly, that he hadn't said that he wanted that someone to be me.

I had foolishly told him to make himself at home. Foolishly because he took me at my word with no concession or compromise. He sprawled everywhere. I was used to my own space – despite my travels to my brother and parents over the previous seven or eight weeks. I excused him by excusing myself for not being used to living with someone.

And Jesus he was so bloody SLOW. Everything he did he did in his own time, in his own way, oblivious to the fact that he was sharing space – and life – with someone else.

I'm not going to say it was an easy time for him. I am fully aware that he hadn't expected to be living with someone who was suffering from insomnia and anxiety. As he told me – more often than he needed to? – it was 'a lot'.

But dear God he didn't help himself. He had started running in lockdown and wanted me to go with him. Running is not, and never has been, my thing. Off we went one morning. I had a debit card and my phone in the flat pocket on the side of my leggings but gave him the house keys as they were bulky. As we got to the park I said I was done and would head home. I was less than thirty seconds up the road when I realised I didn't have the keys. I called his mobile but no answer. He was running and I guess hadn't heard the phone. I messaged and said when you pick this up can you head back to mine as I can't get in. I walked the thirty minutes home very slowly, picked up provisions at Waitrose, and then sat on the steps outside my block waiting. And waiting. I waited almost two hours. His excuse? By the time he'd realised he had the keys he'd got lost and decided to spend some time looking at the trees! I excused him that once – he was evidently the sort of man who had his mind on other things.

Then it happened again. Parking around Primrose Hill had been opened up so we stopped there and set off. Not far into Regents Park I decided I would walk and pointed out – very clearly – where I would meet him in thirty minutes. The café at the Open Air Theatre was doing take out coffee. The bliss of a slow return to normality. I picked up two coffees and waited. And then I called him. He didn't pick up. At least the house keys were in the car and I had the key to that! I slowly made my way back to the car, keeping my eyes peeled. As I got into the car it began to rain. I waited. And waited. The time on the ticket had run out. I gave it one more minute. He showed up. I was trying not to be grumpy and talk to him like a child. And he knew it.

Suffice to say the next few weeks were not a bed of roses. I still don't entirely understand how it came to be but one day we were driving down to the house where he used to rent a room to collect all his worldly possessions as he was 'moving in' with me. If we were honest I don't think either of us truly wanted it, but we both had different reasons for there not being any viable alternative at the time.

I crammed six black bin bags full of clothes and shoved them in a storage cupboard. And he filtered his stuff so there were another six bin bags and a selection of what I thought were awful paintings of foxes and squirrels that went into a very cheap storage facility off the north circular.

I think I was generous. He had a hideous old lantern that he would put a tealight in at night that sat near the television, and one of the fox prints went on the wall in the spare room that doubled as what I had thought was my home office but evidently had become his. I didn't complain but he was overtaking and it irked me.

But let's go back to the room he had been renting in a flat somewhere ninety minutes' train journey outside

London. This marketing consultant hadn't worked for months. He blamed lockdown but people I knew who were working from home had never been so busy. I tried to re-write his CV but there was little to put on it. The role as coach and mentor to men who had been abused seemed to be no more than a Zoom call once a week with an on-line group he belonged to. He had come to mine with six hundred pounds in his bank account not having paid any child support to his ex-wife for his two children for nine months. How had he thought it was a good idea to lie? When did he think I would find out? I properly found out the extent of his lack of money after a shopping trip to Tesco when the cashier rang the bill up and he looked at me expecting me to pay even though it was his turn.

I can't say I was giving him, at that time, any of the things he had hoped for. Apart from his secret hope that I would cover him financially I was probably not much else that he'd wished for when we first spoke about his coming to stay. My sleeping had become worse. Partly because he slept in the middle of the bed, arms akimbo, one hand behind his head the other resting on his genitals. Just bizarre. I regularly found myself on the sofa. Partly because he was becoming increasingly unsympathetic. Was he doing it do be perverse? Was some residue of his past exploitation at the hands of his abuser showing up in his behaviour towards me? I was emotionally volatile. Not in a passive aggressive way, more that I would have moments of extreme anxiety and become clingy. He wanted to have sex a lot and when I didn't go along with it he could be, well, a bit cruel I suppose.

Little by little, as the powers that be determined that covid was supposedly under control, life was opening up. I found an acupuncturist fifteen minutes' walk up the road. She was lovely. And I doubt hadn't expected someone to turn up with the long list of 'stuff' that I had going on and that I hoped – oh how I hoped – she would be able to alleviate. Talk turned to Hector and without saying anything she helped me to see all was not what I needed.

There are two specific events that, if I'm honest, raised the alarm so loud I couldn't ignore its ringing. Every morning, after his run, whilst the rest of us had already been logged on and working for an hour or two (yes – I was still trying to hold down my job – the last outpost of un-needed behaviour and patterns that I still need to let go once and for all), he got back and wrote his 'Morning Pages'. I had done the same for several years previously. They are meant to be a way of dropping stuff on to no more than two or three pages, without thinking about what you are writing, as a way of getting stuff out of your head and enabling your creativity during the day. Except when he wrote it was slow, considered, drawn out. He drew pictures. He wrote carefully. Never rushing. It was painful. So bloody painful. Could the man not just go out for an early run, come home, have a shower, do half an hour's writing and then start to look for work?

It was of course my fault that he didn't get going early enough in the morning. To this day I can't fathom that one. He was the one who stayed up late watching TV whilst I tried to sleep next door, would wake me up when he came to bed, and then go out like a light. I swear there was no gun at his head pleading with him not to get out of bed at half seven in the morning. But increasingly I was to blame .

He felt these pages were so acutely observed and written that they merited a book. We had found ourselves in the position where I offered to order them in a way such that specific topics, feelings, were collated and perhaps would provide a structure to the book. To this end there were piles of A4 pages lined up in front of the television for days.

One day I decided, whilst he was doing something in the other room, to have a read. Forget whatever else he had written there was one thing that stood out. A page he had written admitting he was staying with me in the hope there would be some business opportunity. I read on. There was no love for me, no affection. He needed money and I had seemingly become a transaction.

When I mentioned it to him he was angry. I shouldn't have read them. But how was I going to help with the book, as we had agreed and as he had asked, if I couldn't read them? Apparently he was going to go through them first, to decide what I could and couldn't read. The argument drifted towards nothingness. I was still frightened at the prospect of being alone again so it was an easy ask to capitulate.

The second was a day that I felt truly grim. I mean, absolutely, scarily ill. I had pins and needles starting down one arm. He told me to go to bed. Took my phone away. Raised his voice at me. Told me I was being ridiculous. I lay there thinking I must be an awful person. Why couldn't I be better? And the more I thought about it the worse the pins and needles got. I got out of bed, got my phone and called 111. The usual rigmarole that I had become increasingly used to. A doctor would call me back. I explained everything to him. He didn't think I was having a heart attack or a stroke but agreed that it was alarming. He would get an ambulance out to me.

I told Hector the paramedics would be there soon. He was unimpressed. I was being inconsiderate because it would remind him of when his mum's lodger – the abuser – died. What the actual fuck!

Two wonderful women showed up, in full paramedic gear. My heroines. They did some tests and then took me out to the ambulance for more tests. He didn't say a word. After yet another ECG, blood pressure tests and whatever else they thought was appropriate they said they would take me to hospital to be sure. I went back in the flat to get a bag, some bits and pieces, in case I was a while. He hadn't even realised the ambulance was still there.

I knew the covid set up at the Royal Free A&E department so well by then. Was this my fourth visit in fifteen months? Or my fifth? Or even sixth?

That year and a half was nothing more than a frenzied blur and yet so many details remain etched in my memory. I think I am writing to forget. I am writing to deal with the dealing with it once and for all. Maybe not forget. Maybe to rake over all those horrible moments one more time to let myself feel the things I couldn't let myself feel at the time, and thereby to give myself permission to be sad, to grieve, to let it all go. All of it.

I was probably only there an hour. I sat in the waiting area trying my damnedest not to cry, and then cried buckets in front of the nurse who wired me up for yet another ECG. Anyone who showed me any care in that time was then subject to an overdose of gratitude from me. It became trickier when the doctor came to talk to me. I think an appropriate description of my state would be hysterical. She must be able to do something? To give me more sleeping pills? Something. Anything. Just don't send me home. Don't leave me with nothing to look at but this vast landscape of fear.

But there was nothing she could do and nothing she could offer. Speak to my GP about sleeping pills. But the doctors at my local surgery were at the limit of the three months they could carry on prescribing zopiclone - regardless of any extenuating circumstances.

Was there anyone at home? Reluctantly I mentioned the 'boyfriend' I had been so proud to have a month ago but who now made me shudder. I had texted him twice from the hospital but he took an age to reply.

The paramedics had explained that when you have a panic attack if it is extreme it can cause pins and needles.

I had a week or so back been prescribed an old-fashioned beta blocker called propanalol on the basis it would help with the panic attacks. Instead it left my body and brain at odds, one speeding like a formula one car the other beating calmly as if nothing were wrong.

Hector eventually replied to my text message. He would walk up and meet me. How gracious of him. I was already walking home and we met half way. I was starving. He had brought me a banana. Hardly top of the treats list if you've been taken to A&E in an ambulance worried you are having a stroke!

Am I being too harsh?

I think he knew the end was on the horizon. I imagine my behaviour, my language, had changed. I needed him out the way for a day. Didn't he want to go and see his children? Apparently the ex wasn't keen, worried about covid. I imagine she may have had other reasons but that would be nothing more than speculation on my part. Didn't he have friends? He had ONE. They arranged to meet up.

Finally some space.

I had another prescription of zopiclone to collect. Having made it past the first line of defence with reception a doctor had agreed to one more prescription. The pharmacist passed her judgement by asking if I hadn't just collected a prescription. The criticism I heard in her voice stabbing me hard as if I didn't feel enough of a failure already.

As I queued, two metres apart, into the street, waiting for the little pills to be packaged up and ready to take home I called my mother. I couldn't live with him any more. He was manipulative. Another critic. Judging me without walking a step in my shoes. Throwing his all in to get what he wanted – a roof over his head and someone to live off – with scant regard for the other person.

It wasn't my fault he had no money. It wasn't my fault he had lied to me. It wasn't my fault if I told him to leave that he would, in all likelihood, be homeless.

I was angry. Anger felt good.

I messaged a couple of friends. I needed affirmation that I was about to do the right thing.

Had I let him down? Had I let myself down? Was there any right or wrong to be had here or just a need to do what needed to be done?

*

It's taken so long to get here. But I couldn't have told it any other way. I feel I should apologise, ask for forgiveness. For what? For not knowing? For not seeing? But it could only have happened the way it happened. I am telling the story to let it go – I keep reminding myself. Almost there. One more week until the end and the beginning. One more week until my life began again.

For the first time in what felt like a lifetime time slowed that afternoon and evening as I waited for him to come back. I was so sure of what I needed to do. I had questioned it over and over but always came to the same answer – for my sanity he couldn't stay. I burnt sage and palo santo in every corner of the flat. I tried to meditate, still too twitchy to switch off completely. I cleared the spare room and blew up the inflatable mattress, finding the spare pillows and making up the bed with clean sheets.

Of course he was late. And then later still. I wondered if he would return at all. But he had to – he had nowhere else to go and no-one else to turn to. He wouldn't reconcile with his mother – she was somehow the evil one in his relationship with her lodger – and wouldn't ask for her help.

When he eventually arrived and I heard the key in the door I was calm. It didn't last long. He said he'd thought I might have locked him out. We sat on opposite sides of the room and my carefully constructed reasoning tumbled out in a mess of accusations. He was manipulative. He was only here because he thought I was good financially. He had used me. He asked me to give him examples, to justify what I was saying but I lost the ability to think straight. At the end of the day it came to this, it wasn't working, at the very least we needed a break.

He had nowhere to go. He told me he would end up sleeping rough on Hampstead Heath. I wanted him out so badly. I asked him how much money he had – two hundred pounds. That was all he had to his name. I had already researched accommodation nearby that was open during lockdown. There was a place ten minutes' walk away. It was eight hundred and something for two weeks. I would pay. He insisted he would pay me back. He insisted it was no more than a loan until he got back on his feet, until his 'business' took off.

Okay, so I still took a zopiclone, but for the first time in ages I lay in. I didn't wake up until after nine. He complained the inflatable bed was uncomfortable. I had slept on that bed when my parents had come to stay at Christmases. It was perfectly fine. He was hang dog and sorry for himself but rather than spending the morning actively thinking about logistics and work and money he went out for a run and wrote his bloody morning pages until after midday.

I transferred the money to his account and booked the room up the road on his card. He would move out the next day. He seemed non-plussed. Worried about himself but not willing to make any concession about his relationship with me. I was going down the road of wondering whether, with some time out and a kick up the arse, things might work out after all. I told him I still loved him. I don't think I did but I felt guilty about what I was doing – even though I wasn't entirely to blame.

The place he would be staying was nice. Clean. Comfortable bed. Ensuite shower room. Little kitchenette with a fridge, oven and sink. It was thirty four degrees the day he moved out. He insisted on taking a large holdall full of all his morning pages all the way there in the heat as he dripped with sweat from carrying it. I was walking with him. I remarked that he was literally carrying the weight of his past on his back. I don't think he appreciated the irony.

We sat on the bed next to each other. I told him I loved him again. I didn't. He was a self-obsessed narcissist with unresolved relationship issues. I try not to judge people, to make judgements – we all have our own paths, our own reasons for who we are and how we are, what we do and what we say – but he was. Sorry.

We met the next day for coffee on a green outside the church at the top of West End Lane. I was going for another acupuncture session. He complained about the room being hot. About it being small. Not a shred of gratitude. Just a sense of entitlement beyond his means. He had been for iced coffee that morning. I don't begrudge a man a drink but if you only have two hundred pounds to your name and your now ex-girlfriend has paid for you to stay in an apartment in north west London for two weeks and packed you off with half the kitchen cupboards – including a jar of Nescafe – I wouldn't have thought £2.80 on an iced coffee was the best use of funds.

Am I being mean?

He was still an arse. Talking to me about love, about connection, about finding a relationship that was special, about his aspirations, all despite his having told me just four weeks ago, before it all turned sour, that I was the answer to all those things.

Over the next few days I met him occasionally to hand over more food, or some other item he had left at mine pending collection 'when he got himself settled'. He was as useless as ever with being where he said he would be at the time he said he would be there.

Emotionally I drifted away from the need for him. The weekend rolled around. People were allowed to meet now – albeit with restrictions. I planned a weekend – much like I might have planned a weekend before the world went to hell in a handcart. I met a friend, James, in the park for coffee. The loos were open now – hallelujah. We walked part of the way back to mine until my trainers had rubbed and we jumped on the bus for the last few stops. I talked about Hector not just to get it out my head but also for validation. James was the down to earth, matter of fact human being he had been since I'd known him. How different would the past few months, as I dealt with the trauma, have been if I had been able to meet friends, to talk to them, to cry with them? Pros and cons. Always pros and cons.

Does it all sound too factual, too clinical? If it does then it wasn't. But I was on a sort of auto pilot. Agitated. Over-emotional. Over-thinking yet unable to order those thoughts. My priority was to survive. I got up. I functioned, barely. Every tiny part of daily existence was an attempt to do something to make me feel 'better'. If I made a cup of tea (if I could face the kettle) would that help? If I sent a text message to someone would that help? If I went out to get a coffee would that help? If I lay on the bed listening to a certain piece of music would that help? If I logged on and did some work would that help? What, if anything, for fuck's sake, would help?

Nothing could permeate this vast cloud of anxiety that had engulfed me, that had spread through the flat and that surrounded me wherever I went and whatever I did. Whatever this was it had me firmly in its grasp and, weak with the effort to simply stay alive, I couldn't shake it off.

Natalie was going over to Leila's for the night to sit in the garden and drink wine. I wasn't sure. I loved the girls and it was always fun – too much fun. But that came with copious amounts of wine and I didn't know if drinking would be kill or, at last, the company of close friends would be cure.

To anyone else I must have looked 'normal' – that awful word again. In white jeans and a sloppy joe style gold knitted top I walked around to the local M&S and bought a bottle of prosecco and a packet of ciggies still un-sure if I was going to go through with it. James left me at the tube station and I ordered an uber. James, if you are reading this, I know you know, but you are one of that small group of people who I consider helped save my life.

Melodramatic? Knowing what I know now that is an under-statement.

I arrived at the girls'. It was a relief to see them. But the contrast with what was going on internally, with how I used to feel when we went out, was jarring. I decided not to drink. There was no pressure from them, but the question wasn't one of whether or not a couple of glasses with them would make me feel better, rather if I had a couple of glasses I couldn't resort to a sleeping pill later.

Leila's boyfriend, a chef, had cooked. By nine when we sat down to eat I was so conscious of the fact that whatever we talked about my mind kept dragging me back to 'it' that I said to them I need to try and not think about 'it' for twenty minutes. If I succeeded I would see how I felt about a glass of wine. And then a curious thing happened – I began to talk about other things - I began to enjoy myself. Was that laughter? A lightness?

I made it to twenty-five minutes before I looked at my watch. I had somehow proved a point that it was possible to switch my perspective. If it could switch for twenty-five minutes then I could surely work on the same for longer. I decided it was time for a small glass of wine. I felt optimistic.

However just as my anxiety had been heightened for these months so that optimism became heightened. I got over-excited about the possibility of feeling 'better'. I started to have too much fun. I drank too much. A bottle of Tequila came out at some point. We sat in the little courtyard off the kitchen and I made them laugh with stories about Hector. He was due to come round to collect the rest of his stuff and Leila's boyfriend offered to come round and be the protection if things got out of hand. It felt so good to have friends, so good to have friends who cared, that I could share anything with. Well. Almost.

I woke up in Leila's bed, fully dressed, with Natalie lying next to me in some fancy pink pyjamas, as motionless as a corpse under the covers. It was half ten. I felt like absolute shit. I had a vague memory of having wobbled to the bedroom at some un-godly hour. Had I done half a line of coke with them? The cat, Luciano, came in. How different the past few months might have been with another consciousness around the place to distract me from my own, a furry friend to act as therapist and therapy, to listen without judgement, to love without condition and to cuddle, to hold on to and know that in any moment I wasn't alone.

Leila materialised, waking Natalie up, and we sat on the bed, talking about the night before and who knows what. I went to the place next door for take-away coffees and croissant. I had to get home as I had acupuncture at one o'clock. I was already so hungover it felt like the world would end.

After showering, changing and eating the giant sandwich they packed me off with I walked the fifteen minutes to the acupuncture clinic. How many times had I seen her now – three? I told her he had moved out. I probably told her I was hungover. It was the same routine as the previous times I had been to see her – lots of acupuncture points for release of emotion. I lay there, once she had left the room, crying, wanting to scream, wanting to get off the therapy table and run. But I was worried about standing up with the needles in. And I didn't have a clue where I would run to. Wherever I might run the monster would run with me.

Did I feel worse when I left the acupuncture? Probably. But the hangover was reaching its crescendo and taking me to some precipice of unbearableness.

I don't know why the rest of the day played out the way it did. Was it the hangover tipping me over the edge, was it the acupuncture, was it seeing friends and, oh so briefly, having a 'good time', or was it a perfect storm of alignment, some part of me realising I wanted a life back, a life without the crippling anxiety, fear, insomnia that I had been living with, and another part of me understanding that I had run out of solutions, of places to go or people who might help?

At some point I spoke with my mother, crying, lost, wishing she could make it all go away.

I had reached that point. I don't know whether I asked her, or she suggested it, but by some process of guilt-laden (on my part) communication we agreed she would come up and stay for a couple of days whilst I waited to go in The Priory.

I was out of options. I had called them again – the third time now I think, always third time lucky – and they could probably take me in on Wednedsay the 1st of July. Looking back, emotionally I still don't really understand how it could have reached that point. Logically I am fully aware of how bad things were and how much I needed help. But emotionally it makes me so sad – so almost unacceptably sad – that my life had reached a point where that felt like the only thing to do. I'm not even sure it 'felt' anything. There was a hopeless acceptance that that was the only path left to travel.

We found a car to drive my mother up to London the following day, the Monday and who would drive her home after dropping me at The Priory on the Wednesday. A call was scheduled with a psychiatrist for the Tuesday morning. There were no female psychiatrists available, did I mind? I don't think at that point I really cared about anything except the disbelief that I had ended up here.

I worried about everything. About how my mother would cope with the journey, about how my father would cope having to fend for himself in the kitchen for two days and his penchant for fried onions with everything. And about whether I was truly mad and this was it for ever more.

I spent that Sunday night numb, lying on the sofa in front of the television, already counting down.

Monday morning I had to be a busy bee. I wiped out my savings to pay for a two-week residential stay, transferring the money to my current account. I set the blow-up bed up in the spare room and changed the bed linen in mine. I spoke with my boss and told her I needed to take time out, six weeks, to get better. I was still shocked that she had chosen to share the details of my trauma with her other direct reports. What had the pandemic done to us that we were all panicking and over-sharing about everything? I told her that yes, I did envisage coming back to work and I would email her the week before to work out how we pick things up.

My mother arrived. Life became very inert. I lay on the bed with her or on the sofa. I was like a child again. This contrasting relationship of her needing to look after me at the same time as I needed to look after her now she was getting a bit creaky. Lockdown hadn't been kind on the elderly. I ordered a delivery Monday evening for dinner. Did I still have an appetite? Probably.

Tuesday morning she went to lie on my bed for an hour whilst I had the zoom call with the psychiatrist. My abiding memory of that call is seeing myself in the little box at the top right of the screen and not recognising the worn-out woman wearing an old purple sweater with no make-up who couldn't be bothered to do her hair and who cried endlessly.

I had never spoken with a psychiatrist before. I had an expectation of him being some Freudian style parody of a shrink. He turned out to be incredibly matter of fact. He asked me a number of questions. I answered. He asked if I was sure I wanted to do the residential stay rather than a day patient and I told him yes, regardless of the cost, I couldn't bear the thought of having to cope at home on my own. I think he told me I had complex PTSD, chronic anxiety, severe depression and chronic insomnia. If he didn't tell me then I certainly saw it on a letter he wrote regarding his assessment not long afterwards. He told me that he would put me on some medication – anti-depressants – that would help. I don't know why but that filled me with terror. Was it a sense of failure I related to the need to take any medication, or the fear of putting anything in my body that might affect my mind which I had spent so much of my life training to walk an increasingly fine tight-rope to keep me from falling, unbalanced by the weight of the past?

Did I brush my teeth? He asked. Of course I did. Then you already put chemicals in your body every day. I couldn't argue with that. And I was due to arrive Wednesday? Yes. Try to get in A Wing, it's just been re-furbished, much nicer. I would. And pack as though you are off to a health spa for a few days. I would do that too.

He would see me Thursday morning.

I 'would be fine' he told me. Within a few weeks I'd be 'feeling back to normal'.

The call ended. I was relieved. Terrified but relieved. Exhausted but relieved. I don't think I registered the 'feeling back to normal'. I was too far away from that for it to be comprehensible.

*

There are so many metaphors – supposed clichés – that come to mind as I approach the end, or is it the beginning, or the end of the beginning, or the middle, of this story. How do we refer to the events preceding, during and after, any momentous stage of our lives?

I feel the weight – psychologically and physically – starting to fall away. I sense a space around me that was once dense with an unidentified something. I thought I was done with all of this. I hadn't realised I wasn't yet 'done done', that there was the possibility to embrace the freedom I thought I had found these past couple of years more closely.

But dear God I am so frigging tired. There is a dull ache in my head. Tension? Too much thinking as I remember? A bruising from the release of pressure? I have given myself permission to cry more than I cried during these almost-three years since I imploded. Because to cry I have to permit myself to cry. I have to say to myself 'let go – it's safe – I've got you'. I need to know that I am crying for the past not the present.

My mother may not have been as terrified as me but she was certainly more apprehensive. I remember I chewed gum – something I rarely do – all the way from home to The Priory. The car was a Mercedes. It was luxurious. We sat in the back and somehow I tried to explain, and downplay, to the driver why we were going to a psychiatric hospital, in an attempt to both excuse and justify where I was going and why he was driving me there. I can't recall what I said to him but it was no doubt a very poor version of the truth.

We pulled up outside the place. In another world, another time, I could have been off for a few days at a spa. But I wasn't. The only thing keeping me going as I got out the car, took my suitcase and thanked the driver was the urgency to get help. My mother came in with me to use the bathroom. I went up to the reception, gave them my name and was told to wait and someone would be with me shortly. The despair I felt as I hugged my mother goodbye and watched her, with tears in her eyes, walk slowly, leaning on her walking stick, back to the car was matched only by the guilt I felt at putting her through all of this at her age. How could I make her suffer so much? There was no answer to that. I still didn't really understand then everything that I understand now about trauma.

A woman came through a door carrying an ipad and asked 'Elle McCormick?'. Yes. We moved around the corner from reception into a quiet room with high ceilings. 'Water?' Yes please. There were some perfunctory administrative questions. She told me I would be in the wing above where we were now. It couldn't be. I panicked. I had to be in A Wing where Dr H had told me to be. I told her as much. I was crying. Crying over a room. Crying because it wasn't working out the way it was supposed to. She told me the room was very nice. That A Wing was full. But I couldn't calm down. I asked her what the room was like. 'Does it have wooden walls?' Yes she told me. And some panic rose up in me again, and I couldn't stop the flow of the tears.

And then, for what I think may have been the first time in my life, something miraculous happened. She said 'give me ten minutes, let me make a call and see what we can do.' And as she disappeared the only words I heard her say to whoever she was speaking to were 'sexually abused as a child …. Can we find another room …' . For the first time I saw and heard someone doing something to help me because they believed I had been sexually abused and was traumatised as an adult. Another human being, right in front of me, had listened, had heard me and was trying to help me.

It was over-whelming. I was as frozen by this act of kindness. Quietened. A flicker of hope somewhere inside me.

Many years ago I ran a 5km race. A friend asked me to sign up with her. I had to travel with work for ten days before the race so was horribly unprepared. I got home to find she hadn't got any training in so wasn't going to go. I made myself - a sucker for punishment. After the run you could access a video of yourself crossing the finishing. I felt like I'd flown over the line, fluid, at pace. Instead when I saw the video back there was this slow, lumpy person wearily trudging to the end. That's how I feel now. Inside it feels like a race. I must get to the end as quickly as possible, rush, rush, rush but to the rest of the world I must look like a worn out old boot hobbling onwards hoping, just hoping I can make it.

The joy when this kind, sympathetic woman came back and told me that they could fit me in A Wing was equally overwhelming. I waited some more until a nurse came to get me and walked me over to this shiny new home where surely everything would be okay.

I did what I always did. Pretended everything was fine. The sun was out. I had new sandals on and the grit from the path kept flipping under my feet and the straps at the back kept coming off.   Security let me in to the building. He carried my suitcase upstairs for me. As always I had over-packed, wanting to bring as much of home as I could with me to make me feel safer.

I hadn't registered the fact that I would be in an 'obs' room for one night until a better room came free.   I didn't know what an 'obs' room was. It took me a couple of hours before it dawned on me that this was a room for severely ill people with a window in the door and absolutely nothing that resembled a bedroom at a health spa. There were no taps – a push button built in to the sink and the shower that gave you twenty seconds or so of water, a colourful foam door hinged to the wall, no doors on the cupboards, no mirror, no lamps, no curtains, nothing that you could pull off or tie anything to to inflict physical damage on top of the mental damage that was the reason you were there in the first place.

The nurse came with me to the room.   So many questions.   Administrative stuff and then a tonne of medical stuff each question filling me with more terror than the last worried that my responses could only mean that I was completely insane and there was no hope or help for me, worried, as always, that they would think I had done something wrong, that I was a bad person.

A doctor came.   Yet more questions.   Then medical tests – blood pressure (through the roof), weight, height, blood tests, a covid test.   Another nurse came and went through my suitcase. I couldn't imagine what for until the penny dropped and I understood that this wasn't the luxury spa I'd imagined and I was in fact in a psychiatric hospital and under scrutiny for the first twenty four hours. I was so out of it that it took another day before I twigged that the people roaming the corridors and sitting writing in books were in fact 'observing' me every fifteen minutes. And observing everyone else according to whatever progress and easing of restrictions were determined by the medical staff over the course of their stay.

My phone and laptop charger cables, along with the glass pots containing my face creams, and a lighter, were locked under my bed. Again, the logic escaped me until the next day.

I sat there. I simply sat there. I don't think there was a thought in my head, just a vast sea of numbness and confusion. Dinner was early – half five or six. I went through to the communal area and found a seat. A group formed at the table and people were talking. Others sat on their own or took something to their rooms. What was my name? Was it my first day? I wish my vocabulary could extend beyond lost, numb and overwhelmed, but that was the sum of it. I cried over dinner. The woman next to me was lovely – Emily. After dinner she asked me if I wanted to go outside for a cigarette. That was when I discovered I wasn't even allowed outside un-supervised. As we stood outside and smoked Emily, who had arrived almost a week before me, explained the house rules. I needed to ask my psychiatrist, when I saw him the next day, to get them to relax my regime so I could come and go. Noted.

Bed time came around. Some people take comfort from the structure of institutional life. I didn't, and don't. We had to collect our meds from a little room off the main hallway, queueing up obediently, standing there whilst someone watched us knock back whatever pills we had been given. I had been prescribed Mirtazapine – an anti-depressant that makes you drowsy so is good to be taken at night if insomnia is your thing.

There was a long discussion with the nurse who would be doing my night time observations about how to minimise any possible disturbance given my fractured and obsessive thinking around sleep. He would come in and check on me every fifteen minutes. Jesus. I had insomnia! How was that supposed to help me sleep! I was like a panicky child, afraid of the dark, afraid of monsters. Yet no-one – NO-ONE - treated me like a fool. A grown woman, acting like a petrified child, but it was somehow okay.

We hung a small towel or some sort of cloth over the top of the door so there would be no noise from opening or closing the latch. I lay there, jimjams on, eye mask, Hercules the travel bear who I took with me everywhere to cling on to in the night, waiting for this Mirtazapine stuff to work its magic.

Except it didn't! Shane, another Priory patient who had quickly normalised things for me and become a Priory-friend, had told me it would knock me right out. No-one had foreseen the power of my chronic anxiety levels to over-ride the drugs. I learnt ages ago that when you can't sleep its best not to look at the clock because then you freak out more either at how long you have been lying awake or how little time you have before you have to get up. I don't know how long I lay there but at some point I told the observation nurse I needed something else to knock me out. I think they brought me a Valium but I couldn't tell you what the other pill I took was. Steadily I grew more floppy and un-focused but still I didn't fall over the edge into sleep. Finally, after a trip to the Wing's reception when the rest of the floor was silent, a nurse came in with another pill.

The next thing I knew it was the morning. I was alive. I had made it!

*

Time, perspective, the very constructs of life, all were different in hospital. After a very long time in the shower pressing the button for more water I cleaned my face (my products having been returned), put some clothes on and went for breakfast. The two distinct groups remained – those who wanted to talk and those who didn't. I wanted to talk.

At some point my new room was ready and I trundled down the corridor. The relief … it was indeed a room that looked like a room not a hospital ward. With the exception of the door-less cupboards, un-detachable hangars, and the curtains that were held up with magnets – which I discovered, not knowing my own strength, when I drew them the next day and the whole weight of them ended up on top of me. We were on the second floor and I looked over the main drive and front gardens. The room was sort of green and brown. Brown furniture and headboard, pale green heavy curtains, a pale carpet, white walls with a hint of green. I unpacked. I had my charger cables back and plugged the mobile in. There really wasn't much else to do. I was allowed out for a smoke with Emily again.

I was waiting for Dr H to arrive and talk to me, and for one of the in-house staff to talk me through my programme for the week. At over a grand a night I intended to make the most of this and consume whatever was on offer. It turned out there wasn't much. The cinema was shut due to covid. And the gym. Attendance at group therapy sessions was reduced for the same reason and due to a lack of available staff. It was Thursday and the first class I could get signed up for was Saturday afternoon. I was expecting a one on one session with a psychologist but she couldn't give me a date for this. Fingers crossed it would be sooner rather than later.

When Dr H arrived we sat in a large reception area in armchairs on opposite sides of the room. He was fully masked but having been tested on arrival none of the patients were obliged to wear them. He asked me how I was, did I sleep well? On looking at my notes he rather perfunctorily read through, under his breath, the list of medication I had been given and commented that whatever they had given me at half two in the morning would have been enough to fell a rhino. To this day I have no idea what it was. 'Old Me' would have needed to know, would have requested it be written down for me, to google and find out all the contraindications so I could know, so I could worry. 'New Me' (for that is what I was becoming) didn't give a monkeys!

We agreed my obs could be reduced during the day and to four hours at night which gave me two reasonable windows of sleep if I was woken up and meant my sleep-anxiety levels didn't need to ne un-necessarily raised. We agreed I could be allowed outside un-supervised. In fact, if I wanted to leave the premises it was okay. It was the first time in months that I thought to myself 'bloody hell, you can't be doing too badly'. It's all relative.

One thing I appreciated about Dr H was his immaculate dress. The chinos, the beautifully cut navy blazer, the suede ankle boots and the navy face mask with his initials embroidered on the edge. Bespoke from his tailors in Saville Row – I had asked. Seeing him like that somehow reminded me of who I was. Who I had been. Not the expensiveness of the clothes, but the attention to detail, the dressing as though you were a canvas on which to paint each morning and your clothing an expression, in art form, of your state of being and feeling. If you had looked at the way I presented myself these past months there had been no care. Hair permanently up – not because I couldn't be bothered to wash and blow dry it rather because to have it down, coiffed, would not have been a reflection of my mental and emotional state. No make up – what was the point in painting a face when my emotions had felt so bare, so exposed. And the same bloody uniform every day – jeans and a t shirt – just as every day had been groundhog day in my head. When I saw Dr H a switch flicked briefly and a memory of something registered somewhere in my subconscious. Little steps. Little signposts on a long journey.

After he left that was it, the excitement was over, and I settled into a routine of smoking, talking to my new friends and eating when it was breakfast, lunch or dinner. Reflecting on it now I am surprised how quickly I accepted and adapted to this new routine and these new people. How 'normal' (there is that word again) it seemed to have to wait at the reception at the end of the corridor if I wanted anything, or to wait to be buzzed in or out of the building, or how 'normal' it was to see other patients lying on their beds all day, depressed, agitated, seemingly unable to cope with this thing called life. When a new high risk patient came in and was placed in the critical obs room next door to the reception it seemed perfectly 'normal' to see a nurse sitting at the end of her bed 24/7 and hear her talking throughout the day and night, in that unforgiving space where time becomes an irrelevance.

That was the biggest blessing from my stay in this bizarre hospital – extracting myself from my life, removing any responsibility I may have had for looking after myself, taking myself out of the equation of how a life is supposed to be, and understanding, at the deepest level of my being, that how I was feeling, what I was experiencing, was 'perfectly normal'.

Perfectly normal.

My reaction to the effects of disclosing my trauma were an entirely appropriate response to that disclosure, to the trauma.

Amen.

Some things at The Priory weren't at all 'normal'. Apart from the gym and cinema being shut because of lockdown group therapy class sizes were scaled back for social distancing. And some therapeutic staff wanted to work from home. Essentially there was fuck all to do. I arrived on a Wednesday and it was Saturday before I attended that first group session. I joined another Sunday and one more Monday, and had my first direct individual session with a psychologist on Tuesday. Getting into therapy classes was a bit like getting tickets for the hottest gig in town – if you weren't in the queue at least an hour before they went on offer you didn't stand a chance, and even then you probably wouldn't get the seats you wanted.

I wanted it all. Given the chance I would have been in two group sessions and one individual session a day. I wanted to rush at myself head on and confront the past, punch my way through it and come out the other side still running. Because that was, if I'm truthful, how I'd lived my life. Running repetitively away from the past and this fear of the past in the present Running like a mad-woman to find a future where the past didn't exist.

Slow didn't feel like the answer but slow was what I got. So goddamn slow. Perhaps slow is the only way. All those moments in the past, with the numerous and varied 'therapists' I'd paid my money to for them to 'fix' me, where a moment of epiphany had proved to be no more than a moment and the epiphany proved to be just another insight that kept me going until I needed my next fix.

It was a curiously life-affirming place. Life affirming in the sense of completely supporting my belief that the story we have told ourselves about how we should live our lives is no more than a story that so-called civilisation adds another chapter to every year. Thou shalt go to school, thou shalt get a job, get married, buy a house, get a car, have children, work hard to earn a living, go on holidays, talk about your kids to other people with kids, have hobbies (or not), try to stay fit and healthy so you don't die young, retire, look after the grandchildren, die. In today's world if you're lucky your 'job' may be something that does in fact define and fulfil you, or under that vast banner of 'celebrity'. Or you may end up like so many of us, going through the motions each day dreaming of your freedom from something you surely must have chosen to do at some point in the past.

It's all just a story. All of it. There is no reason we could not, over the millennia, have determined another version of how 'a good life' should be lived. How easier might my life had been if I could have studied things that interested me rather than pursuing subjects towards a career that – according to some un-inspired beliefs about societal norms held by the staff at my school who were surely more motivated by their own egos that a desire to nurture my dreams – would be more appropriate. How much easier my life if the world might not have considered it so daunting that I drop out of further education to follow my heart. How less dull the past thirty years if I had spent ten hours a day doing something I felt passionate about rather than a job that leaves me painfully unfilled and exhausted. How much less tragic if I hadn't spent my thirties and early forties answering all those questions about when I was going to meet someone and didn't I want children. How much younger might I have got help if society hadn't, for so much of its history, held the belief that mental illness was shameful, a disgrace, not to be talked about, to be swept under the carpet whilst we all pretended nothing was wrong.

Because this stupid story we have about how life should be, how a 'normal' person should behave, about what's 'right' and 'wrong', about the things we should aim for, the things we should learn to put us in good stead for a 'better' life hasn't worked. If it had worked I wouldn't know so many people who were sexually abused as children. If it had worked more people in the world could, hand on heart, say they found their lives – all of their lives – fulfilling. And it seems to be getting worse. There seems to be a growing ground swell of people in their teens and twenties questioning the foundations of existence. Question away I say. I ask just one favour – do it with kindness, respect and compassion for every living person, every living being. We are all trying to do our best even if it doesn't always look that way.

My first full day there I found out some more about of my Priory friends. A woman who had tried to kill herself just a few weeks ago. Some part of her wanted to hang on to life enough that she rang 999 just before she passed out from all the alcohol and pills she had taken. She was a joy. A beautiful soul. In terms of that ridiculous story about how to live your life she had a successful job, two children, a house, ... And yet here she was, full of life but coming to terms with what she had done and re-defining what it meant to be her and to live with mental illness. A guy who had been pushed to the limit by a scheming ex and was suffering from such overpowering anxiety that he was still shaking two days after he started to take anti-anxiety drugs. An ex-drug addict who had been at The Priory over a decade earlier to get clean but had found herself, during lockdown, struggling - a lockdown romance having turned into a lockdown nightmare when he moved in and she found herself using again. I was not alone.

These were the beautiful people I spent most of my time with. There were others. An older chap who spent all day sitting in his room in a chair by the window. He came in to eat when everyone else had finished. I could see and feel the quiet suffering inside him. If it could have helped – if he would have let me – I would have wrapped my arms around him and held him until whatever was hurting had gone away.

There was another woman with a high-profile corporate job who was there to be monitored whilst they changed her anti-anxiety medication. A model-esque woman, all long legs and Vogue photo shoot looks in her denim cut-off shorts and little vest tops, whose depression was so bad she could barely get out of bed - a loving husband and son at home who she missed badly.

We pottered along. Doing next to nothing. I might walk out the premises to a local newsagent to buy cigarettes. It didn't even cross my mind to buy alcohol. I think it was just day two, on the phone to my mother, that I heard my voice come back. I heard how I used to sound. For a few seconds I knew that I was still in there somewhere, and I knew that the disconnect of these past few months could be sorted out, that I would be okay … whatever the hell 'okay'might mean! The next morning I woke up and put on a full face of make-up – something I hadn't done for months. Halle-fucking-lujah!

Then things got a bit weird. It's strange how life – time – plays out. Strange how sometimes even when something truly frightening, horrific, happens you know that it really couldn't have happened any other way.

*

Time had been passing like a slow train for the first few days of my stay. We went to bed by eleven, got up around eight, had lunch around midday, dinner around six. We talked about anything and everything - we talked about why we were ill, how we were ill, the meds we were on, the psychiatrists, the lack of available therapy, all with a freedom that didn't exist 'outside'. It was a language I'd not known and yet one that I easily and happily adopted because it made sense. Because I fitted in. For the first time in my life it was acceptable to talk about how I felt, what had happened to me, and I talked, and people listened, and I cried and people cared, and it was all perfectly 'normal'. It was normal because it was the reality of where we were and who we were at that point in time. Curiously it's a language I miss. I still get to use it sometimes, but it's acceptance in the world outside isn't readily there. Conversations about divorce, sex, work, relationships, break-ups, people moaning about the government, the cost of living, your ex, the state of the world … but bring a conversation around to depression, sexual abuse, admitting yourself to a psychiatric hospital, the last conversation you had with your psychologist, and somehow you are lowering the mood, talking about a subject that for no understandable reason is off-limits. I do my best to try to normalise it all. I am doing my best as I remember. I am learning how to use my voice.

A young chap moved onto our ward on the Saturday morning – Callum. Having completed four weeks getting clean the other side of the hospital he had been transferred over to A Wing. He was young, a gypsy traveller and, according to Shane who I realised in hindsight liked a bit of drama, had been talking about how many people he had cut up in the past. He was only nineteen. Shane put the fear of God in me and I asked to talk to a nurse in private, shared my fears and had to be assured that he was quite safe and I was quite safe. Yes I was being a snitch but a part of me was very much stuck at seven years old, especially the part of me that was reacting to fear and anything I saw as a threat.

On the Sunday consultants and therapists were all on a day off and the place was run by the nursing and security staff and the shift-manager. It was visitor day and as I didn't know many people either nearby or who drove I had asked my brother if he would come and visit. He said yes but out of a sense of duty I think rather than a desire to see me and check I was doing okay. I assumed that he would be fearful of coming to a place like The Priory – for the same reason so many people would, not a fear of the patients, rather some innate suppressed anxiety regarding the unknown. Most people can't make sense of bi-polar disorder, schizophrenia, depression, PTSD, chronic anxiety, insomnia, because they don't understand it, because these things aren't talked about in a way that makes them understandable, and because you only truly. deeply know if you have experienced them yourself. They get a cursory mention these days – soundbites on social media, words used to describe what someone is 'struggling with', the occasional television programme. But they are so much more than words. They impact all your life, your very existence. And, tragically, they impact so many of us – one in six children have been sexually abused. Why isn't this something we talk about over coffee or tea with friends or colleagues? Why doesn't this come up as frequently as conversations about other things that affect more than one in six of my friends? Why the fuck aren't we talking about it? And talking about how we stop it, first off, and how we make sure there is a network of support for people who have been sexually abused?

My brother arrived and I met him at his car so he wouldn't have to come into the property. We walked up to Richmond Park, got a coffee and wandered around for about forty-five minutes. In the absence of any questions I talked about myself for a while and then I heard about his girlfriend's on-going problems at work, about the snagging in his new home, about all sorts of things. Why couldn't he ask me about me? Why couldn't he ask if I was okay, tell me how brave I had been, ask if I needed anything? What was missing? I love my brother. We can still make each other laugh ridiculously. But we don't talk about this stuff.

So we got back to The Priory earlier than I'd forecast. My brother left and I changed into a sundress as it was a warm, sunny afternoon. I sat on the lawn watching all the patient's families, the kids so happy to see mums or dads they hadn't seen all week, the brothers, sisters, parents who had come to visit, and I felt sorry for myself. There was nothing to be done – I couldn't magic my own version of these people out of nowhere – so I skimmed through the Sunday papers, looked at the pictures in the magasines and started on the word games.

There was an American guy on our ward. I was going to say again I can't re-call his name but still there is so much of it that is lost in the farthest recesses of my mind. Is that because there was too much that happened over that short period of time for me to have filed it somewhere at the front of my mind or is that because my subconscious selectively chose what was important and it would retain and what it could chuck in the archive bin for deletion? In any event, I can't remember what his name was, other than it was unusual and we all seemed to pronounce it differently.

He was a strange chap. I had spoken to him several times but he always took the conversation down the road of conspiracy theories, politics, or some such similar subject that none of the rest of us were interested in. Three or four of us might be sitting around a bench outside, drinking tea or with a can of pop, smoking (as usual), talking about ourselves, sharing, having conversations that felt salutary and he would sit down. Slowly, diplomatically, people would start to peel off citing conversations with the nurse, needing to go and lie down, needing to make a call, until one of us was left with him, being polite for as long as possible until, for our own well-being, we also had to make our excuses and absent ourselves.

He came and sat next to me that Sunday on the lawn. He seemed more agitated than usual. He was talking about a girlfriend back in the US who none of us actually thought existed. He talked to me about the US military, about service he'd seen – although I'm sure someone had told me he had been a US army chef rather than front-line forces – and there wasn't a lot I could say. I listened, I tried to maintain a sympathetic expression on my face, I asked the odd question, at some point I disagreed with him, and after half an hour or so he took his leave and moved on to the next person. Something was definitely not okay with him that afternoon. Anyone who had spoken to him could see it.

Later that evening a group of the girls, plus Callum and Shane, were sitting in the open plan TV area watching some rubbish on the box. Word began to go around that the staff were panicking because someone was missing.

It was the US military guy. I don't think we thought much of it until there was screaming and shouting at the end of the corridor. The staff were running to the entrance door and I sat there glued to my seat, overwhelmed by a feeling of terror. Shane sprinted back to his room, next door, to better listen in I assume, but Callum stood, outstretched, across the arch way to the TV area where we were sitting, suddenly seeming taller, bigger, and in the most matter of fact way told us that he would protect us.

Never, ever, judge a person until you know them!

He was so sure of himself, so certain of his role, as a man, to make sure that none of the women got hurt even if that meant putting himself in the line of danger. I'm not sure I've met many people who would do that.

The noise from just down the corridor carried on. The US military chap was shouting racial abuse at the two petite black nurses who were covering that night shift. At some point the night manager arrived at our wing. He tried to assure us that everything was under control but I didn't believe him. As he disappeared to go and support his colleagues we moved round the corner from the open plan lounge area to the communal kitchen dining room and seven or so of us sat there dissecting the events of the evening and questioning our own safety if this guy was left on the ward. The staff stuck their heads around the door and suggested we go and get our meds and go to bed but we were having none of it.

The night manager, with support from another member of staff, tried to convince us that we were perfectly safe. Were we?

I was worried he would get into my room. Can I lock the door?

No.

But you told us half an hour ago that he had locked himself in.

No response.

So he didn't lock himself in?

No. We can lock you in if you want.

No, I don't want - how the fuck is that supposed to make me feel safe? What the fuck! If he comes out of his room the night shift nurse sitting at the end of the corridor who can intervene. Really? That's your idea of appropriate security? What if they miss him? What if he goes the other way? I mean, how did he even go missing for the whole evening – who was supposed to be monitoring his whereabouts?

The problem, we were told, is that there was nowhere for him to go.

Send him back to the other ward.

There are no rooms available.

Well he can't stay here – it's not fair on the rest of us, he's the one that's out of order so he needs to go.

On and on it went, round in ever-decreasing circles, repeating the same arguments and counter arguments using different words.

By eleven o'clock there were just three of us sitting in the kitchen. Me, Callum, and the woman I thought must be a model. Callum vowing he wouldn't go to bed until the two of us were safe. It didn't even occur to me at the time that everyone else had drifted off to their bedrooms, or that some patients had not even come out to see what the hullabaloo was about in the first place. We were at a stalemate with the night manager and his sidekick.

They were urging us to go to bed. We were becoming a problem ourselves. Out of nowhere I blew up! I stood up, and as I fussed to re-tie my dressing gown and collect some water to take to my room I accused them of putting the other patient before me.

Didn't they know why I was there? Didn't they understand I had been sexually abused as a child and was terrified of the dark, terrified that someone would come and get me? But oh no, as expected, put the other person first. What I needed, how I was feeling, didn't matter.

And I opened the door, with its rectangular window, took off down the three steps and headed up the corridor to my room, shuffling along in my towelling Priory slippers talking out loud to myself 'Is anyone going to follow me? Of course not. That's right, stay in the fucking kitchen, ignore me, I'm being too difficult ....' But I wasn't being difficult ... And then the weirdest fucking thing happened. I turned around and marched back up to the kitchen, opened the door and, very matter of factly, asked 'isn't anyone going to bother to follow me, to check that I'm ok?' Silence. I did another one eighty and left again, crying.

I sat on my bed and sobbed, not loudly but not quietly – audibly.

The sweetest nurse in the hospital wing tapped at my door and came in. She stood there against the wall and let me cry. And talk whatever words needed to come out. I repeated, like a mantra 'no-one came, they just left me, no-one came, no-one fucking came, no one-came, ...' until, gently, I came to a stop and began to laugh.

I came into the Priory for therapy, for the trauma recovery that I needed and that I hadn't been able to find anywhere else during this lockdown. Yet here I was, having a powerfully cathartic moment on the back of a situation with a drunk American and poor security in a psychiatric hospital. Forever my own keeper.

They called his military base in the end and insisted someone drive the two and half hours to collect him there and then. He would be gone by the time we woke up. The nurse and I talked, she said how hard it was, because of Covid, not to be able to hold patients when they were upset. She bought my Mirtazopine and sleeping pill in bed, stood there whilst I swallowed them down and wished me goodnight.

When I woke the next morning I knew it was time for me to go home. I didn't need to be here for two weeks. I showered, dressed, put some make-up on, went for breakfast and then headed outside to sit at a bench in the sun, have a smoke, and think about my decision before I did anything. There was a secluded spot near A Wing with a couple of benches, not far from the gravel drive and entrance to the grounds. As I walked out there, in clear sight, was a multi-pack box of red stripe lager, three or four cans left in the bottom and one, half-empty, discarded under the bench. I looked up at the cleaner sitting on the bench the other side of the grass talking on her phone. How had she missed these? How many people in there, going through treatment for alcohol addiction, might have stumbled across these if I hadn't? I know shit happens but surely security would have spotted these as they did their rounds that morning. I took a photo of the box under the bench, emptied the can on the grass, and handed the box to the cleaner to dispose of. I went back inside and told the team at reception. The yank had gone but not before he had been out boozing all day and sitting outside nursing the last cans until he needed to stumble to his bed and consequently all hell had broken loose.

I checked what time my next meeting with Dr H was and called my mother. It was time to go home. I had taken myself out the equation, asked for help, normalised how I was feeling, let someone else look after me for a few days, had a surreal cathartic moment, but now I needed to go home, to start to live life again, with whatever psychiatric and other support I needed to get me out the other side of this trauma recovery 'stuff'.

*

People are a funny lot aren't they. When I'd said to friends and family and even my GP that I needed professional help and was going to check myself in to The Priory the question hanging in the air from some of them was 'are you sure?' Now I had decided to leave it was the same. Either these people knew me far less well than I thought they did – or I felt that they should – and didn't trust that I knew my own mind and body, or they were internalising their feelings about it and externalising their related doubts, fears and incomprehension. Or …. they were somehow worried that my going in to the The Priory put them in a place that made them feel uncomfortable, at a loss as to what to say to me, and my leaving The Priory risked the same. It's a curious thing that when human beings don't know what to say they say nothing. They don't even proffer an 'I don't know what to say' or a 'I'm in shock' in response to the sad, tragic or unexpected news about someone they know and even someone they love. Is it a British thing? Have we no capacity for empathy when confronted with it face to face? I'm stunned every time I hear, at work, the news of someone's parents, grandparents, uncles, close friend's death and watch as very few people manage to find the wherewithal to overcome their own fear and say anything. It may not make me feel comfortable to say it, I may feel very self-conscious, but the absolute least I can do is to reach out to them and say I am so sorry to hear what has happened. And when I am next on a call or in a meeting with them to ask how they are. Fuck me, you don't even have to mean it but make the effort and get over yourselves.

And you know what would have been especially nice … someone, outside of family and a small number of close friends, saying to me 'well done – you must be so pleased you were brave enough to bite the bullet and check yourself in because look how far you've come in the that short week.'

Except for one person. I felt that, in the truest sense, from one person. A neighbour. Often that true validation of who you are, how you are, that impeccable empathy, comes from the unlikeliest of places.

The one person who, of course, was utterly pragmatic about it was Dr H. Was I sure? Yes. Why? Because I can her my voice, stronger and stronger, because I have lost the fear of being lost, because I have re-found myself, because I know I have a support network of professionals who know how to help me.

Did I have someone who could come and stay with me for a couple of days when I got home? I would sort that out.

He would check in with me a couple of days after I got back. He knew a psychologist who he could recommend to work through the trauma with me. He'd contact her and if she could fit me in would pass on her details. And how did I feel about sonic reset therapy?

He thought it could be really useful for me. I'd never heard of it, had no idea what it was, but you see, he was the medical professional, he knew far better than me what was the best thing to do, so yes I'd give it a go. But for the first time in my life I think I was starting to realise that I didn't have to say yes. I might have felt some fear about stepping into the unknown with all this trauma therapy, but curiously there had never been any fear of Dr H as a doctor. How did he manage to do that?

Fear in itself is a curious thing. A bungee jump, rollercoasters, scuba diving, … the thought of having to do them scares me, makes me feel fearful. The idea of trauma therapy, delving into remembering and somehow – and I didn't appreciate then how long this would take – accessing and letting myself feel all the feelings that I had buried at seven and that I had buried since, I had been at that start line for months, perhaps even years, waiting for someone to fire the starting pistol and let me at it.

I don't think I give myself credit sometimes for my strength, resilience and determination. I keep going. I trust myself. It's what I've always done. I am reminded, by Ally, of how much hard work I have put in to every aspect of my life. How committed I have been to every part of the process. How I have never shied away from going to places that, in absolute and complete honesty, were tough, so tough, to go to. Places that left me wrung out and dripping with the tears of decades old emotions. Places that have been so dark that without her guidance I may not have found my way out.

At one of only three group sessions I made it to before I left Zoe, the ex-drug addict who had generously indulged me in frisbee one evening when I was bored of doing nothing, who had found herself struggling to cope being on her own during that first, long lockdown when nothing and no-one was accessible, sat across the room from me and admitted that she had been sexually abused as a child.

My heart went out to her. She couldn't go there. Wouldn't. The weight of it was too much. They had suggested EMDR – eye movement desensitisation and reprocessing. As they had explained to her how it worked all she had heard was that it might not work, and that it might feel difficult going back to the traumatic event, stirring up those buried emotions. I get it. I get that fear of not going there. I had been so afraid of remembering that my subconscious had hidden the rape from my conscious for years, the veil slipping occasionally to give an ambiguous glimpse of something in the shadows. And when the effort of hiding, of coping, of living in this complex and restrictive world of not feeling that I had created for myself, to avoid the horror of it all, became too much and it flooded back into the front of my mind it took years before I found the courage to tell anyone. It took getting to the point when I was afraid I had lost my mind, afraid I might harm myself, to finally give in and ask for help.

We all want to feel that we are doing okay. Society has instilled in us a need to feel like we belong to some community. Biology has made us gravitate towards whatever will give us the strongest possibility of evolution, of survival. It was no different in a psychiatric hospital. Conversations with my new friends – however short-lived those friendships might have turned out to be – were enlightening and reassuring. Everyone else was on some sort of anti-anxiety medication or anti-depressant or anti-psychotic. Some people took sleeping pills. More people were in need of medication three times a day compare to my once before bed. It was affirming. I didn't feel like the odd one out – a feeling that had trailed round after me like a stray dog all my life. I had found my new normal. We were the sane ones because we had seen the light, seen and experienced the insanity of the world through whatever 'journey' our trauma had taken us on, be it addiction, self-hatred, fear, depression, ... I am romanticising of course. I didn't understand then that nurture as well as nature is a building block of a confident, happy, fulfilled life. I thought that the problem with 'the rest' of the world was that they didn't understand what it was to suffer, didn't have some intellectual drive that gave us this deep, powerful perspective of all of life, not just the easy bits.

But then I didn't understand much back then. I certainly didn't understand that life could in fact be and feel happy, that I could feel confident, that I could not hate myself and that there was the possibility that my life might actually feel fulfilling.

*

The irony of my first one on one therapy session with a psychologist being on my last day at The Priory was not lost on me. We talked for fifty minutes. I cried but understood why I was crying and what I was crying about instead of crying feeling like a storm of unquantifiable craziness was washing over me until it abated and decided to move on.

The psychologist was nice. She was, however, no Dr H, my new benchmark for how I wanted to be treated – sympathetically, pragmatically, and as an intelligent, articulate woman not solely an unknowing child for whom love and affection alone might save the day. I did not want to be patronised. I did not want to be spoken to as though I didn't know myself. I did not want to be educated, in simple terms, about concepts that I clearly already grasped. I needed someone with emotional and intellectual intelligence who saw the whole of me when we spoke and didn't just hear the words. It was a tall order but somehow it was working itself out.

I had bought chocolates for the staff on the ward. Not much to shout about as it was slim-pickings at the local seven/eleven. I hoped they appreciated the thought. Do other people do this? I don't really know. I am just always so grateful. And it is such a little thing. Such an easy thing to do. Once when I had a mole removed from the top of my right arm I rang the hospital the next day, concerned it was bleeding through the plaster, and they said 'come in, we'll re-do the dressing'. I stopped and bought four cupcakes in a box as a thank you. I was so grateful. So grateful they hadn't thought I was wasting their time. Grateful they hadn't turned me away. Grateful they hadn't ignored me. Grateful they had listened. I see the pattern, now. I see where that desperate gratitude came from and it makes me sad. Giving thanks to another is a beautiful thing but in the past I often took it to a place where it fulfilled some need in me to feel lesser, to feel at fault, to feel subservient to the other. It reinforced that belief that grew to huge and complex proportions as the years, the decades, passed that I counted for nothing, should never be seen. And so if anyone ever did see me, even if it was their job to help, even for a moment, a minute, I was deeply grateful.

It makes me very sad. But now, now I see it for what it was, I am grateful - it allows me to appreciate how touching, powerful even, thanks can be for the person who is receiving them. A thank you has the ability to change someone's day.

So I thanked this psychologist, politely took her number knowing I probably would not be calling and went back to my room for the last time. Money, phone, keys, money, phone, keys, money, phone, keys. I checked I had everything and shut the suitcase. The nurse who had checked me in what seemed like another world ago, walked me out the building. He offered to carry my suitcase downstairs and I said yes – something I wouldn't have done before never wanting to put anyone else out or be a burden to them. See, you have to understand how all-pervasive the effects of trauma can be ... as a result of my being raped as a child I would not let anyone carry my suitcase for me, because they didn't really mean it, because they were only pretending to offer to help. Because I had to 'cope' on my own.

Do you see? Do you see the layers and layers of complex nonsense that had woven their way into my thinking all because of those forty-five minutes. Do you see how clever the brain is in trying to protect the person, keeping an eye out for anything that might be a threat, trying to avoid any scenario which might trigger that same awful feeling that they felt when they were raped? My mother told me about a friend of hers, Margaret, in her late eighties, a very religious woman who one would assume was all about Christian charity and goodness. When she asked after me and my mother told her what I was dealing she said, outright, with no apology or warmth 'it happened so long ago, it's all a fuss about nothing'. Well fuck you. And fuck your fake friendship, your supposed christian love. I bet you'd be the first to preach about forgiveness as well.

I walked to the end of the path, away from the buildings, towards the entrance to the property and called for a taxi. I smoked a last cigarette. The driver would be late so I smoked another last cigarette. Eventually he pulled up, put my suitcase in the boot and off we set. I don't think we spoke a word from behind our masks as the car wound its way through south west London, across the river and through Westbourne park on its way to mine. Pubs and cafes had been allowed to open up in the past few days and the sight of people sitting outside in the sunshine having a drink echoed the joy and the sense of new beginning that I felt inside.

How did I feel on that journey home? Apprehensive for sure. My thoughts couldn't comprehend how the woman who had arrived in such a hideous mess just a week ago could be leaving feeling so differently. Logically, of course, I could point my finger at things that had happened and why I felt better. But emotionally, psychologically, there were no short answers. Getting from A to B was a long, circuitous journey of whats, whys and wherefores. It still is if I'm honest although my vocabulary to explain these things when others ask is becoming more concise, more adept.

I am certain I cried when I walked through my front door. Out of sheer relief to be alive, to have re-found myself and to have finally acknowledged little Elle, the seven-year old me, and given her the chance to speak and to heal.

I must have wandered around to the local mini M&S to get some provisions because there was nothing in the flat. I walked there seeing the world completely differently yet knowing that no-one I walked past would look at me, know what I had been through or see any difference from the last time they had seen me walk by.

I ate dinner and I called my mother. I gave up on reading Wolf Hall, the book I had taken in to The Priory, and watched it on television instead. The stillness of Mark Rylance's acting resonating with the stillness I felt inside and that I wanted to hang on to for as long as I could.

I got in to bed. I had what seemed like an armoury of drugs that I put in the top drawer of the table next to the bed. In response to my question as to whether it was okay to keep taking the sleeping pills if I needed them Dr

H had basically told me I had other fish to fry at the moment and not to worry about it. I read for a while, took the Mirtazopine, put the light out and lay there. I decided not to take a sleeping pill. Well, not immediately. I'd see. If I didn't nod off I could always take one later. But I didn't have to get up in the morning, I was off work for five more weeks, I had a support plan in place with Dr H, it all felt as though it was all going to be okay.

It was the first night I slept soundly, on my own, unassisted, in five months. Hallelujah. I was so grateful. Grateful to an indefinable god, grateful to Dr H, to the staff at The Priory (well, most of them), grateful to my family and friends for being there for me (even if sometimes it was very much in their own way and had felt, at the time, like more of a hindrance than a help). But mostly, I was grateful to myself. Grateful for being the bravest person I knew and asking for HELP. Grateful that little Elle had remained like a light somewhere deep in my heart and soul that hadn't gone out, waiting, patiently, for the time when she – we – could be set free.

*

I was going to end this story there. I was naïve, impatient, thought that having had my moment of catharsis, having had my breakdown, having cried all those tears, I could stroll out the other side and everything would be ticketyboo. I had no idea. No idea how long the process of trauma recovery can take, especially given the decades that had passed. But equally no idea about how beautiful life would become because of how differently I would start to see myself and feel about myself.

I had, as I said, just five weeks before I needed to resume my work contract but, more importantly, before my money would run out. Thank god I have had the money to fund this myself even if it has made a significant dent in my savings and wiped out any plans to pay some of the mortgage off over the last two years. It has not been cheap. But what is that expression – 'you can't put a price on freedom'?

Those first couple of weeks I spoke with Dr H a couple of times. He had spoken with Ally, who has become my biggest ally these past few years as I work on eviscerating every trace of the trauma from every aspect of who I am, what I believe about myself and my place in the world, and how I live my life. And finally, to complete the trinity, an impressive man called Edward who provided me with and guided me though Sonic Reset Therapy (SRT).

It all sounds lovely doesn't it. So positive, so structured, such a path through fear and loathing to the glorious fields of eleutheria.

It wasn't. To recover from trauma you have to revisit trauma. I cried. Oh dear god I cried. Great sobbing, dribbling, tears. Other times gentle tears and watery eyes that often came from nowhere as I spoke and the memory of something – a word, an image, a feeling – pricked me.

How on earth to describe my SRT experience? This eccentric, incredibly erudite man sitting in an armchair somewhere in what I imagined was a beautiful house in the country. A feeling of complicity as he rather dismissively told me he had had 'what used to be called a nervous breakdown' a couple of times. An explanation that he would give me access to the SRT program on my laptop, I would put headphones on and listen to it, whilst he left the room so I didn't feel watched – much as he would have done if, in different times, I had visited him in his consulting rooms in London. I would listen once, we would reconvene and talk about what had happened and ask any questions, then I would listen again, the expectation being that the impact of listening would be diminished second time around. It would be a lie to say I didn't feel uneasy about this step into the unknown, but I was invested in the process and trusted Dr H who had recommended it.

We checked the play button worked, I put my headphones in, Edward left the room and the screen went blank.

Show time!

Those first weeks after I returned from The Priory any emotional, psychological or physical impacts of the trauma recovery therapy were off-set by the sheer bloody joy of sleeping and being happy to be alive. I made sure I had a few close friends around me and got plenty of exercise. I did my best to keep talking to those same friends about what had happened and how I was feeling.

I tried to be kind to myself. Mostly it was heaven to have allowed myself to take time out of work. The weather was glorious and with the feeling that some part of me had been liberated and all was well in the world they were, for me, halcyon days.

I don't really think, at that time, I appreciated what was happening to me, how long and complex recovery would be and the impact that process would have on me, my inability to meet my own needs at every level of my being after years of believing I was value-less, and how hard it would be to let go of decades of ingrained thinking and behaviour to uncover the true me, the person I always was and should have been.

I struggle to explain how Sonic Reset Therapy works. It somehow gets rid of the worst of the storm, calms the eruption, brings some order to the thousands of thoughts and feelings fighting for space in your head. Edward suggested I listen to it regularly. Somehow, within seconds of this non-descript noise beginning to play I would find myself crying hard. Strong emotions would come up and my brain would work its way, in no particular order and very rapidly, through multiple times in my life when I had experienced those emotions, processing something, clearing something, moving it into a bucket clearly marked the past rather than allowing it to continue to live in my present. I saw Edward on and off for a couple of months. We talked about art one day. I explained that I was going to paint a picture. I had never really painted anything before other than a term or two of evening classes at a local art school but in the day or so before the car came to take me to The Priory I very clearly had an image come into my mind of a painting I needed to start and finish. Edward's advice was 'Don't overthink it. Everyone tries so hard to be perfect, whatever that it is. Have fun with it.' And so I did. Loud music on, slapping paint onto the canvas, painting over it again and again and again until I thought 'yep, that'll do'.

The painting is called 'What I Saw When I Thought How I Felt'. My little work of art. Work of life.

The trauma recovery therapy with Ally was gentler. Slowly, very slowly, over eighteen months we went back over the past and its impact on the present. Every week or two for eighteen months. I was of course back working by now, thankfully mostly working from home because of the pandemic so it was easier to fit all these 'medical' appointments in between meetings.

I don't think, even now, I realise how tough it was. To have to go back to something that brought up such powerful emotions, something that I'd buried for decades, over and over again. I sat on the sofa, the laptop resting on a cushion on the coffee table, with a mug of tea or glass of water and a pile of tissues next to me. But I never questioned what I was doing. I trusted Ally. I trusted the process. I wanted to be out the other side, to be free.

It was a safe space and each session was always brought round to the present, to something else, so I was never left stuck in the past. I couldn't count how many times Ally has said to me 'you're doing brilliantly … I'm so proud of you'. For a long time they were hollow words and meant nothing to me. Because for a long time I hadn't thought anything anyone said to me meant anything. I didn't believe compliments were compliments because I was unimportant, I didn't count. Words were just lies. And yet I'd clung to friends' and lovers' words for years, believing them, until the truth came out. We talked about the rape. We found a new vocabulary for talking about what had happened. We even talked about how I would refer to what he did. Rape – a word that to me had seemed so extreme, an exaggeration, calling attention to something that surely hadn't been so bad – was the word I chose. Rape, a brutal word that reflects the brutality of what happened to me that day.

We talked through the shame, the guilt, the details, how I felt about him and the two bitches, what I would say to them if I met them, what I would tell little Elle, how I would hold her tight and never let her go.

But there is so much, so so much, and that is surely another story, for another time.

In working our way through the rape itself and everything associated with that I often found it hard to access those emotions that the rest of the world might consider perfectly 'normal'. Anger was the first to come. I was so angry. So incredibly fucking angry. SO INCREDIBLY FUCKING ANGRY. An anger I had never allowed myself to feel about anything. So fucking angry.

'But don't you feel some sadness?' asked Ally, numerous times, trying to coax me to see if I did or could.

'No'. Always no.

I had started dating – along with the rest of the world that was single or bored during lockdown. I'd met an Italian guy twice. I'm not sure I even found him attractive but putting myself out there on a dating app and thinking I might actually be able to have a relationship was new territory for me. Twelve years earlier, in an effort to let down a friend who I didn't want to let down and explain why I didn't want to sleep with him or get involved romantically, I had told him I had decided to remain celibate for a year. I ended up talking myself into it and discovered it was easier to cope with my life emotionally and psychologically if I was single and celibate – even if it was lonelier. Yet again I was managing to fulfil my own prophecy of how un-loveable I was.

Anyhow, this Italian went off to his lake house for a month. He asked me to go out for a week or two but, wisely I thought at the time, I declined the offer. He messaged me constantly, sent me photos of himself and the mountains, and lake Como. He was going to his Milan apartment after the lakes. He wouldn't be back for a while. More photos, more messages, more 'can't wait to see you'. More 'baccios' at the end of his messages. He sent me photos of his place in London that he was having re-furbished. It really wasn't my cup of tea (lots of dark wood!) but in an effort to be polite I told him it looked great and yes, I couldn't wait to see him either.

His date for coming back to London kept getting moved out. I didn't buy it but I couldn't let it go. Was I trying to prove that I would never meet someone who treated me with love and respect, was I still trying to show the world that look, I am 'normal' because a man wants to go out with me, or was I still, at some level, hoping that someone else could take some responsibility for me so I didn't have to cope on my own.

He got back to London and we were supposed to meet on a Sunday. I didn't hear from him Saturday so messaged him. No reply. No reply Sunday either. The angry voice I'd found sent him a last message telling him he was selfish and rude, I had no idea what he'd been playing at these past months, and he could 'fuck right off'.

Ally asked me if I was sad. Nope. Angry, yes. Get over it and move on I said.

It happened twice again. Two more men. In hindsight narcissistic, putting themselves on a pedestal, full of their own successes. One went quiet on me after he'd cajoled me into having sex with him. I finally asked him to at least explain himself. He'd lied he said. When he had gone out of town the other weekend he had stayed with an ex and had realised he had feelings for her. Then why the fuck did he have sex with me the angry voice shouted by text. He hadn't had sex with her yet. So apparently it was ok. My parting shot across was that I was fairly sure if some man treated his daughter like that he wouldn't be impressed.

The third one was even worse. Months it went on. God he was vain, self-absorbed, selfish. I thought, when I first met him, that he had told me he had twelve thousand followers on Instagram. I was impressed in a way that I shouldn't have been. He said I could 'follow' him, as though he were giving me permission. The next morning, along with sending my links to songs with cryptic lyrics, he told me where to find his Instagram profile. In all truth I should have got out then – not twelve thousand followers, twelve thousand posts! Almost all of them of himself. I'd mis-heard! And still I didn't listen to my intuition.

At some point, in the middle of all of this, whilst I took on a new, intense and very stressful role at work managing elements of a major divestment, I began to acknowledge there were things that made me sad. I remember the first time I felt sad. I got into bed one night, thought about the way the man who had posted twelve thousand photos of himself on Instagram had treated me, and this violent feeling of something – of despair, despondency and loss - came over me. I realised it was sadness. I was feeling sadness. But the awful thing was it felt utterly unbearable.

Ally explained it. I was like 'a little alien', learning things that other human beings had learnt as children, growing up, for the first time. Sadness would get easier. All the emotions would feel easier. One of the primary goals of therapy, she said, was that people were able to feel and deal with their emotions. Here I was, very much a grown up, learning to feel for the first time. I won't deny it was tough, and weird, and very much like learning a new language. But having spent so much of my life in darkness my appreciation of the light is immense. It's a beautiful thing to be able to see and feel and know how much of a gift life actually is when your life, your truth, was stolen from you as a child.

After eighteen months of tears, laughter, learning to live again and learning to live my life as it would have been before someone swapped my story for another one, more violent and more desperate, Ally told me that I didn't need active trauma therapy any more.

In spite of the past I can't believe how lucky I am to be where I am today. So many people who were sexually abused as children end up with drug or alcohol addiction problems. An unacceptably high percentage of people who are homeless were abused as children. So many people who were sexually abused never disclose their abuse. They carry on coping as best they can, living, at best, a partial life. Not many people who do disclose their abuse get the treatment they need. Organisations and resources that can provide appropriate help and counselling to victims of childhood rape and sexual abuse are few and far between and very much underfunded and the alternative of paying for your own treatment, is, as I have found these past few years, not a cheap investment. Even fewer people who do get to start trauma recovery therapy decide to finish it and come out the other side.

So often, when Ally said to me 'you are a miracle', I don't think I understood the depth of those words. Now I do. It is a miracle that I am here, alive, living a life that feels more and more my own every day. It is a miracle that I kept myself alive and coped for all those decades, that somehow I fashioned a career and forged friendships and relationships, and pursued hobbies and got a mortgage, and, and, and … . It is a miracle, and a privilege, that I can tell this story – that I have the strength, emotionally, physically, spiritually, to tell this story.

It didn't end there of course. There is no neat full stop. I still see Ally. More often than not when something from the past has been triggered for the first time and a new thought or a feeling knocks me for six, but sometimes just when work has been very stressful and I have managed to get myself lost in old behaviours and need someone to help me find my way out.

I still speak with Dr H every six months. It's re-assuring to know that even if I can swim there is a life raft within reach of the tips of my fingers just in case.

I still haven't lost most of the weight I put on through the insomnia, the break down and taking the mirtazapine. At some point it will disappear.

But it's okay. Everything is okay. That little light that I knew hadn't gone out burns bright now. I am that light. That feeling like I was walking around covered in tar? It's gone. I used to cry myself to sleep not knowing what's wrong with me. Now I cry when something makes me cry.

Trust me, I'm not invincible. But if someone had tried to explain how free life would feel I couldn't even have grasped what they were saying. I used to wonder how people were happy. I was perplexed by the way people went about life – their family, friends, jobs, everything – and seemed to enjoy it. It has sometimes felt like a slow process but it couldn't have played out any more quickly. Every few months Ally and I would reflect on how I was doing and how far I'd come and I would always say I had never known it was possible to feel the way I feel.

It's been hard work. She has to keep reminding me that everything feels different, everything has changed, because of my hard work. I may be a miracle, but the way I feel about myself and my life is not. It has been tough. So many times I thought 'that's it … I've made it' until I realised that it's not a finite process. After I finished active trauma therapy I didn't see Ally for a few months. But it proved too soon. I might have finished active therapy to deal with the trauma but I had four decades of living the wrong life to un-ravel and put back together. I still talk to her, once a month, sometimes about something, sometimes, it feels, about nothing. Sometimes I need someone to help me see what I can't see, to ask me the question that I've been avoiding asking myself, to make me see the positive where I've got myself stuck on the negative, or, quite simply, to make me feel better when I've been feeling crap.

But life is infinitely better. The depression has gone. I get the odd day or two when I might feel down but some part of me, the observer, will eventually see what's making me feel that way, help me work out why and ask me how, in that moment, I could be kinder to myself. Having spent a life in fear I am seldom anxious. Or if I do find myself feeling apprehensive or fearful that same observer will work out whether the root of that apprehension is the present or something in the present that has triggered the past.

As for sleep … I'm not quite there yet. Some nights – possibly most nights – I do or could sleep like the proverbial log, but I have a fear of being tired that I am yet to fully work my way through. I'm not afraid of the dark any more, and it doesn't take me two or three nights to lose the fear of the unknown when I go on holiday and stay in a room I've never slept in before, but I worry that if I'm tired I won't be able to do my job, if I can't do my job I may be sacked and if I am sacked how will I pay the mortgage on my own. There's a lot packed in there. And I know the answers to all the questions: I can do my job just fine when I'm tired – look at the past decade when I seem to have been endlessly tired because of work; if this company terminates my contract it will give me a chance to take a break for a couple of weeks, reset, and find another role – I am exceptionally good at my job and will find something else no problem; I will find a way to pay the mortgage and worst case I will sell the flat and move somewhere cheaper (and no doubt bigger!) outside London. Let's face it – corporate life has never fulfilled me so I very much doubt the opportunity to change my life and do something else would be a hardship. It might involve some change that other people would struggle to get their heads around, but what the heck.

Jump in.

Both feet.

So … life is not perfect, not always how we want it to be. There is always something to do, money to earn, things that frustrate us. But, ultimately, life is a blessing. Lying on my back on the grass or sand, staring at the sky or the sea, I couldn't be happier. I know there are infinite possibilities out there just waiting for me. I am ready. I am.

And if you're reading this story and there is some truth buried deep inside you I know the idea of letting go of the secret may seem impossible. I know you were told not to tell anyone. I know it may be a long, hard road to travel from there to here. But please, please, let it go. Be brave. Be courageous. Ask for help. Or talk. Just talk. To someone you trust. To me if there is no one else. I promise you, if I can do it so can you.

*

It's been a long time since I began this story. I'm tired. It's time to move on. To allow myself, metaphorically, to breathe different air, to walk down a different road, to let it all go. I have learnt so much about trauma, about the mind, about myself, as part of this road to recovery and the evisceration of every impact – from the tiniest to the most terrifying – of what they did to me. I know it's unrealistic to think I can work through everything but I am having a bloody good go at getting through everything that had or still has any influence on the way I see myself, the way I value myself, my self-belief, my self-worth, my confidence, my belief about my place in this world and my relationships. We all come into this world equal, we all leave this world equal, anything in between that isn't love or kindness is just judgement or a story. I choose to love myself, to be kind to myself, to love others and be kind to others.

Right back at the start of the process with Ally she would, from time to time, give me 'homework'. Once she also asked me to write a letter to little Elle. Little Ellie. The girl that was silenced, whose life was stolen. Here is what I wrote:

"Dearest, dearest Elle.

I'm so sorry. I know it's not my fault but I am so deeply deeply sorry. How on earth did this happen to you? Oh gosh – if I could go back and stop it or somehow make it never happen I would. If I could have changed anything to make that day never happen.

You are truly the joy of life.

I just want to wrap my arms around you and tell you over and over again how loved you are, how very loved.

These are just words, but I want you to know it's all okay. It happened, and I will do everything I possibly can to make sure you know that it never was and never will be your fault. I don't know how anyone could do what they did to you. There are truly evil people in this world. And I'm so sorry you came into contact with people like that, that they screwed your life up. But please please please know, in your heart and soul and every fibre of your being that this was not your fault. It happened but it was not your fault. I hate that man for what he did to you and I hate those women for the way they treated you, for abandoning you in the hour of your greatest need. I will never abandon you. I am here whenever you need to talk to me, whenever you are feeling afraid, alone, un-heard and un-seen. I will be here to hold you tight and keep you safe. All day every day. For the rest of time.

You can cry and shout and scream – it's all okay. None of that will ever change how much love I have and feel for you.

Whatever it takes for you to have the life you desire I will do or be for you.

Know that whatever happened doesn't affect who you are. You were, are and always will be enough. You were, are and always will be the most beautiful person I know.

Never forget how kind, beautiful, fun, wonderful, lovely, loving, special, unique and amazing you are.

You always shine my beautiful little girl, please, please let that light shine as bright as bright can be. You deserve it. You deserve to show the world how wonderful and joyful and amazing you are.

You were, are and always will be my miracle, my bundle of joy, my heartbeat. My love will be in you, around you and with you, now and forever.

There are no words to express the depth or my love and admiration for you and my gratitude that you are here and will always be a part of me.

Elle xxxxxxx"

Maybe one day I will be able to read it without crying. Maybe.

But I think that is what I have been doing, every day, for the past three years - doing everything I possibly can so that I can be the me I was before it happened. Once, talking to Dr H about how much I was having to learn from scratch or re-learn, he likened what had happened to someone uploading the wrong operating system, and now that programme has been deleted and the original, correct operating system had been re-installed. It's not terribly romantic imagery but I like it. Sometimes it just feels like that re-boot is taking longer than I'd hoped. I hope it doesn't take too much longer – it seems to be hanging at that last two percent.

I remember my parents telling me about that flight to Paris, when I was such a happy baby. When they sat the carry-cot that my father had made on the table in front of them. Everyone that went past commented on what a beautiful, happy baby I was. The French exclaimed 'comment elle rigole!'.

Where did that laughing, smiling little girl go? She's still here. Growing. Listening. Taking it slowly, not trying to run before she can walk. Asking for help when she needs it. Learning.

Last year I visited Paris one weekend with a friend. We arrived late Friday. Saturday morning we walked down to the Rue de Rivoli and as we crossed onto the Place de la Concorde I began to cry. I walked ahead – in part so my friend wouldn't see me and in part as it felt like a very private moment. For the first time in my life a wave of nostalgia for the past hit me. We had had some wonderful times in Paris when I was a kid. All those last minute weekends away. Running around town in my uncle's Citroen with the crazy suspension. Sunday lunches at a Moroccan restaurant or pizzeria with a pizza oven in the middle of the room – things that were exciting because they simply didn't exist in 1970s English suburbia! The coffee religieuses. I swear if I ate one now it would be through tears. Because I realised that it hadn't all been bad. That underneath the fear, the gradual shutting myself off from feeling, the constant invisible need to protect myself, I had had 'a good life'. There were happy memories. Everything in my life had been coloured by the trauma and as the years passed that sense of blackness became darker and more all-pervading. But there have been adventures, there has been love, and laughter, in abundance.

Can you imagine that? Can you imagine having lived so long and never felt any sentimentality for the past? Never had a moment of longing for another time? It blew my mind away. In that moment I understood that my life hadn't been a failure, that it hadn't all been worthless. I just hadn't been able to see the moments of joy through that bloody curtain of fear.

I still don't really remember much of my childhood before I was seven. How awful to have not just your life but your memories of your childhood wiped away. Sporadically some fleeting image or feeling or memory comes into my head of laughing with my parents, of feeling safe and happy. Perhaps I will see more. It's all locked in there somewhere, filed somewhere safe on the very last shelf at the very back of my mind. Even as I write this I can feel some warmth of that love around me.

If I turn my thoughts to it I can feel the warmth of my own love, the warmth of love of good friends, the love that runs through all people of the world, but sometimes takes a bit of finding.

And at other times, still, I feel an overwhelming sense of grief. And powerlessness.

What happens next? I think I know. I certainly know what I want now – what I always wanted, since I was a child. It never really changed, just got a bit more sophisticated. And I never believed in myself or anything enough before now to know that it was possible. I saw the infiniteness of possibility but never felt it was accessible to me.

I thought I might be apprehensive about finishing this story but find I'm not. In any event apprehension no longer brings with it a sense of foreboding.

Have I found my voice? Yes. From time to time I catch myself not speaking up, not saying what I mean, not standing up for myself, but I am, like everyone else, a work in progress.

Am I happy? Broadly, yes. I feel more fulfilled. I spend more time doing things I want to do rather than going along with whatever anyone else wants to do. I allow myself to be more vulnerable which makes it easier to recognise when I don't feel okay. There is a feeling of contentment that runs through the simple things of my days. Whereas in the past I needed to have done something, brought something, been somewhere, to feel a sense of achievement or some bizarre sense of accomplishment, now I find that the smallest things of creation give me a feeling of one-ness that over-rides any need to 'do' anything.

And do I feel 'normal'. Do I feel like I fit in? Do I feel like I am 'fixed'? To be honest I don't really care. What the heck is 'normal'? And why would I want to be 'normal' if it isn't the definition of the way I want to live. Why do I need to 'fit in' and who should I 'fit in' with? As I become more and more comfortable with myself, as I have understood what it means to have boundaries, I find that the people who are meant to be in my life at that point in time arrive and others leave. And am I 'fixed'? To the extent that I have finished trauma recovery therapy yes. To the extent that I am, gradually, living my true life, yes. But did 'I' need fixing? No. What needed fixing was the fall-out from the abuse, the after effects of living with the lie for so long, the impact on the beliefs that 'I' held about myself and everything that came from living for so long with fear.

How do you end a story? Especially a story that isn't over? If I was out with a friend, things had been feeling too much recently, and I had cried over dinner, or brunch, or a glass of wine, there would be some well-timed segueway into something else, or a waiter would bring something to the table and create a natural pause that would mean we might take another path when conversation resumed.

I was hoping for some great words. A great insight that might change the world. I have neither. Sometimes the most appropriate and most powerful words are clichés that are easily discarded because they seem trite. I will, however, leave you with something along those lines …

BE KIND TO YOURSELF. AND TO OTHERS. THE WORLD NEEDS MORE KINDNESS.

Epilogue

It wasn't my fault.
It was never my fault.
I have nothing to be ashamed off. They lied.
I did my best.
Don't apologise for something I never did.
If it's how I'm feeling it's how I'm feeling.
Don't compare myself to other people.
Life isn't a competition or a race.
People aren't always careful with their words.
Don't judge someone or their life solely on what you can see.
Sometimes the people you expect to be right are wrong.
The gift and joy of life truly is in the small things.
Live by my values – but above all things be kind.
If it will hurt me it will likely hurt someone else.
People's actions say more than their words. Too many people put their egos first.
Not enough people appreciate the power of gratitude.
It's okay to be vulnerable.
If I am tired rest. If I am upset cry.
No-one really knows how to talk about sexual abuse.
Be kind.
If I need to talk find someone to talk to, but make sure it's someone I trust with my feelings, that I know wants the absolute best for me.
Find out where to find the help that I need.
What works for one person may not work for me. And vice versa.
It's okay not to know what to do next.
Try not to shut off from the rest of the world.

We all need other people. But make sure they are the right people.

If people don't understand or don't want to help or don't want to listen it doesn't mean I am wrong, or have done something wrong.

Do what I love. And do it again and again and again if it makes me happy.

Celebrate my successes.

Listen to music.

Dance. Who cares what I look like!

Love. Love your life. I don't have to love everyone else's.

Live. But live the way I want to live. Live a life that means something to me.

Write a love letter to myself.

Be honest. Honesty isn't just about not lying. It's about being honest with how I feel. And if people flinch at that honesty, if they don't want to deal with how I feel, find people that do.

Friends may come and go, but don't be afraid of losing friends who don't treat you the way a friend should. You will make new friends.

And be kind. Above and beyond everything else be kind. With words, thoughts and deeds.

And, in any moment, when everything is said and done that needs to be said and done know when it is time to move on …. to the next chapter, the rest of the story.

ACKNOWLEDGEMENTS

There are, of course, people to thank and people without whom I probably wouldn't have had the courage to send this book out into the world. I thought, when I got to the end of trauma recovery therapy that I was 'there'. Then I realised that wherever 'there' was I was still some way off. A year or so later I felt compelled to write this story and thought that revisiting events and emotions would release whatever I thought was 'stuck'. But still something wasn't 'right'. I finally decided to publish the book and things seemed to get worse before, eventually, after feeling like I was falling apart again, I gave in and broke the ties with the negative emotions and patterns of negative thinking that had been stuck, like silt, caked in the hardest to reach corners and that hadn't been washed out even during the previous three years. The final piece of the jigsaw was the realisation that I had a voice and (something that would have filled me with terror in the past) I wanted to use it.

Thanks to Ally. Thank you everything these past 3 years and ten months (I am still counting). I don't know where I'd be without you. Thank you for taking the time to read this book, thank you for your feedback and thank you for believing in me. Thanks to Dr H. Undoubtedly the right person at the right time. Thank you to my parents and especially to my mother, Eileen, for the countless evenings over the decades when I have cried down the phone and you have been there to listen. Thanks to the small number of close friends who have been there in some way shape or form over the past four years or so. You know who you are.

What happened to me was horrific but I know that I am lucky to have survived, to have somehow found the wherewithal to disclose my abuse, to have been able to find the help I needed to heal and to have had the determination to keep going. It is another cliché I know but I hope this story may help someone who is struggling like I was to find another way to live and a way to love themselves.

Thank you so much for reading my book.

Printed in Great Britain
by Amazon